Law and Truth

Law and Truth

Dennis Patterson

OXFORD UNIVERSITY PRESS
New York   Oxford

Oxford University Press

Oxford   New York
Athens   Auckland   Bangkok   Bogotá   Buenos Aires   Calcutta
Cape Town   Chennai   Dar es Salaam   Delhi   Florence   Hong Kong   Istanbul
Karachi   Kuala Lumpur   Madrid   Melbourne   Mexico City   Mumbai
Nairobi   Paris   São Paulo   Singapore   Taipei   Tokyo   Toronto   Warsaw

and associated companies in
Berlin   Ibadan

First published in 1996 by Oxford University Press, Inc.
198 Madison Avenue, New York, New York 10016

First issued as an Oxford University Press paperback, 1999

Oxford is a registered trademark of Oxford University Press

Library of Congress Cataloging-in-Publication Data
Patterson, Dennis M. (Dennis Michael), 1955–
Law and truth / Dennis Patterson.
p.   cm.
Includes bibliographical references and index.
ISBN 0-19-508323-7
ISBN 0-19-513247-5 (Pbk.)
1. Jurisprudence.   2. Law—Philosophy.
3. Truth.   I. Title.
K230.P378L39   1996
340'.1—dc20   95-17515

1 3 5 7 9 8 6 4 2
Printed in the United States of America

For Sarah

Acknowledgments

Many people have contributed to the writing of this book. As their number is embarrassingly large, I must refrain from detailing their individual contributions to my work. However, they are all, I trust, aware of the depth of feeling I have for them and for their support of and contribution to my work. Thanks to Robert Ackermann, Anita Allen, Jack Balkin, Guyora Binder, Philip Bobbitt, Sherry Colb, Jules Coleman, Anne Dalesandro, Michael Dorf, Neil Duxbury, Kent Greenawalt, Dick Hull, Richard Hyland, Peter Koller, Brian Leiter, Thomas Morawetz, Nancey Murphy, Bill Powers, Paul Robinson, Roger Shiner, Allan Stein, Jim Tully, Ernie Weinrib, and Vincent Wellman.

Richard Morrison, Barnett McGowan, and Diane Graham provided research assistance.

Rutgers University, and in particular Roger Dennis, dean of the Law School in Camden, provided research leaves and other financial assistance in support of this work.

Portions of some of the chapters of this book first appeared in professional journals. I thank the Columbia, Cornell, Iowa, and Texas law reviews as well as the *Canadian Journal of Law and Jurisprudence* for permission to reprint these previously published works.

Thanks to Simon Blackburn for permission to reproduce figure 1 from his *Spreading the Word* (Clarendon Press, 1984) in my introduction.

Thanks to Robert Rauschenberg for permission to reproduce *Express* for the cover for this book. This painting, which hangs in the Museo Thyssen-Bornemisza, captures well the spirit of this work.

My greatest debt is to my immediate family, Barbara, Sarah, and Graham, who have endured my absences and supported my work in ways large and small. I also wish to thank my parents, who sacrificed much to send their boys to good schools, and who are responsible for whatever measure of quality one finds in these pages.

Contents

Law and Truth

Philosophy may in no way interfere with the actual use of language; it can in the end only describe it. For it cannot give it any foundation either. It leaves everything as it is.

Ludwig Wittgenstein

1

Introduction:
Realism, Anti-Realism,
and Legal Theory

Even the debate about the nature of law, which has dominated legal philosophy for some decades, is, at bottom, a debate within the philosophy of
language and metaphysics.

Ronald Dworkin[1]

This book addresses the following question: "What does it mean to say that a
proposition of law is true?"[2] On the surface, the current jurisprudential literature provides what appear to be radically divergent answers to this question. For
positivists, a proposition of law is true if it accords with certain institutional facts.
Some contemporary natural lawyers argue that a proposition of law is true if it is
consistent with principles of morality that put the law in its best light. Still others
claim that "truth" names a convergence in interpretive assumptions about law.

Perhaps it is best to begin with a defense of the question to which this study
is directed. We are comfortable in saying that empirical claims (claims about some
state of affairs in the world) are "true," but can the same be said of legal assertions? Are legal propositions the sorts of things about which we can be "right"
or "wrong"? Do legal propositions admit of the characterizations "true" and
"false"?

The following claims are examples of legal propositions:

The First Amendment prohibits prayer in the public schools.
No contract is enforceable without consideration.
Manufacturers are strictly liable for injuries caused by their products.
Insanity is a defense to murder.
Payments to creditors within ninety days of the filing of a petition in
bankruptcy are voidable as preferential transfers.

1. Ronald Dworkin, Introduction to *The Philosophy of Law* 1 (Ronald Dworkin ed., 1977).
2. I do not intend any technical meaning to attach to the word "proposition." I take the
word to mean nothing more than a sentence with a sense. A proposition of law is a claim about the
content of law or, put differently, a claim about what the law requires, prohibits, or makes possible (e.g., power-conferring rules).

3

I take the task of jurisprudence to be that of providing a philosophical account of what it means to say that propositions of law are true and false. This entails spelling out just what is involved in saying something is true as a matter of law. In addition to detailing truth, some account must be given of disagreement and the resolution of disputed cases. Perhaps some propositions of law have no truth value; perhaps legal statements are not bivalent (admitting always of truth and falsity). These are some of the issues that will concern us.

Before we turn to the specifics of jurisprudence, it is perhaps best to get a sense of how these issues are of general philosophical concern. I begin with a broad description of the current debate over realism and anti-realism. To understand the debate, consider the following figure:[3]

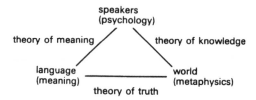

The realism/anti-realism debate is over how best to characterize the relationship between the theory of meaning (semantics), the theory of knowledge (epistemology), and the theory of truth (metaphysics). The debate looks at questions like the following:

> Can there be truths of which we are unaware?
> Does language reflect the world?
> Do we have knowledge beyond our senses?
> What is the ground of knowledge?
> What is the nature of "truth," "language," "the world"?

I begin with a discussion of the larger context of realism and anti-realism because I believe that this discussion helps to frame what is at stake in contemporary jurisprudential debates over justification. In law, we want to know whether a judge "got the law right," whether a lawyer's claim about the law is "true," and what it means to say that another's view of the law is "mistaken." The broader context helps to sharpen our perceptions of what acceptable answers to these questions might look like.

After a brief survey of the broader philosophical terrain, we take our first look at the landscape of current legal theory. This introductory discussion is prefatory: my goal is to get the reader interested in the issues under consideration.[4] To do that, I have to show how any of these questions matter to our reflections on the nature of justification in law. In particular, I want to signal, albeit broadly, what it is in the accounts of others I find flawed. In this way, I hope to justify these questions and anticipate my own responses to them.

---

3. This is taken from Simon Blackburn, *Spreading the Word* 3 (1984).
4. Thus, in this introduction I do not consider all the views taken up in the following chapters.

Realism/Anti-Realism

Our understanding of the current debates in jurisprudence over the truth status of legal propositions can be enhanced by considering equally contemporary debates in philosophy over the nature of meaning. These debates are a cluster of controversies to which the terms "realism" and "anti-realism" attach.

Realism and anti-realism are two different approaches to the nature of the truth of propositions. For the realist, the meaning of a sentence[5] is given by the conditions that make it true. So, for example, the sentence "My car is parked in front of the house" is true if, and only if, there is a car, it is my car, and it is indeed parked in front of the house. Now this example may seem confusing, for it appears to conflate the meaning of a sentence with the truth asserted by the sentence.[6] For the realist, one knows the meaning of a sentence when one knows what it would take for that sentence to state a truth. Hence, the proposition is true if the conditions that would make the proposition true obtain. In this way, we see that, at least for the realist, truth depends on a certain sort of approach to meaning, which may be characterized as truth-conditional in nature.

Realism's opposite, anti-realism, does not dispute the contention that truth is a matter of conditions. Where realists and anti-realists part company is over the question whether truth conditions may be "recognitionally transcendent." For realists, the truth conditions for a proposition may lie beyond our capacities to recognize them (a lack of epistemic access). This is of no moment to the realist, for she believes that propositions may be true quite independently of our ability to recognize and discern their truth. This is precisely what the anti-realist denies. As one defender of anti-realism puts it,

> [T]he case for anti-realism rests on the proposition that speakers grasp the meaning of, or understand, a sentence when they know which conditions warrant its assertion. This proposition will be supported by reflection on the

---

As stated, my interest here is to focus the reader's attention by providing a sense of the issues involved as well as some of the positions in the literature.

5. A sentence is the linguistic unit that expresses a proposition.

6. D. W. Hamlin does an excellent job in succinctly summarizing the relationship between the meaning of a proposition and what makes it true. See D. W. Hamlyn, *Metaphysics* 28–29 (1984): "Realism involves at least the claim that there is a reality independent of us and our minds, and that what we think, understand and recognize does not necessarily exhaust what reality involves. The facts may go beyond anything we are capable of ascertaining, but the truth is so by virtue of those facts and that reality. In recent times, however, philosophical concern with realism has had to do with its connexion with theories of meaning, because it is taken to be the case by many philosophers that the meaning of propositions is a function of what makes them true or false. The question at issue, therefore, is whether what is to be understood in any proposition lies simply in what sort of fact makes it true—in other words in its truth-conditions. Anti-realism holds that what has to be understood is more than that. To understand a proposition we need also to know its verification-conditions; we need, that is, a recognition of when the truth-conditions apply, and when we are justified in holding that they do. It follows, given this view of what it is to be understood in a proposition, that there is no sense to be attached to the idea of facts going beyond what we are capable of ascertaining."

sort of training in language use which speakers can receive. If understanding consists in a grasp of warranting conditions, truth cannot transcend what can be warranted. And anti-realism is correct.[7]

Another line of demarcation between realism and anti-realism is the question of objectivity.[8] Realist philosophers of science, for example, are of the view that propositions about the natural world are true in virtue of the way the world is. Scientific theories are true to the degree they comport with facts of nature. Of course, realists see no necessary connection between natural states of affairs (facts) and our ideas about nature (beliefs). Nature is what it is, quite apart from anything we may believe about it. It is in virtue of these natural facts that propositions about nature are either true or false.

Realism is not limited to the realm of naturalistic inquiry. Some moral and legal philosophers posit the existence of moral facts, which make our moral assertions true and false. This thesis, which is metaphysical in nature, is an account of the nature of truth in morals. Recalling the connectedness of truth and meaning, the moral realist affirms that a moral proposition is true if the conditions that render it true (moral facts) obtain. Again, as with the scientific realist, the moral realist unpacks "p is true" in terms of the conditions (facts) in virtue of which p is true.

The anti-realist in morals denies the existence of moral facts. One form of moral anti-realism, emotivism, characterizes all ethical statements as expressions of personal preference or desire. Thus, for the emotivist, a statement of the form "Killing is wrong" merely states a preference for a world in which there is no killing. Because there are no moral facts, there is nothing in virtue of which "Killing is wrong" might be true or false. Thus, the proposition "Killing is wrong" can never be objective.

This account of realism and anti-realism cannot purport to be an exhaustive survey of what are several debates in ethics, philosophy of language, and metaphysics. Much in these debates is of little concern to the present endeavor, concerned as it is with matters of jurisprudence. However, the broader problems raised in these debates figure directly in matters of current concern to jurisprudence. Let us now turn to these.

Jurisprudential Realism

To get a sense of why legal philosophers have paid attention to the question of truth in law, let us look at how one of the leading figures in modern jurisprudence views the matter. Ronald Dworkin has developed and sustained a position in jurisprudence by returning his critical attention to legal positivism, specifically

---

7. James O. Young, "Meaning and Metaphysical Realism," 63 *Philosophy* 114, 115 (1988).

8. For an excellent discussion of the objectivity of law, see Brian Leiter, "Objectivity and the Problems of Jurisprudence," 72 *Tex. L. Rev.* 187 (1993) (reviewing Kent Greenawalt, *Law and Objectivity* (1992)).

the version of positivism formulated by H. L. A. Hart. In an introductory essay[9] for a collection of essays on the philosophy of law edited by himself, Dworkin discusses the relationship of philosophy of law in ways that show why the issue of truth is of such importance. His account of the philosophical importance of truth for jurisprudence is perspicuous and persuasive. We shall consider his argument in some detail.

Like his fellow positivists Hans Kelsen and John Austin, Hart advocates the view that "propositions of law are propositions about laws."[10] And "propositions of law are true when they correctly describe the content of laws or rules of law; otherwise they are false."[11] So, on the positivist account of the matter, "truth" means "accurate description." A direct corollary of this view is that "no sense can be assigned to a proposition unless those who use that proposition are all agreed about how the proposition could, at least in theory, be proved conclusively."[12] This, Dworkin maintains, is not a matter of legal theory but a thesis in the philosophy of language:

> [M]any positivists rely, more or less consciously, on an anti-realist theory of meaning.
>
> . . .
>
> Lawyers are agreed, according to positivism about how the existence of a law or a legal rule can be proved or disproved, and they are therefore agreed about the truth conditions of ordinary propositions of law that assert rights and duties created by rules. But controversial propositions of law, which assert rights that do not purport to depend upon rules, are another matter. Since there is no agreement about the conditions which, if true, establish the truth of such propositions, they cannot be assigned any straightforward sense, and must therefore be understood in some special way, if at all.[13]

As Dworkin reads positivism, when it comes to controversial propositions of law, there are two choices: there is no truth of the matter about the propositions in question, or the truth conditions for controversial propositions of law are "special," that is, different from the truth conditions for ordinary propositions.

Dworkin disputes the positivist account of the truth of legal propositions, claiming that the positivist argument rests on a controversial philosophical view of the nature of truth:

> Some readers may object that, if no procedure exists, even in principle, for demonstrating what legal rights the parties have in hard cases, it follows that they have none. That objection presupposes a controversial thesis of general philosophy, which is that no proposition can be true unless it can, at least in principle, be demonstrated to be true. There is no reason to accept that thesis

9. Dworkin, *supra* note 1.
10. *Id.* at 6.
11. *Id.*
12. *Id.* at 8.
13. *Id.* at 8.

as part of a general theory of truth, and good reason to reject its specific application to propositions about legal rights.[14]

Dworkin's dispute with positivism connects jurisprudence directly with philosophy of language.[15]

> There can be no effective reply to the positivist's anti-realist theory of meaning in law, however, unless an alternative theory of propositions of law is produced. That theory must assign a sense to controversial propositions of law comparable to the sense that controversial propositions in science, history, literature, and academic awards are supposed, by those who use them, to have. It must at least show how disagreement about such propositions may seem genuine to lawyers and not, as the anti-realist position would insist, illusory.[16]

Dworkin's alternative to what he terms the positivist's "anti-realist" theory of meaning is an account of legal discourse that shows that the truth of legal propositions is not completely settled by legal practice. Dworkin wants the truth of what we say in law to be independent, at least in part, of the ways in which we agree that a proposition of law is true. In short, Dworkin wants to make the case that the truth of (at least some) legal propositions transcends our current practices. Whether Dworkin is successful in his endeavor will depend on the extent to which he provides an account of truth that is independent of legal practice.

Dworkin's position, at least in the form sketched above, is a version of realism. He seems to be saying that any adequate account of truth in law must explain how beliefs about what law requires can be true apart from mere *belief* or *agreement* that they are true. What is needed here is a philosophical account of the distinction between "seems true" and "is true."[17]

One clear impetus for realism about propositions of law is the belief that there is some "fact of the matter" about legal discourse. We want to know that what we say about the law is true. However, realists want "is true" to mean more than anti-realists do; for the latter, "true" means the satisfaction of intersubjective criteria. For the realist, there must be something more to "is true" than the fact that with respect to a given proposition of law, everyone believes that proposition to be true. Of course, what some realists—call them "metaphysical realists"[18]—seek is an account of the nature of truth wherein "the meaning of 'is true' is given by the correspondence of some sentences to some mind-independent and convention-

---

14. Ronald Dworkin, *Taking Rights Seriously* 81 (1977).

15. Dworkin, *supra* note 1, at 1. In fact, Dworkin goes so far as to say that jurisprudential questions concerning the truth conditions for propositions of law can only be settled by the philosophy of language.

16. *Id.* at 8–9.

17. I owe this way of putting the question to Brian Leiter.

18. Because each may properly be referred to as "naturalists," it is important to state that the positions of Ronald Dworkin and Michael Moore are rather different. Moore seems better described as a "metaphysical realist" because of his unwavering commitment to ontology as the engine of metaphysics and truth. Dworkin, on the other hand, speaks in the language of realism but eschews metaphysical commitments like Moore's. Moore, of course, thinks Dworkin is a "deep conventionalist" at best and, thus, no realist at all. See Michael S. Moore, "A Natural Law Theory of Interpretation," 58 *S. Cal. L. Rev.* 277, 299 n.35 (1985).

independent state of affairs."[19] For the metaphysical realist, legal language *simpliciter* is an incomplete and, thus, inadequate ground of truth (hence, an inadequate justification for a claim to truth). The realist is not satisfied until and unless the language of the law is itself shown to reflect the ways things "in fact" are.[20]

The aspirations of realism are, of course, completely understandable. When we claim that certain things are "the law," we are interested in getting it (the law) right. But, as Donald Davidson reminds us, we do not want to make truth a function of our epistemic powers. As he puts it, "[B]elieving something does not in general make it true."[21] How, then, does the realist move from mere belief to truth? What is it that transforms an intentional state into a judgment worthy of the name "correct" or "true"?

Michael Moore advances a capacious answer to precisely this question:

> A realist theory asserts that the meaning of "death," for example, is not fixed by certain conventions. Rather, a realist theory asserts that "death" refers to a natural kind of event that occurs in the world and that it is not arbitrary that we possess some symbol to name this thing. (It may be arbitrary what symbol we assign to name this class of events, but it is not arbitrary that we have some symbol to name it). Our intentions when we use the word "death" will be to refer to this natural kind of event, whatever its true nature might turn out to be. We will guide our usage, in other words, not by some set of conventions we have agreed upon as to when someone will be said to be dead; rather, we will seek to apply "dead" only to people who are really dead, which we determine by applying the best scientific theory we can muster about what death really is.
>
> Further, on a realist theory of meaning fact will not outrun diction. Continuing with the example of "death": finding out that not all persons who have lost consciousness and who have stopped breathing, have also had their hearts stop, will not leave us "speechless" because we have run out of conventions dealing with such novelties. Rather, either "dead" or "not dead" will have a correct application to the situation, depending on whether the person is really dead or not. Whether a person is really dead or not will be ascertained by applying the best scientific theory we have about what death really is. Our present scientific theory may be inadequate to resolve the issue, but a realist will assert that there are relevant facts about whether the person is or is not dead even if we presently lack the means to find them. A realist, in other words, believes that there is more to what death is (and thus what "death" means) than is captured by our current conventions.

19. Michael S. Moore, "The Interpretive Turn in Modern Theory: A Turn for the Worse?" 41 *Stan. L. Rev.* 871, 878 (1989).

20. It is important to notice that I have not made the *demonstration* of the truth of a proposition of law a requirement of the realist. I do this so that I may bring under the rubric of "realism" the position of Ronald Dworkin, whose claim that there is a right answer to every legal question has always carried with it the tag that the truth of his metaphysical claim about the truth of propositions of law depends in no way on a demonstration that, in a given case, any given answer to a legal question is "right."

21. Donald Davidson, "The Structure and Content of Truth," 87 *J. Phil.* 279, 305 (1990).

Finally, a realist theory of meaning will not view a change in our conventions about when to apply a word as a change in its meaning. If we supplant "heart stoppage" with "revivability" as our indicator of "death," we will do so because we believe revivability to be a part of a better theory of what death is than heart stoppage. We will not have changed the meaning of "death" when we substitute one theory for another, because by "death" we intended to refer to the naturally occurring kind of thing, whatever the true nature of the event turned out to be. Our linguistic intentions are constant, on the realist theory, even if our scientific theories change considerably.[22]

The picture of knowledge presented by the metaphysical moral realist seems to rest on the assumption that the world makes a contribution to the content and character of our knowledge. This contribution comes by way of language. Somehow language is affected by—and may "reflect"—"the way things are" in the world. Thus, no matter what we may *believe* about the world, our *use* of language (not "our language") will be correct or incorrect relative to the way the world *is* not the way we *take* (believe) it to be.

How does the world perform its guidance function?[23] That is, how is it that the world—even a world that, as Moore puts it, "really is"[24] as we take it to be—guides our usage? Moore's answer is that the world makes its informational contribution[25] through our theories. We know, for example, that someone is "really" dead "by applying the best scientific theory we can muster about what death really is."[26]

But does resort to scientific theory meet the realist's burden of proof? The whole point of metaphysical realism is that the truth of language is a function not of anyone's beliefs (including collective beliefs, i.e., theories) but of "the way the world is." In the case of death, the burden of proof cannot be met by the production of evidence that is not *independent* of language. To move from one form of language (law) to another (science) seems not to solve the problem, only change the venue.

Moore is careful to state that he is making no epistemic claim of direct access to reality. To the contrary, Moore embraces a coherence epistemology, one in which "[j]ustification of any belief about anything is a matter of cohering that belief with everything else we believe."[27] The problem with this approach to coherence is, of course, how to square it with Moore's metaphysical moral realism. If the essence of one's metaphysics is appeal to "the nature of . . . things,"[28]

22. Moore, *supra* note 18, at 294.

23. Again, Moore's expression is important here: "We will guide our usage, in other words, not by some set of conventions we have agreed upon as to when someone will be said to be dead; rather, we will seek to apply 'dead' only to people who are really dead, which we determine by applying the best scientific theory we can muster about what death really is." *Id.*

24. *Id.*

25. I label the contribution "informational" because it is the world that is informing us of its actual state or condition.

26. Moore, *supra* note 18, at 294.

27. Michael S. Moore, "Precedent, Induction, and Ethical Generalization," in *Precedent in Law* 183, 198 (Laurence Goldstein ed., 1987).

28. Moore, *supra* note 19, at 882.

then one is committed to the view that the truth of propositions that ostensibly refer to things is a matter of word and world hooking up in a way *that provides a normative check on our linguistic practices*. Moore fails to illumine this crucial connection. Instead of providing some account of how it is that "the real nature of death" underwrites the truth of anything we say, we are directed to another body of talk whose truth claims are equally tendentious. It seems that the realist, at least in the person of Moore, has failed to meet his burden of proof. Unless he can show how, as John McDowell puts it, that "a conception of facts could exert some leverage in the investigation of truth,"[29] it seems the claim "the world makes what we say true and false" is, at best, a platitude.

In the end, a nagging problem for realism, of whatever stripe, is its failure to provide a plausible account of how evidence-transcendent conditions constrain linguistic behavior. It is simply counterintuitive and implausible to argue that something that plays no role in our practices of assertion and justification can, in any meaningful sense, be said to limit what we can say and do.[30] Because meaning is normative,[31] nothing that fails to influence meaning can have any normative role to play in the activity of justification. And yet, realists continue with their talk of limits and right answers as if these alleged constraints had normative force.

Varieties of Jurisprudential Anti-Realism

There are varieties of anti-realism in legal theory, just as in mainstream philosophy. Broadly speaking, for the anti-realist in jurisprudence, it can be said that when it comes to semantic constraint, the strictures are either minimal or fanciful. Again, as with realism, the problem is to come up with an account of seman-

29. John McDowell, "Projection and Truth in Ethics," Lindley Lecture, University of Kansas, Department of Philosophy 11 (1988).

30. See P. M. S. Hacker, "Language, Rules and Pseudo Rules," 8 *Lang. & Commun.* 159, 164 (1988): "It is, therefore, an essential feature of rule-governed behaviour that the normative activities of teaching and training, guiding conduct by reference to rules, justifying, explaining, evaluating are part of the standard context of behaviour. In these normative activities rules are cited, formulated, referred or alluded to. They are *used* as standards of conduct, guides to behaviour and norms for its evaluation. There is no such thing as a rule which has no role, *a fortiori* no such thing as a rule which *could have* no such role. . . . For a form of words or a sign to be the expression or 'representation' of a rule is not an *intrinsic* feature of the sign, but a feature of its employment in a complex activity (just as being a ruler, a sign-post or a model is not an intrinsic feature of an object but a feature of its *use*). Just as sounds or marks on paper, slate or sand do not constitute symbols and are not expressions of propositions unless such sounds or marks have a standard use in the behaviour of symbol-using creatures against a complex context of a form of life, so too nothing can be said to be an expression of a rule unless it is *used* as a rule."

31. See Crispin Wright, *Realism, Meaning and Truth* 24 (2d ed. 1993): "Meaning is normative. To know the meaning of an expression is to know, perhaps unreflectively, how to appraise uses of it; it is to know a set of constraints to which correct uses must conform. Accordingly, to give the meaning of a statement is to describe such constraints; nothing has a claim to be regarded as an account of a statement's meaning which does not succeed in doing so. The argument is now that the realist's truth-conditional conception has indeed no such claim."

tic constraint that has metaphysical bite. The realist wants to say that what we say has to be true in virtue of something beyond the agreement of fellow practitioners. Anti-realists deny that any such constraints exist, or that the whole notion of anything limiting what can be said "truthfully," is an illusion.

Anti-realist arguments come in both strong and weak versions. Before we look at examples of each of these, we would do well to consider just how it is the anti-realist position gets its start. Many in modern jurisprudence see the later work of Wittgenstein, particularly his remarks on rule-following, as providing the best argument for anti-realism. What is Wittgenstein's argument? Let us have a look.

Imagine a scene in which a father is attempting to teach his daughter how to "add." He starts off by showing her the following series of numbers: "0, 2, 4, 6, . . ." He says, "This series shows what it means 'to add.' In this series, the number 2 is added to the number that comes before it. Now, why don't you try to continue the series." The daughter then writes "10." Dad then says "You've made a mistake. I gave you the rule 'add 2' and you failed to follow it."

The *philosophical* problem posed by the example is one of normativity. We can state the problem thus: "What does it mean to say 'You have made a mistake'?" The philosophical problem is about what we mean when we say that someone is or is not "following a rule." By what criteria do we make this judgment? If the judgment is disputed, how can we go about settling the dispute? Are there criteria for deciding the dispute that are "neutral" or "objective"? Is there a "right answer" to the question "Did *X* follow the rule?"

Father claims to have given his daughter a rule, one which, in his view, she has misapplied. Suppose she replies to him "Well, yes, I know what *you* mean by 'add 2.' But I understand the locution 'add 2' to mean 'add 2 up to the number 6 and thereafter 'add 4.'" Dad replies "You don't understand what it means to add." Daughter rejoins "Oh yes I do, I just don't understand it in the same way as you."

Put another way, we might ask "Does the rule itself answer the question 'Who is correct—father or daughter?'"[32] But what do we mean by "the rule"? Surely the bare figures on the page or the sound that emanates from the mouth of the father cannot point the way: they are just scratches and noises. We do not glean the meaning of "add 2" from its material instantiation, either written or oral. But if not, then how is it we understand the locution at all?

Wittgenstein himself, in the voice of his interlocutor,[33] asks this question: "But

---

32. The outstanding English-language interpreters of Wittgenstein, Gordon Baker and Peter Hacker, believe that "the rule itself" answers this question. See G. P. Baker & P. M. S. Hacker, *Wittgenstein: Rules, Grammar and Necessity* 171–72 (1985): "The pivotal point in Wittgenstein's remarks on following rules is that a rule is internally related to acts which accord with it. The rule and nothing but the rule determines what is correct (PI § 189). This idea is incompatible with defining 'correct' in terms of what is normal or standard practice in a community. To take the behavior of the majority to be the criterion of correctness in applying rules is to abrogate the internal relation of a rule to acts in accord with it."

33. The sentence that I quote next appears in Wittgenstein's text as the first of two sentences, both of which are contained within a single set of double quotation marks. As many readers are no doubt aware, many remarks in Wittgenstein's numbered paragraphs are the words of an imaginary

how can a rule shew me what I have to do at *this* point?"[34] An immediate observation is then made: "Whatever I do is, on some interpretation, in accord with the rule."[35] Clearly, by "the rule" the interlocutor means the material inscription that is understood to state the rule. In the form of a verbal command, the rule "add 2" tells us nothing: we need to know what "add" and "2" (and, possibly, their combination) *means*. The rule *itself* does not tell us what it means: the meaning of the rule is not "self evident."[36] What is one to do?[37]

The interlocutor has an answer. We can "interpret" the rule, thereby generating a meaning to which we might then appeal as a ground for our claim to have followed the rule correctly. But this will work neither for father nor for daughter (nor for anyone else) as the interlocutor well knows. The upshot of his remark is that whatever is done (2 is added [father's interpretation]) (or 4 is added after reaching 6 [daughter's interpretation]) is correct if by "correct" one means "consistent with one's interpretation." The point is that, in our hypothetical, the daughter could have written any number for the next number in the series and, under *some* interpretation of the rule, the choice of that particular number would be correct.[38]

This, then, leads to Wittgenstein's statement of the paradox raised by these considerations: "[N]o course of action could be determined by a rule, because

---

interlocutor. In the *Investigations*, the interlocutor plays the role of the philosophical naif, whom Wittgenstein sets right by showing the varied ways in which the interlocutor's questions prescind from philosophical confusions of various sorts.

34. Ludwig Wittgenstein, *Philosophical Investigations* § 198 (G. E. M. Anscombe trans., 3d ed. 1958).

35. *Id.*

36. For discussion of this point, see John Searle, "The Background of Meaning," in *Speech Act Theory and Pragmatics* 230 (John Searle et al. eds., 1980): "It is a fact about human practices that we count certain moves as good arithmetic and certain other moves as bad arithmetic, but there is nothing in the content of the representations that, so to speak, forces us to accept only one set of moves to the exclusion of all others. The representations are not self guaranteeing, and we do not eliminate this dependence by grounding representations in principles, for the principles are further representations which will have different applications relative to different practices and assumptions. Any set of such principles is grounded in practices which are themselves ungrounded." For elaboration of the specifics of Searle's account of the relationship between meaning, representation, and the "background of meaning," see John Searle, *The Rediscovery of the Mind* 175–96 (1992).

37. As we shall see, all of these questions are designed to suggest that something is wrong with the interlocutor's entire line of inquiry. See Meredith Williams, "Blind Obedience," in *Meaning Scepticism* 104 (Klaus Puhl ed., 1991): "In this passage [§ 198] all the key elements of Wittgenstein's alternative have been introduced. First, we need to change our way of looking at the problem, to ask different questions, for the very way we have posed our problem has directed us towards an intellectualist solution, namely a solution in terms of some interpretive act or decision or the like. Secondly, training into a custom or social practice is the way in which we come to follow rules. The process of learning is crucial to our understanding of understanding. Thirdly, meaning is a social phenomenon and so the individual cannot be radically isolated from the community. And finally, in being so trained, the individual has come to master a technique: '. . . and now I do so react to it' (PI § 199)."

38. The paradox from which this example is drawn owes its existence to Nelson Goodman, *Fact, Fiction and Forecast* (1965).

every course of action can be made out to accord with the rule."[39] By itself, the rule determines nothing: "If everything can be made out to accord with the rule, then it can also be made out to conflict with it. And so there would be neither accord nor conflict here."[40]

So how does the anti-realist propose to resolve the paradox and, armed with an account of truth, answer the question "Who (father or daughter) is correct?" Weak anti-realism is neutral on the question. The weak anti-realist simply points out that there is no "correct" way to understand addition, and that "correct" cannot mean anything more than agreement in use with one's interpretive community. This view,[41] which is defended variously by Stanley Fish,[42] Sanford Levinson,[43] and others, received its first expression in the philosophy of Nietzsche:

> "Everything is subjective," you say; but even this is interpretation. The "subject" is not something given, it is something added and invented and projected beyond what there is.—Finally, is it necessary to posit an interpreter behind the interpretation? Even this is invention, hypothesis.
>
> In so far as the word "knowledge" has any meaning, the world is knowable; but it is *interpretable* otherwise, it has no meaning behind it, but countless meanings.—"Perspectivism."
>
> It is our needs that interpret the world; our drives and their For and Against. Every drive is a kind of lust to rule; each one has its perspective that it would like to compel all the other drives to accept as a norm.[44]

The central idea many take from this paragraph is that our understanding of the world is built on some interpretation of it; that all views of the world are a matter of one or another "perspective."[45] Interpretation is, so to speak, the "bridge" between rule and action. Of course, the weak anti-realist does not disagree that propositions of law can be "true." All the weak anti-realist requires is that "true" be understood to mean an interpretation that comports with interpretations others have of the rule.[46] The interpretive version of anti-realism has obvious appeal. If nothing else, it seems to allow one to have some account of truth without the metaphysical baggage of realism, in its several manifestations. But weak anti-realism is not without its problems. If truth is defined as consen-

---

39. Wittgenstein, *supra* note 34, at § 201.

40. *Id.*

41. One expression of weak anti-realism, that of Stanley Fish, is the focus of chapter 6. I focus on weak anti-realism, and Fish's particular expression of it, because his view represents the anti-realist position as it is most commonly understood.

42. See Stanley Fish, *Doing What Comes Naturally* (1989).

43. Sanford Levinson, "Law as Literature," 60 *Tex. L. Rev.* 373 (1982).

44. Friedrich Nietzsche, *The Will to Power* 267 (W. Kaufmann & R. Hollingdale trans., 1968).

45. This view is given its fullest expression in Alexander Nehamas, *Nietzsche: Life as Literature* (1985). For a thorough critique of Nehamas's argument, one that persuades that Nehamas's reading of Nietzsche is seriously flawed, see Brian Leiter, "Perspectivism in Nietzsche's *Genealogy of Morals*," in *Essays on Nietzsche, Genealogy, Morality* (Richard Schacht ed., 1994).

46. For a similar sentiment, see Donald Davidson, "Thought and Talk," in *Inquiries into Truth and Interpretation* 157 (1984) ("[A] creature cannot have thoughts unless it is an interpreter of the speech of another.")

sus among the members of an interpretive community, then it seems that the community can never say anything that is not true. In short, whatever the community says is true. What if the entire community agrees that the earth is flat? Or that 2 + 2 = 6? Is the community correct? Are these "truths"? Avoiding the relativistic implications of anti-realism must be of the utmost importance. If one is to live without the metaphysical comforts provided by realism, an alternative to realism has to show that the relativistic implications of interpretive anti-realism can be avoided.

Strong jurisprudential anti-realists have none of these worries. They see the entire range of issues from truth, meaning, objectivity, and the like, to be little more than a collection of philosophical antiquaria. A familiar version of strong anti-realism is the claim from critical legal studies that the law is "indeterminate." In its sophisticated form, the indeterminacy argument sees legal justification as the outward expression of deeper political commitments. As Roberto Unger, the doyen of critical legal studies, puts it: "[E]very branch of doctrine must rely tacitly if not explicitly upon some picture of the forms of human association that are right and realistic in the areas of social life with which it deals."[47] And why is it necessary for one to have a political theory? "Without such a guiding vision, legal reasoning seems condemned to a game of easy analogies."[48]

One could easily take Unger to be saying that there is no content to law apart from that contributed by some political theory. But Unger is saying something more subtle than this crude reading allows. In words that remind one of Kant's famous lines about intuition and content, Unger states that one should neither accept doctrine blindly nor reject it as a whole. This leaves one in the difficult position of deciding just what to include and what to leave out. To make these choices, "you need a background prescriptive theory of the relevant area of social practice, a theory that does for the branch of law in question what a doctrine of the republic or of the political process does for constitutional argument. This is where the trouble starts."[49] The "trouble," as Unger sees it, is the Achilles' heel of the legal reformer: "No matter what the content of this background theory, it is, if taken seriously and pursued to its ultimate conclusions, unlikely to prove compatible with a broad range of the received understandings."[50]

Unger sees no necessity to the present structure of law.[51] His program of "Deviationist Doctrine" is advanced in the hope of expanding the range of materials that are to count as "doctrine" while increasing the likelihood of social transformation. In short, Unger sees legal doctrine as subject to the play of larger political forces, but not so in the ways one finds in the cruder versions of historical materialism. In short, for Unger, the "truth" of law is a product of a political vision, and nothing more.

47. Roberto M. Unger, *The Critical Legal Studies Movement* 8 (1986).
48. *Id.*
49. *Id.* at 9.
50. *Id.*
51. Nor does he see any "necessity" to the present structure of society. For sustained discussion of this point, the so-called context-smashing perspective, see Roberto M. Unger, *Politics* (1987).

Unger's subtle mix of doctrine and politics contrasts with other versions of the indeterminacy critique. In a much-discussed article in the *Yale Law Journal*, Joseph Singer argues for two seemingly contradictory conclusions.[52] First, he claims that legal doctrine is "indeterminate." How does Singer understand "determinate"? He advances an answer in the context of what one can rightfully expect from a legal theory:

> We cannot expect the new to emerge phoenix-like from the old. Traditional legal theorists have assumed that theory is, or should be *determinative*—that the goals of theory is to *generate answers*. For this view to make sense, we must believe that it is possible to find out what to do by thinking in the right way.
>
> . . .
>
> But in the end, all the sophisticated versions of theory that seek to describe it as a decision procedure based on a sure foundation are supremely unconvincing; they cannot convince precisely because they are so sophisticated. The dilemma comes down to this: For a theory to generate answers, it must be mechanical, yet no mechanical theory can render an adequate account of our experience of legitimate moral choice. We cannot even escape the dilemma by trying to make some of our choices (the "core") mechanical and some (the "periphery") open-ended: *No* mechanical choices appear to be unequivocally valid.[53]

This states the first horn of the apparent contradiction: the law is indeterminate. Thus, legal doctrine "does not fully constrain our choices";[54] "The arguments therefore do not determine the result."[55] If doctrine does not generate choices, what does? This brings us to the second horn of the dilemma. The law is predictable because lawyers and judges share the same legal culture.[56]

> To the extent legal decisions are predictable, they can be explained by legal culture. This does not mean that legal decisions are completely predictable. On many issues, no conventions are available. Many other issues are outside mainstream political controversy and therefore we cannot predict what individual judges will think about them. It is precisely because of these uncertainties as well as gaps in the legal rules, and because legal reasoning is indeterminate and manipulable, that judges often surprise us by using existing arguments to justify results we did not expect.[57]

The essence of Singer's account of the coherence and consistency of legal doctrine is not normative but sociological. Lawyers and judges see the world through the same categories. It is in that seeing—not in anything to do with the categories—that the stability of doctrine resides. Singer does not deny that there is a truth of the matter about law: what he denies is that legal truth is normative.

---

52. Joseph Singer, "The Player and the Cards," 94 *Yale L.J.* 1 (1984).
53. *Id.* at 61.
54. *Id.* at 14.
55. *Id.* at 16.
56. *Id.* at 19–25.
57. *Id.* at 24.

That is, the stability and regularity of law is to be explained *empirically* (e.g., by the methods of sociology), for that is the only form of regularity the law can enjoy. The normative regularity of law is an illusion. Again, no theory can generate answers to legal questions, for to do so "it must be mechanical, yet no mechanical theory can render an adequate account of our experience of legitimate moral choice."[58]

For Singer, legal reasoning is best understood as a sociological phenomenon. The basic form of Singer's account of law is empiricist or social scientific. He asks the question "How is it that we can accurately predict the outcomes of cases?" His answer is causal in form: lawyers and judges are all responding to the same cultural cues. They are not "deciding" cases, because the rules do not compel outcomes. The behavior of lawyers and judges is to be explained as responses to cultural stimuli—shared vocabularies, presuppositions, and so on—and nothing more.

Singer's mistake is classic: he seeks to substitute a causal account of a phenomenon for a normative account.[59] To see the mistake, consider the following from H. L. A. Hart:

> If, however, the observer really keeps austerely to this extreme external point of view and does not give any account of the manner in which members of the group who accept the rules view their own regular behavior, his description of their life cannot be in terms of rules at all, so not in terms of the rule-dependent notions of obligation or duty. Instead, it will be terms of observable regularities of conduct, predictions, probabilities, and signs. For such an observer, deviations by a member of the group from normal conduct will be a sign that hostile reaction is likely to follow and nothing more. His view will be like the view of one who, having observed the working of a traffic signal in a busy street for some time, limits himself to saying that when the light turns red there is a high probability that the traffic will stop. He treats the light merely as a natural *sign that* people will behave in certain ways, as clouds are a *sign that* rain will come. In so doing he will miss out a whole dimension of the social life of those whom he is watching, since for them the red light is not merely a sign that others will stop: they look upon it as a *signal for* them to stop, and so a reason for stopping in conformity to rules which make stopping when the light is red a standard of behavior and an obligation. To mention this is to bring into the account the way in which the group regards its

---

58. *Id.* at 61.

59. Philip Bobbitt, whose position is the subject of chapter 7, diagnoses the problem with characteristic succinctness. See Philip Bobbitt, *Constitutional Interpretation* 24 (1991): "Although most people may to some extent hold the view . . . that there *must* be some sublime explanatory mechanism that allows our ideas to interact with the world—there is no reason to think so. . . . Law is something we do, not something we have as a consequence of something we do. Sometimes our activities in law—deciding, proposing, persuading—may link up with specific ideas we have at those moments; but often they do not, and it is never the case that this link must be made for the activities that are law to be law. Therefore the causal accounts of how those inner states come into being, accounts that lose their persuasiveness in contact with the abundance of the world, are really beside the point. If we want to understand the ideological and political commitments in law, we have to study the grammar of law, that system of logical constraints that the practices of legal activities have developed in our particular culture."

behavior. It is to refer to the internal aspect of rules seen from their internal point of view.[60]

Hart's point here is one about normativity. One cannot understand the nature of justification without investigating how individuals in a practice *use* rules as justifications in appraising another's behavior. Singer thinks that if a rule does dictate results "mechanically" it can play no justificatory role. This is absurd. Were it true, we could not understand how rules govern everything from cello performance, to chess, to traffic regulations. Are all these activities, which we see as governed by rules, to be dismissed as merely behavioral responses to cultural stimuli?

Beyond Realism and Anti-Realism

Some philosophers argue that the realism/anti-realism debate in philosophy is a pseudodebate. Put succinctly, the problem with the debate appears to be the terms on which it is conducted. The central difficulty is that the participants share a dubious premise about the nature of truth. Both realist and anti-realist alike believe that the truth of propositions of law is a matter of truth conditions. Each believes propositions of law can be true; the disagreement is over what (conditions) in virtue of which propositions of law are true.

Jurisprudential realists and anti-realists share with their philosophical brethren the belief that issues of meaning and truth start from the distinction between beliefs and truths. A belief that some proposition of law is true does not make the proposition true. The belief is true if and only if some state of affairs obtains that makes the proposition true. It is that state of affairs which, when accessed by the lawyer, licenses the attribution of knowledge. What the lawyer has knowledge *of* is a fact of some sort. The relationship of that fact to the asserted proposition is one of truth or falsity. Thus, jurisprudential realists and anti-realists each subscribe to the following account of legal knowledge, meaning, and truth:

1. Take the following legal proposition: "Lawyer *L* knows the meaning of *P*";
2. The meaning of *P* = the truth conditions of *P*;
3. The truth conditions of *P* are *TC*;
4. *L* knows that the truth conditions of *P* are *TC*.[61]

Jurisprudential realists and anti-realists agree that the meaning of legal propositions is given by their truth conditions. What they *disagree* over are, at least, the nature of those truth conditions. Realists maintain that the truth conditions for propositions of law are or may be given by states of affairs to which we do not have direct epistemic access. Anti-realists deny that we lack access to the truth conditions for propositions of law. Additionally, and perhaps more importantly,

---

60. H. L. A. Hart, *The Concept of Law* 89–90 (2d ed. 1994).

61. This is adapted from Richard Rorty, "Pragmatism, Davidson and Truth," in 1 Richard Rorty, *Philosophical Papers (Objectivity, Relativism, and Truth)* 147 (1991).

anti-realists affirm that the truth conditions for propositions of law are entirely social in nature.[62]

Recall Dworkin's criticism of legal positivism. Positivism asserts that a proposition of law is true if the requisite social facts obtain that make the proposition true. Dworkin denies the plausibility of the positivist account with his claim that a proposition of law may be true even if there is no legislative fact of the matter that, on the positivist account, would make the proposition true. Dworkin wants to tell a different story about the truth conditions for propositions of law. For him, "propositions of law are true if they figure in or follow from the principles of justice, fairness, and procedural due process that provide the best constructive interpretation of the community's legal practice."[63]

Dworkin shares with positivism the premise that the debate over the nature of truth is a struggle over the "correct perception of the true grounds of law."[64] This is the premise I wish to dispute. Further, I believe that the truth of propositions of law depends not at all on the existence of conditions, factual or otherwise. The truth of a proposition of law is not a matter of the relationship of the proposition to something (e.g., a social fact) that *makes* the proposition true. Rather, the truth of a proposition of law is shown through the use of forms of legal argument. It is in the use of these forms of argument—the grammar of legal justification—that a proposition of law is shown to be true.

The heart of the position I advocate, one that goes "beyond realism and anti-realism," is in the denial of the truth-conditional account of propositions of law. "True" does not name a relationship between a state of affairs and a proposition of law. "True" is best understood disquotationally. For example, when a statute becomes law, it is true that the legislature has done something. But the *meaning* of what the legislature has done is not given by the fact of their having done something. The meaning of their corporate act—what the act amounts to—is given by the practice of statutory interpretation. Apart from the forms of legal argument appropriate to the reading of statutes, the promulgation and passage of a statute has no meaning at all. Only in a practice of reading statutes do we know what the legislature has done. We cannot say that the legislature has done anything (and, thus, we cannot say anything about what the law is) apart from our practice of statutory interpretation. Let us consider an example.

In *United Steel Workers of America v. Weber*,[65] the Supreme Court considered the question whether Title VII prohibits voluntary affirmative action in training activities. One focus of the Court's attention was the following statute:

> It shall be an unlawful employment practice for any employer, labor organization, or joint labor-management committee controlling apprenticeship or other training or retraining, including on-the-job training programs to dis-

---

62. For example, Hart argues that the existence of social facts about legislative action are the truth conditions for propositions of law. Stanley Fish argues that propositions of law are true just in case there is a convergence of interpretational presuppositions.

63. Ronald Dworkin, *Law's Empire* 225 (1986).

64. *Id.* at 6.

65. 443 U.S. 193 (1979). This case is discussed in more detail in chapter 4.

criminate against any individual because of his race, color, religion, sex, or national origin in admission to, or employment in, any program established to provide apprenticeship or other training.[66]

On its face, the statute would seem to preclude the type of plan at issue in *Weber*. The form of argument at work is textual argument, which involves appeal to the ordinary meaning of the words of the statute. The force of the appeal of textual argument comes out in the words of Justice Rehnquist, who dissented from the majority's decision approving the affirmative action plan: "Were Congress to act today specifically to prohibit the type of racial discrimination suffered by Weber, it would be hard pressed to draft language better tailored to the task than that found in § 703 (d) of Title VII."

In affirming the legality of the affirmative action plan, the majority in *Weber* appealed not to the language of Title VII but to the history surrounding the promulgation and passage of the statute. The majority set up the historical argument with a doctrinal argument.

> Respondent's argument is not without force. But it overlooks the significance of the fact that the Kaiser-USWA plan is an affirmative action plan voluntarily adopted by private parties to eliminate traditional patterns of racial segregation. In this context respondent's reliance upon a literal construction of §§ 703 (a) and (d) and upon *McDonald* is misplaced. See *McDonald v. Santa Fe Trail Transp. Co.*, *supra*, at 281 n. 8. It is a "familiar rule, that a thing may be within the letter of the statute and yet not within the statute, because not within its spirit, nor within the intention of its makers." *Holy Trinity Church v. United States*, 143 U.S. 457, 459 (1892). The prohibition against racial discrimination in §§ 703 (a) and (d) of Title VII must therefore be read against the background of the legislative history of Title VII and the historical context from which the Act arose.[67]

Having set up the need to consult history, the majority then shifted to the historical form of argument. After recounting the motivations of Congress in promulgating this legislation, the majority concluded that "[t]he natural inference is that Congress chose not to forbid all voluntary race-conscious affirmative action."[68] The majority uses three forms of legal argument—textual, doctrinal and historical—to show that the proposition in question[69] is true. The forms of argument are the means by which the Court appraises the proposition in question. Truth and falsity are not properties of legal propositions, nor are the forms of argument truth conditions for propositions of law. They are the means for showing that propositions of law are true or false.

---

66. 78 Stat. 256, 42 U.S.C. § 2000e–2(d) (1976).
67. 443 U.S. at 201.
68. *Id.* at 206.
69. The proposition was stated by the majority in the form of a question: "The question for decision is whether Congress, in Title VII of the Civil Rights Act of 1964, 78 Stat. 253, as amended, 42 U.S.C. § 2000e et seq., left employers and unions in the private sector free to take such race-conscious steps to eliminate manifest racial imbalances in traditionally segregated job categories." 443 U.S. at 197.

Plan of the Present Work

This introduction began with the question of how three concepts are related: meaning, truth, and knowledge. I introduced the realism/anti-realism debate to relate the contemporary philosophical discussion of these issues to similar current debates in contemporary legal theory. I have suggested that in law, legal forms of argument constitute the terms for appraising the truth of propositions of law. Nothing *makes* our legal utterances true. Truth in law is neither a property nor a relation. Truth is not an explanatorily useful concept. Likewise, meaning is not to be explained as a matter of conditions. One cannot say something meaningful in law without using the grammar of legal argument. Getting a clear surview of this grammar is the task of jurisprudence.

We now have a context for the question this book addresses, namely, what it means to say that a proposition of law is true. The last chapter presents an answer to the question, albeit one that departs significantly from the answers provided by other commentators who have devoted themselves to this question. Despite my disagreements with their views, my position develops both directly and indirectly from interaction with, and criticism of, their positions. Each view has much to recommend it. At one point or another, something in each has attracted my attention and, in some cases, I have adopted the point of view as my own. But after sustained thinking about the question of truth, I have departed decidedly from almost all the positions discussed here. This in no way undermines the fact that I have learned much from the work of those whom I criticize.

The book moves through each of the major positions with an eye on the final chapter which presents my account of what it means to say that a proposition of law is true. While much of the book is critical, the position I ultimately develop emerges out of the arguments and positions of those other views. Without this background, the alternative nature of my position could not be appreciated.

2

Legal Formalism:
On the Immanent Rationality of Law

Those who dismiss legal formalism as a naïve illusion, mistaken in its claims and pernicious in its effects, do not know what they are in for.

Roberto M. Unger[1]

The genuine refutation must penetrate the opponent's stronghold and refute him on his own ground; no advantage is gained by attacking him somewhere else and defeating him where he is not.

Hegel[2]

Formalism is the most maligned contemporary approach to jurisprudence. Yet, after countless dismissals, formalism survives. One explanation for its survival is that, at some level, it appeals to our deepest intuitions about law. If anything is to be ordered, structured, or internally coherent, law should be a prime candidate. But if there is a structure to law—a form—what is it? If the law embodies a certain form, an intelligible order, is the order there to be found or is it we who put it there? These are some of the questions at issue in the formalist approach.

Ernest Weinrib's defense of legal formalism[3] is the most sophisticated articulation of a formalist jurisprudence in the literature. The central claim of Weinrib's argument lies in the primacy of what he refers to as *immanent intelligibility*.[4] Weinrib believes that the only way to maintain the dichotomy between law and politics is to understand law on its own terms or, as he puts it, "from the internal point of view."[5] Fundamental to Weinrib's argument for formalism is his belief that an enterprise such as law can (indeed, must) be understood strictly on its own terms.

1. Roberto M. Unger, *Knowledge and Politics* 92 (1975).
2. G. W. F. Hegel, *The Science of Logic* 581 (A.V. Miller trans., 1969).
3. The most succinct articulation of Weinrib's general jurisprudence is Ernest Weinrib, "Legal Formality: On the Immanent Rationality of Law," 97 *Yale L.J.* 949 (1988) [hereinafter "Legal Formality"]. The fullest expression of his position is Ernest Weinrib, *The Idea of Private Law* (1995) [hereinafter, *Private Law*] (In this latter work, Weinrib defends the proposition that formalism provides the best account of the nature of private law.).
4. Weinrib, "Legal Formality," *supra* note 3, at 955 ("[F]ormalism postulates that juridical content can somehow sustain itself from within.").
5. *Id.* at 951 ("Formalism postulates that law is intelligible as an internally coherent phenomenon.").

This chapter is a presentation and critique of Weinrib's unique approach to formalism, which he has championed over the course of the last two decades. First introduced in the context of tort law, the course of Weinrib's development of formalism culminates in his recent book *The Idea of Private Law*.[6] In that work, Weinrib defends the notion that private law has an internal, conceptual structure that cannot be grasped by "external" critiques of law,[7] such as one finds in virtually every other contemporary jurisprudence.

The plausibility of the formalist enterprise depends upon the success of its metaphysical claims, specifically that law has a conceptual and normative structure independent of the play of external, usually political, interests. In this structure, which thought and critical reflection are capable of disclosing, lies the nature of law.

Apropos of our question concerning the truth of propositions of law, formalism asserts that a proposition of law is true if the stated proposition is consistent with the structure of private law, correctly understood. The structure of private law is dependent in the first instance on Aristotle's distinction between corrective and distributive justice. This distinction is a necessary one: to mix the forms of justice is to embrace incoherence. In short, truth for the formalist is a matter of coherence.

The formalist account of coherence and truth depends ultimately on the degree to which we may ignore Aristotle's distinction between corrective and distributive justice. Traditionally, when a concept or distinction is one which cannot be ignored, the notion may be said to be *necessary* to the enterprise in question. In the course of this chapter, I spell out formalism's claims for the juridical necessity of the distinction between corrective and distributive justice. Further, I seek to show that those claims are not successful, in part because the alleged necessity is simply asserted but not shown. Additionally, I argue that formalism's account of human understanding is defective because it fails to take human interests into account. Thus, what is trumpeted as a virtue turns out to be a defect.

The Formalist Account of Legal Understanding

If Weinrib's account of legal formalism is correct, then virtually every other jurisprudence is misconceived. In other words, were Weinrib's claims for the necessity of understanding law from the "internal" perspective to turn out to be correct, then virtually every competing description of legal activity could amount to nothing more than a failed attempt at accurate representation of the true nature of law. The justification for this sweeping characterization is clear: any attempt

6. Weinrib, *Private Law, supra* note 3.

7. The meaning of "external" will be enhanced and clarified later in this chapter. Briefly, external approaches to law (economics, sociology, philosophy) attempt to explain law from the point of view of another discourse. For example, tort law might best be explained as the pursuit of efficiency or distributive justice.

to understand law from anything but a perspective "internal" to law is necessarily a defective account of the enterprise. Why? Because, according to Weinrib, only an internal account of law's intelligibility can guarantee the separation of law from politics.[8]

Weinrib's formalism is premised on the claim that law is an "immanently intelligible enterprise."[9] The nature of law is such that it can only be (fully) understood from the internal point of view. As Weinrib puts it, the "internal standpoint cannot be ignored: Only by reference to it is legal philosophy assured of having made contact with its subject matter [law]."[10]

The subtlety of Weinrib's argument lies in his ingenious synthesis of the metaphysics of Aristotle, Aquinas, Hegel, and Kant.[11] Following Hegel, Weinrib links the intelligibility of law to the immanence of the subject (the self) in legal discourse. While the meaning of immanence in Hegel may be somewhat opaque, Weinrib's use of the term is clear. "Immanent" to law means "inside" legal discourse. To understand the structure (form) of law it is *necessary* (but not sufficient) to have a thorough acquaintance with legal subject matter.

The necessity of examining law from the internal perspective is grounded in the requirement of reflection.[12] Again, the inspiration is Hegel for whom the idea of philosophical method requires not reflection upon an object merely as it appears in sensory experience but rather a method that "by contrast, does not behave as an external reflection, but takes what is determinate from its object itself, for it is itself its soul and immanent principle."[13] Reflection is a process of thought that is triggered by the situation in which the reflecting subject finds herself. It is the

8. In Weinrib's view, the importance of critical legal studies lies in its highlighting the importance of keeping separate the political and legal spheres. See Weinrib, "Legal Formality," *supra* note 3, at 1016: "For the formalist, the salutary contribution of Critical Legal Studies is to show that once we step outside the most rigorous notion of internal coherence, the slide to nihilism is swift and easy. In this sense, Critical Legal Studies captures the essence of contemporary scholarship by accentuating—and then exploding—its makeshift compromises. The significance of Critical Legal Studies is that it forces us to confront anew the problem of coherence in law. It raises the eternal question of legal philosophy, and presents us with its own skeptical answer."

9. As Weinrib states, "Immanent intelligibility is not a subclass but a paradigm of intelligibility." Weinrib, "Legal Formality," *supra* note 3, at 963. The importance to Weinrib's account of the necessity of understanding from the internal point of view places his account of knowledge within the tradition of Hegel: "Immanent criticism must give up the deeply felt epistemological need to impose its own standards upon the subject matter. Any such external input, what Hegel calls 'our addition' (*unsere Zutat*), must be avoided by the philosopher, who is allowed only to observe (*Zusehen*) consciousness. There is no point, then, in trying to determine a priori rules of evidence for what is to count as knowledge or how it is to be verified. The idea of an immanent critique, or phenomenological self-reflection, means rather that we need only test knowledge against itself." Steven B. Smith, *Hegel's Critique of Liberalism: Rights in Context* 153–54 (1989).

10. Weinrib, "Legal Formality," *supra* note 3, at 952.

11. The thought of Aristotle, Aquinas, Hegal, and Kant runs throughout the entire body of Weinrib's work, but is most explicit in Ernest Weinrib, "Corrective Justice," 77 *Iowa L. Rev.* 403 (1992).

12. "Juristic activity includes reflection on its own self-understandings and aspirations." Weinrib, "Legal Formality," *supra* note 3, at 952.

13. G. W. F. Hegel, *Wissenschaft der Logik* 491, quoted and translated in Michael Rosen, *Hegel's Dialectic and Its Criticism* 89 (1982). In terms of the dichotomy between subject and object,

promise of formalism to render experience intelligible as an idea: if you think about (reflect on) what is going on you will come to see that (legal) experience not only "makes sense," but must make sense *in a certain way.*

The fundamental problem with all current attempts at legal theory, so the formalist argues, is that they merely take account of law from one or another external perspective.[14] Because these perspectives are external to (the Idea of) law, they are at best *partial* perspectives and thus *necessarily* defective.[15] Likewise, positive law (what we *call* "law") may itself be defective because it fails to conform to the Idea of law understood from the internal point of view.[16]

The Idea of Form

Law is constituted by form. Form renders juridical relationships intelligible as such. Form is what makes something intelligible, making it what it is and distinguishing it from all other things.[17] In other words, form makes the object or idea intelligible to a subject capable of cognition.[18] As an object of consciousness, form must be grasped as a unity, that is, as a unity of content.

For Weinrib, form and content "are correlative and interpenetrating."[19] Form determines content, and content determines form. A form without content "would not be a form *of* anything"[20] and a content without form would be unintelligible: it would simply be a congeries of particulars. Form gives content to an ensemble of particulars by organizing them into a coherent notion.[21] Content is what form renders intelligible, such that it can be recognized as a something.

---

reflection takes "consciousness as its own object, thinking about thinking, examining (as opposed to employing) the understanding." Robert Solomon, *In the Spirit of Hegel* 282 (1983).

14. For example, critical legal studies sees law as a discourse that imports politics. Law and economics conceives of law as an expression of nonlegal values such as efficiency.

15. For a thoroughgoing critique of the partiality of modern contract theory from the Hegelian perspective, see Peter Benson, "Abstract Right and the Possibility of a Nondistributive Conception of Contract: Hegel and Contemporary Contract Theory," 10 *Cardozo L. Rev.* 1077 (1989) (a critique of the theories of Michael Sandel, Charles Fried, and Anthony Kronman).

16. Weinrib's principal example of such an analytical failure is the incorporation of strict liability into tort law. See Weinrib, *Private Law, supra* note 3, at 171–203 (asserting that strict liability is incompatible with corrective justice).

17. As Weinrib puts it, "When we seek the intelligibility of something, we want to know *what* the something is." Weinrib, "Legal Formality," *supra* note 3, at 958.

18. In short, form is both causal and normative. See Ernest Weinrib, "Why Legal Formalism?" in *Natural Law Theory* 341, 353 (Robert George ed., 1992): "When applied to law, form refers to the structure of justification immanent in a juridical relationship. Formalism focuses on the ensemble of concepts and institutions that gives a specific juridical relationship its character. The coherence of the juridical relationship consists in the participation by these concepts and institutions in a single justificatory structure. Generic differences between juridical relationships reflect differences in their underlying justificatory structures. Formalism accordingly elucidates the possibilities from justificatory coherence latent within specific juridical relationships."

19. Weinrib, "Legal Formality," *supra* note 3, at 959.

20. *Id.*

21. It is form that a subject comprehends.

The analysis of form and content, and the necessary relation of one to the other, is enlarged and clarified by Weinrib's discussion of the three interrelated aspects of form and content. They are character, unity, and genericity. The character of a thing is what makes it what it is; those things the lack of which would destroy its uniqueness. This is its essence.[22] The structure or unity of a thing displays the integrative element of form. When we grasp a thing's form, "we understand the thing neither as an aggregate of independently intelligible properties nor as a homogeneous unit consisting of an extended single property."[23] Rather, what we see is one *thing* with a number of *integrated* parts. It is the "oneness" of the parts that is their structure. Finally, the genericity of a thing's character is that by virtue of which we are able "to regard all the instances of the matter in question as having the same character and as being other than whatever has a different character."[24]

To make his point here, Weinrib offers the example of a table, the set of properties of which "is found in all tables."[25] This set of properties "constitutes the genericity of what it is to be a table."[26] He explains:

> The form of a table is the design that guides the artisan to impart to the chosen material a set of attributes (elevation, flatness, hardness, smoothness, and so on) that make something a table. In the classical understanding of form, the representation present to the artisan's mind— . . . "the form, plan, or design of the table"—is the principle that organizes these attributes into the single thing known as a table. The set of properties that embodies this form is what makes something a table. Accordingly, the form of a table is present in all tables and enables us to classify them *as* tables.[27]

For the formalist, form and content are inherently related: one is inexplicable without the other. Form organizes the ensemble of particulars that is its content; but only certain content can cohere under a given form. This is the idea of genericity. A thing's essence is what marks it as what it is, and without which it would not be what it is. Having unpacked the idea of form, we now move from the level of necessary conceptual structure to that of epistemology. Now that we know why things are what they are (conceptual necessity) we need to know how we recognize them as such (epistemology).

Immanent Intelligibility

Let us continue to discuss the notion of "table" as a preliminary to introducing the central metaphysical element of formalism, that of immanent intelligibility.[28]

22. Weinrib, "Legal Formality," *supra* note 3, at 960.
23. *Id.*
24. *Id.*
25. *Id.*
26. *Id.*
27. Weinrib, *Private Law*, supra note 3, at 28.
28. Weinrib, "Legal Formality," *supra* note 3, at 961.

The centrality of immanent intelligibility lies in the fact that it alone guarantees the separation of law from politics. This separation is both conceptual and epistemological. When dividing the world into this and that, it is of the utmost importance that in deciding which things are which, we find them as they *are* and not as we take them to be. Again, this is a matter of getting their form right. In discerning form we need to be wary of the danger of externalism—that in our inquiry we "are not exhibiting anything about the thing but only about ourselves."[29]

So what of the table? In discerning its form, how are we to avoid the dangers of externalism? Weinrib cautions against taking the obvious route and approaching the object "from the outside"—that is, from the perspective of "our external requirements as users, observers, and inquirers."[30] For instance, to see the rectangular shape before us as a table is to see that it fits the purposes for which we have tables.[31] But this, Weinrib urges, is the wrong way to go about the business of intelligibility. Form, on this view, "bespeaks an intelligibility introduced from the outside."[32] Form, Weinrib insists, is illuminated from within.

Why is the external mode of understanding defective? Because it presupposes the existence of "a qualitative disjunction between the inquirer's thought and the object of the enquiry."[33] Objects are not merely given to us in experience, they are, as it were, "constituted" by thought.[34] Like Hegel, Weinrib wants to eliminate the barest possibility that true judgments could be contingent at all.[35] He says exactly this: "Inasmuch as law's nature is to be immanently intelligible,

29. *Id.*

30. *Id.*

31. See, e.g., Stanley Cavell, *The Claim of Reason* 71 (1979) (a Wittgensteinian analysis of the grammar of "chair").

32. Weinrib, "Legal Formality," *supra* note 3, at 961.

33. *Id.* As Michael Rosen points out, the point Hegel makes in this connection is, *contra* Kant, that there is no "distinction between the way things are and the way they appear to the subject." Rosen, *supra* note 13, at 132. See G. W. F. Hegel, *Logic*, Part 1 of *Encyclopedia* 232 (W. Wallace trans., 1975): "To form a notion of an object means therefore to become aware of its notion: and when we proceed to a criticism or judgment of the object, we are not performing a subjective act, and merely ascribing this or that predicate to the object. We are, on the contrary, observing the object in the specific character imposed by its notion."

34. Weinrib makes precisely this claim when he states that "law is *constituted* by thought: Its content is made up of the concepts (e.g., cause, remoteness, duty, consideration, offer and acceptance) that inform juridical relationships." Weinrib, "Legal Formality," *supra* note 3, at 962.

35. The following summary of the positions of Kant and Hegel on this point will make clearer Weinrib's view of the details of understanding: "To sum up: Hegel and Kant agree that sense or intuition are cognitively deficient because of their intrinsic particularity. Their joint position can be expressed as a simple argument: (1) Intrinsically what we receive through our senses is a manifold of particulars. (2) *But* our experience shows order and universality; it is cognitive. (3) *Therefore* our experience contains a further component which is the source of this order and universality. The two disagree, however, about the nature of this source. Hegel rejects Kant's transcendental psychology according to which the synthesis is a subsuming, ordering activity of the knowing subject. The source of order is now a realistically construed component of reality, the Absolute Spirit as *Logos*. The knowing subject comes into harmony with reality not by imposing his order on a received material but because there is present and active in himself (even if unconsciously) the freely self-developing Thought." Rosen, *supra* note 13, at 104–05. Weinrib appears to agree with Hegel

one can grasp this nature without distortion. Just as one can understand geometry by working through a geometrical perplexity from the inside, so one can understand law by an effort of mind that penetrates to, and participates in, the structure of thought that law embodies."[36]

In sum, understanding is internal, coherent, and integrative.

The Truth of Coherence

As we have seen, there are three central, related aspects to the understanding of concepts or notions:[37] character, unity, and genericity. Every notion must have its central elements (character)—those that mark it uniquely as what it is. These elements must go together and must do so "all of a piece" (unity); only then can we see all instances of the notion as being "of the same character" (genericity). Understanding, seeing something as what it is and not as something else, is a matter of seeing the congruence between idea and actuality, the idea of the thing and its instance, the universal and the particular.[38]

Although necessary to it, these three aspects do not complete Weinrib's picture of conceptual understanding. In identifying the essential elements of a juridical notion, it is of the utmost importance to see that not only do the elements of a notion go together in a certain way, they *must* go together in *just* that way if the notion is to be at all intelligible. When we reflect upon law or, more precisely, the nature of juridical notions, we must—if understanding is to be achieved—reach the point where we see the essential elements of a notion cohere in a certain way and, further, appreciate the fact that they must so cohere if we are to make any sense at all of legal relations.

In this connection, consider the concept of negligence. One does not learn the meaning of negligence simply by studying specific contexts in which the concept or word "negligence" is used.[39] One understands the meaning of negligence when one sees the various acts of negligence as "representing broader legal concepts (for instance, duty, cause, and fault)."[40] When we think through the

---

and Kant that it is thought that constitutes the ideas with which we make sense of experience. However, he agrees with Kant rather than Hegel that when it comes to putting ideas and experience together, the process is subsumptive—experience is subsumed under mental categories. See Weinrib, "Legal Formality," *supra* note 3, at 976 ("[I]nclusiveness is achieved not by adding another item to an aggregation, but by subsuming the item under a higher level of abstraction.").

36. Weinrib, "Legal Formality," *supra* note 3, at 961.

37. I shall use "concept" or "notion" interchangeably. Hegel uses the German term "*Begriff*," which sometimes means one or the other, but is usually translated as "notion."

38. Weinrib, "Legal Formality," *supra* note 3, at 959 ("We understand something when form and content are congruent.").

39. Formalism is not about "the meaning of words." See Weinrib, *Private Law, supra* note 3, at 31: "[It is a] misconception . . . that formalism is concerned with the meaning or the use of words like "private law" and "tort law." Under this misconception, questions like "What is private law?" or "What is tort law?" are queries not into the salient features or private law and tort law, but into the entitlement to use the words "private law" and "tort law." The formalist specification of the character of private law or tort law is seen as an attempt to determine proper semantic meaning

categories that constitute tort law, those that make it what it is, we see that it is these notions that constitute the very means of intelligibility, without which we would be unable to make sense of a battery as a tort. Again, this understanding—which is by its nature juridical—can only be achieved through reflection—reflection upon and movement toward recognition of those concepts that, taken, together, constitute the notion of a "tort."

Central to Weinrib's account of immanent intelligibility is the idea of coherence. Not only must juridical notions have certain elements, those elements must be *coherently* related to each other.[41] As he sees it, the central question is: "Do they [the elements] constitute a coherent ensemble?"[42] To continue with the tort example, the elements of the concept of "tort" must be both internally coherent, one to the other, and they must be coherently related to other aspects of the juridical system. For example, in negligence law the internal coherence of the concept of negligence requires a bipolar litigational structure of plaintiff and defendant. Damages, which represent "the remedial expression of bipolarity,"[43] mandate that the defendant and not some third party be the agent responsible for paying compensation.[44] Were some other entity, an insurance fund for instance, required to compensate the successful plaintiff, the coherence of the juridical relation between notion (negligence) and structure (bipolarity) would be

---

or linguistic usage. The upshot is that features of positive law that do not satisfy the formalist strictures are not really what is meant by "private law" or "tort law"—a conclusion that, even if it were at all important, might be confirmed or refuted simply by canvassing the appropriate community of language users."

40. Weinrib, "Legal Formality," *supra* note 3, at 967.

41. A different conception of unity is at work in material objects than one finds in legal notions. See Weinrib, *Private Law, supra* note 3, at 29–30: "A different conception of unity applies to the attributes of tables than applies to the features of a juridical relationship. A table brings together a group of predicates that . . . 'have in their own nature no affinity with one another.' The table may be hard, smooth, and elevated, but hardness has in itself nothing to do with smoothness, nor smoothness with height. These otherwise diverse properties come together in a single object 'only in so far as the form . . . demands the copresence of them all.' Although coexisting in the table, the properties as such are indifferent to one another. A more stringent conception of unity applies to juridical relationships, especially to those of private law. As I have noted, private law values its coherence. The coherence of a private law relationship refers to more than the copresence of a number of otherwise independent features. . . . For a juridical relationship to be coherent, its component features must come together not through the operation of something beyond them that brings them together but because they are conceptually connected in such a way that, in some sense still to be explained, they intrinsically belong together."

42. Weinrib, "Legal Formality," *supra* note 3, at 968.

43. *Id.* at 969.

44. As Weinrib explains, "The idea that money should be exacted from some for the benefit of others in order to spread the burden of a catastrophic loss as lightly and as widely as possible is as pertinent to a non-tortious, as to a tortious, injury. The levies loss-spreading justifies are not confined to tortfeasors. Accordingly, the appropriate institutional setting for loss-spreading is not the bipolarity of litigation, but a general scheme of social insurance or taxation that would spread accidental loss as thinly and broadly as possible. The restrictions arising out of the adjudicative format do not, therefore, correspond to any feature internal to the idea of loss-spreading. Rather, they are imposed on this idea from outside it, so that it is not operationalized to the full extent of its normative reach." *Id.* at 971.

upset. The unity of the various elements must be coherent, with the price of failure being the creation of a "conceptual monstrosity."[45]

But what is the ground of coherence and incoherence? For this, we must return to Aristotle's discovery of private law.[46] Aristotle identified two forms of justice: corrective and distributive. According to Weinrib, Aristotle's two forms of justice are "so inclusive and abstract . . . that [they] apply to any legal ordering of external interaction."[47] In short, taken together, corrective and distributive justice exhaust the possibilities of justice. Additionally, central to the formalist position is the requirement that the forms of justice remain distinct: to mix the forms is to embrace incoherence.

Corrective justice is the structure of private law. Weinrib summarizes the features of corrective justice thus:

> Justice is effected by an award of damages and the consequent transfer of a certain amount of money from one party to the other. The award of damages simultaneously quantifies the wrong suffered by plaintiff and the wrongfulness inflicted by the defendant. It thus expresses the integration of action and injury in the wrong that one litigant has done to the other. This wrong, and the damage award that undoes it, represents a single nexus of activity and passivity where actor and victim are defined in relation to each other.[48]

Under distributive justice, by contrast, the law's task is "to divide the benefit or the burden according to some criterion."[49] Distributive justice is a form of mediated interaction.[50] It is mediated because what it regulates does not come from the form of justice itself but from outside it. Distributive justice integrates three elements:

1. the benefit or burden that is the subject of the distribution,
2. the recipients among whom the benefit or burden is to be established,
3. the criterion according to which the distribution is to take place.

In this connection, consider a decision by a legislature to set up a scheme of worker's compensation that denies a benefit to one group but not others. The benefit in question is worker's compensation. Who is to receive this benefit? All workers? Some? If less than all, by what criterion is the distribution of the benefit to be made? These are the questions with which distributive justice is concerned.

Because corrective justice is the structure of private law, no juridical decision worth the name may prescind from the framework of corrective justice. Form requires that justification proceed from within the form appropriate to the question at hand. If the question is a matter of justice between persons, then private

---

45. Strict liability is just such a monstrosity, for it imposes liability in the absence of fault, thereby joining conceptually a scheme of corrective justice (tort law) with a scheme of distributive justice (loss spreading).

46. This is Weinrib's characterization. See Weinrib, *Private Law, supra* note 3, at 56 ("In the history of legal philosophy, private law is Aristotle's discovery.").

47. Weinrib, "Legal Formality," *supra* note 3, at 977.

48. *Id.* at 978.

49. *Id.* at 979.

50. *Id.* at 980.

law is the appropriate form. If the issue is one of the distribution of a benefit or burden across a population, then distributive justice is the appropriate framework. Incoherence results when the wrong form is employed to solve a legal problem or when the forms are mixed together.

An example of the difference between a coherent ordering and a conceptual monstrosity is found in *Lamb v. London Borough of Camden*.[51] In *Lamb*, the plaintiff homeowner sued a municipality for negligence that caused damage to her residence. In the course of repairing a broken sewer pipe, a contractor hired by the municipality breached a water main, which flooded the plaintiff's house. Squatters moved into the plaintiff's house soon after it became vacant. They were ejected and, despite the plaintiff's boarding up the house, squatters returned, this time damaging the premises. The legal question raised by the case was whether the municipality was liable for the damage caused by the second group of squatters.

The case comes down to the quite specific question whether the damage caused by the second group of squatters was sufficiently proximate to the act of the contractor that the judgment could be made that the negligence requirement of proximate cause had been met. The majority opinion of the court, written by Lord Denning, cast the question as one "of policy."[52] He put the matter this way:

> [T]he criminal acts here, malicious damage and theft, are usually covered by insurance. By this means the risk of loss is spread throughout the community. It does not fall too heavily on one pair of shoulders alone. The insurers take the premium to cover just this sort of risk and should not be allowed, by subrogation, to pass it on to others.
>
> . . .
>
> So here, it seems to me, that, if Mrs. Lamb was insured against damage to the house and theft, the insurers should pay the loss. If she was not insured, that is her misfortune.[53]

In his concurring opinion, Lord Justice Watkins reached the same result as Lord Denning, but did so on completely different grounds. Lord Watkins's framework was not the uncertain realm of policy but the juridical category of negligence. From the juridical perspective, there was only one question to answer: "Was the damage done to Mrs. Lamb's house by the second group of squatters too remote to be a consequence of the council's initial negligent and damaging act which partly destroyed support for the house and for which they had to compensate her?"[54] On the facts before him, Lord Watkins's judgment was based on his "instinctive feeling that the squatters' damage is too remote"[55] and, thus, liability on the part of the municipality is not indicated.

For Weinrib, the approaches to the question of liability in *Lamb* represent paradigmatic examples of the proper use (Watkins) and abuse (Denning) of juridical categories. For his part, by

51. 2 All E.R. 408 (C.A.) (1981).
52. He stated, "[U]ltimately it is a question of policy for the judges to decide." *Id.* at 414.
53. *Id.* at 414–15.
54. *Id.* at 420.
55. *Id.* at 421.

concentrating on the features of the injurious act rather than on a mediating goal, Lord Justice Watkins treats proximate cause as a concept that bears on the immediate intelligibility of the parties' relationship. Proximate cause so treated is one of the set of concepts through which a delictual interaction is understandable as corrective justice. Because corrective justice is conceived as immanent to the transactions that it regulates, its operation is not intelligible independently of those transactions.[56]

By comparison, Lord Denning's judgment fails to illumine the immanent intelligibility of the parties' juridical relationship. Through the imposition of an external purpose on the conduct of the defendant, the *legal* implications of that conduct are never approximated. In short,

> Lord Denning's approach was essentially political. It first required selecting the particular goal of loss-spreading from among the various goals (including general deterrence, specific deterrence and redistribution to the deepest pocket) that his judgment might promote. It then necessitated electing to effect this goal through the homeowner's property insurance, not through the tortfeasor's liability insurance or through the municipality's self-insurance. Loss-spreading, however, like all external goals, is a matter for distributive justice and cannot be coherently achieved within the relationship of doer and sufferer. Nor is its positing the province of a judge, who is neither in a position to canvass the range of possible collective goals, nor accountable to the community for the particular goal chosen.[57]

With the *Lamb* case in view, we can now turn to Weinrib's distinctly philosophical claim for the necessity of the formalist perspective. The reason formalism is the only proper means for understanding the nature of juridical relationships is that it is the most satisfactory account of those relations.[58] The reason the formalist account of juridical relations is the most satisfactory is that it alone satisfies the appropriate criterion for the truth of an account of juridical relations, coherence:

> Coherence is the criterion of truth for the formalist understanding of a juridical relationship. As the loss-spreading example demonstrated, the coherence of an ensemble of justificatory aspects can confirm or negate the essentiality of a given legal feature. The formalist elucidation of legal phenomena is devoted to making explicit the unity possible in juridical relationships, and the disclosure of this unity is the yardstick of its success. The point is not that the positive law of a given jurisdiction necessarily embodies justificatory coherence, but that such coherence is possible, and that positive law is intelligible to the extent that it is achieved and defective to the extent that it is not.[59]

The *Lamb* case presents a question of corrective justice: "Has the plaintiff suffered at the hand of the municipality?" In other words, has the municipality acted negligently such that the plaintiff has been injured? However one decides

---

56. Weinrib, "Legal Formality," *supra* note 3, at 1007.

57. *Id.* at 1006.

58. *Id.* at 963 ("[I]ntelligibility that is immanent to its subject matter is the most satisfactory notion of understanding, and not merely one among many.")

59. *Id.* at 972.

the question of the remoteness of the squatters' conduct (and, thus, the muni-cipality's negligence), Lord Denning's analysis falls completely outside the realm of corrective justice. Denning approaches the case not from the appropriate stand-point of corrective justice, but from the standpoint of distributive justice. He sees the question at issue not as one of a wrong between persons but as a question of allocation of a burden (risk). For the formalist, such an approach can only end in incoherence, for the question at issue is not distributive in nature. To decide a question of corrective justice from the point of view of distributive justice is not only unjust, it is manifestly incoherent.

We now come to the key question to which we have been making our way: "Why is coherence *the* criterion of truth?" Weinrib's answer is as follows:

> The reason coherence functions as the criterion of truth is that legal form is concerned with immanent intelligibility. Such an intelligibility cannot be vali-dated by anything outside itself, for then it would no longer be immanent. Formalism thus denies that juridical coherence can properly be compromised for the sake of some extrinsic end, however desirable. The sole criterion is an internal one. Form is the principle of the unity immanent to an ensemble of legal features, and judgment about intelligibility can flow only from this unity. Because the intelligibility of form is immanent to its content, no other crite-rion is available; and if immanent intelligibility is . . . the most satisfactory mode of understanding, no other is needed.
>
> Not only can no point outside the form vindicate the truth of formalism, but no point or points, atomistically viewed, located inside the form can do so either. Because form constitutes the unity of a set of legal phenomena, no single element has a significance that is independent of its interplay with the others. Therefore, it is not the presence or absence of this or that desirable feature that is decisive for judgment about a juridical relationship, but the extent to which all of its features cohere.[60]

Let us meet the formalist on his own ground and accept that "coherence functions as the criterion of truth."[61] We are now entitled to ask, "What is the proper test of the coherence of legal relations?" From among competing con-ceptions of coherence,[62] how do we know (as opposed to merely believe) that Weinrib's account of juridical coherence is the correct one?[63] The problem for Weinrib is to come up with an answer to this question that avoids begging the question. The strategy is to find the true ground of legal understanding—that which can be understood in itself—without reference to something other than itself. Weinrib's own methodology always entitles us to ask what might be called "the Skeptic's Question": "How do I know (as opposed to merely believe) that my criterion of coherence is the true one?"

60. *Id.* at 972–73.

61. *Id.* at 972.

62. Lord Denning and Lord Watkins are a prime example of differences in judgments about coherence. Of course, Weinrib would not put the matter this way, believing as he does that Lord Denning's approach precludes the possibility of judgment and leads only to incoherence.

63. This question was first raised in Peter Lin, "Wittgenstein, Language, and Legal Theoriz-ing: Toward a Non-Reductive Account of Law," 47 *U. Toronto Fac. L. Rev.* 939, 947 (1989).

To this query, Weinrib responds:

> Circularity is a consequence of the self-contained nature of intelligibility. Because form is the distinct principle of unity that renders intelligible the content that realizes it, no criterion of understanding can exist outside form's encompassing embrace. Provided that the circle is inclusive enough, circularity is here, as elsewhere in philosophical explanation, a strength and not a weakness. For if the matter at hand were to be non-circularly explained by some point outside it, the matter's intelligibility would hang on something that was not itself intelligible until it was, in its turn, integrated into a wider unity. Criticism on the grounds of circularity implies the superiority of the defective mode of explanation that leaves outside the range of intelligibility the very starting point upon which the whole enterprise depends.[64]

Can this amount to anything more than mere assertion? In the end, does Weinrib do anything more than simply stand on his claim that his account of coherence is correct because, as he puts it, "no criterion of understanding can exist outside form's encompassing embrace"?[65]

With this insistence, all Weinrib manages to accomplish is a begging of the very terms of the debate. Intelligibility must rest on coherence. Why? Because coherence is the criterion of truth. How do you know that? Because to claim otherwise "implies the superiority of the defective mode of explanation."[66] But how do you know the other mode of explanation is defective until you have demonstrated the truth of the perspective you advance, which, after *its* truth has been demonstrated, will reveal the false character of the opposing view?

The importance of this question of the criterion for coherence is clearest in Weinrib's discussion of "Justificatory Coherence."[67] In the course of discussing the elements that comprise a legal form, the claim is made that the elements all comprise a unity: the elements "are cognizable only through the unity they comprise, the intelligibility of each simultaneously conditions, and is conditioned by, the intelligibility of all the others."[68] The truth of the claim that the elements of tort are unintelligible apart from the unity they comprise is, of course, normative and not descriptive. No one has any trouble understanding the law and economics literature on tort law: the arguments *are* "intelligible" (i.e., they can be understood). The intelligibility of the arguments is not in question, only their relevance. Weinrib claims that, owing to their external character, the law and economics arguments are incoherent. The efficacy of this claim is directly dependent on the efficacy of Weinrib's prior claim that the formalist account of tort law is the only possible account. Thus, the critical account of the failure of external perspectives stands or falls on the success of the prior claims for coherence as the only defensible criterion of legal truth.

To succeed, Weinrib must show that the formalist account of justice—grounded in the distinction between corrective and distributive justice—is a logi-

---

64. Weinrib, "Legal Formality," *supra* note 3, at 974–75.
65. *Id.* at 974.
66. *Id.* at 975.
67. *Id.* at 970–71.
68. *Id.* at 970.

cally or conceptually necessary feature of legal thinking. For Weinrib, truth in law is a function of first principles. For an account of truth based on first principles to succeed, the necessity of those principles must be demonstrated. For Weinrib's argument to succeed, he would have to show the absolute necessity to legal thinking of the distinction between corrective and distributive justice.[69] This he has not done.

I can only conclude that, in the end, Weinrib's claims for the truth of his perspective are ungrounded assertions and not, as he argues, demonstrable truths. The only way his account of juridical intelligibility gets off the ground is with the assumption that coherence, and in particular his account of juridical coherence, is the correct criterion of truth. His claim is true because it is correct, and it is correct because it is true. No, it does not work, does it?[70]

One Form of Reflection?

I have referred to Weinrib's approach to legal formalism as a "mode of critical reflection." This is in keeping with Weinrib's own view of the importance of reflection in properly understanding the law.[71] For the formalist, the proper mode of critical reflection on the practice of law is immanent intelligibility. The centrality and importance of immanent intelligibility to the formalist project are described as follows:

> Immanent intelligibility is not a subclass but a paradigm of intelligibility. Its virtue is that whatever is immanently intelligible can be understood self-sufficiently without recourse to something external that would pose the prob-

69. For example, Weinrib's formalism places strict liability outside the reach of tort law. Further, it prohibits remedial devices such as market share liability. For the formalist, the justice of a tort system is a function of the degree to which it adheres to the demands of immanent intelligibility. It is not clear how far formalism takes us by pointing out that we are not following the dictates of immanent intelligibility. Again, without the needed metaphysical bite, the formalist critique of positive law is less than efficacious.

70. The problem here duplicates the very criticism Weinrib levels against that champion of the economic approach to legal understanding, Richard Epstein: "Often, those who wish to defend the centrality of these features can do no more than baldly reiterate that what has been impugned is deeply embedded in our comprehension of the situation at hand. For example, Richard Epstein attempts to stave off the implications of the Coase theorem by (1) pointing to the transitive verbs used by Coase himself, and (2) distinguishing between causal reciprocity and the notion of redress for harm caused. Epstein does not explain (1) why linguistic structure overbears economic insight, or (2) how Coase can be refuted by rehashing the very distinction that Coase's analysis challenges. Epstein's assertion that a normative theory of torts must take into account common sense notions of individual responsibility is a conclusion that is consequent on the dismissal of economic analysis, not a reason for dismissing it." *Id.* at 968 n.48.

71. See Weinrib, "Legal Formality," *supra* note 3, at 951–52: "The implications of the formalist claim extend to every aspect of reflection about law. It affects one's view of the nature of legal justification, the limits of the judicial role and judicial competence, the meaning of legal mistake, the relevance of instrumentalism, the relation of law and society, the viability of contemporary legal scholarship, and the place of law among the intellectual disciplines. The scope and importance of these issues attest to the inescapably fundamental nature of the formalist claim."

lem of intelligibility afresh. If something is not intelligible in and through itself, it must, if it is intelligible at all, be intelligible through something else. But unless that other thing is in its turn intelligible through itself, it will merely point to something else on which its own understanding depends. This regression continues until the understanding alights upon something that is immanently intelligible. Therefore, intelligibility that is immanent to its subject matter is the most satisfactory notion of understanding, and not merely one among many.[72]

The entirety of Weinrib's formalism flows from and depends upon his claims for the importance of immanent intelligibility. What, exactly, is the claim Weinrib makes for immanent intelligibility? It is this: As a mode of reflection on law, immanent intelligibility is, as Weinrib states, "a paradigm." In other words, as a reflective activity, immanent intelligibility is not the *preferred* method of reflection, it is "the most satisfactory . . . and not merely one among many."[73]

We are entitled to ask, by what means does Weinrib identify immanent intelligibility as the most satisfactory mode of understanding? Yes, he claims for immanent intelligibility the virtue of self-sufficient understanding, but may we not ask this question: "Why is the intelligibility of something in and through itself necessarily superior to the intelligibility of something through something else?" Put another way, we are entitled to ask the question "What activity of reflection tells us that immanent intelligibility is the most satisfactory activity of critical reflection?"

Weinrib does, indeed, have an answer to this question.[74] Among the many virtues he claims for the formalist approach to legal understanding, none is more important than the assertion that immanent intelligibility—that is an understanding of law from the "internal" point of view[75]—"is not a subclass but a paradigm of intelligibility."[76] Immanent intelligibility is a paradigm, and not one among many ways of understanding, because to understand in this way is to understand something in itself and not by reference to some other notion. Weinrib articulates this claim thus:

> If something is not intelligible in and through itself, it must, if it is intelligible at all, be intelligible through something else. But unless that other thing is in its turn intelligible through itself, it will merely point to something else on which its own understanding depends. This regression continues until the understanding alights upon something that is immanently intelligible. Therefore, intelligibility that is immanent to its subject matter is the most satisfactory notion of understanding, and not merely one among many.[77]

72. *Id.* at 963.

73. *Id.*

74. Again, I must stress that the burden on Weinrib is not to show that the formalist account of law "makes sense." Of course, it does. His claim is that the formalist account is the *only* one that renders the law intelligible. It is with this contention that I take issue.

75. Weinrib, "Legal Formality," *supra* note 3, at 955 ("[F]ormalism postulates that juridical content can somehow sustain itself from within.").

76. *Id.* at 963.

77. *Id.*

Weinrib's argument takes the following form:

Premise 1. If something is not intelligible in and through itself, it must, if it is to be intelligible at all, be intelligible through something else.

Premise 2. Unless that other thing is in turn intelligible through itself, it will merely point to something else on which its own understanding depends.

Intermediate Conclusion. This regression continues until the understanding alights upon something that is immanently intelligible.

Conclusion. Therefore, intelligibility that is immanent to its subject matter is *the most satisfactory* notion of understanding, and not merely one among many.

The core of this argument lies in its first premise. It is at this point in the argument that Weinrib sets out the false dichotomy between internal and external understanding. In an effort to reduce all "external" modes of understanding to some version of functionalism, Weinrib provides the example of an instrument which, he states, "can be understood only by reference to the purpose it serves."[78] Legal forms are not instruments.

But are these the only two choices? That is, must we inevitably choose between immanent intelligibility and crass functionalism? Weinrib apparently thinks as much. He states:

The mere possibility of a non-instrumental understanding renders instrumental understandings of the same legal material superfluous, but not vice versa. This follows from the paradigmatic quality of immanent intelligibility. Instrumental understandings are by their nature imperfect. They first transfer the burden of intelligibility from the subject of the inquiry to the external end this subject serves and then, in turn, require that end to be grasped somehow, presumably by reference to some further external end. Unless this endless shifting of ends can be arrested at a point of non-instrumental stability, the understanding is caught in a game of musical chairs, in which it seems to know everything only because it knows nothing.[79]

The conclusion Weinrib draws from these considerations is crucial and can be read as a further conclusion to the argument recited at the beginning of this section: "[I]nstrumental and noninstrumental understandings do not have an equal footing."[80]

There are, so Weinrib argues, two ways to understand legal materials: instrumentally and noninstrumentally. This expression of the modes of understanding is but a rephrasing of premise 1 in the argument given above. This premise, as

78. *Id.* at 964.
79. *Id.* at 965.
80. *Id.*

well as the distinction between instrumental and noninstrumental understanding, rests upon an assumption implicit in Weinrib's account of understanding and intelligibility, which premise is both unargued and problematic.

Weinrib holds out the possibility that the same legal material can be understood *either* instrumentally or noninstrumentally. What is the assumption that makes the dichotomy possible? It is none other than the assumption that "material" can be identified as "legal" apart from some mode of understanding. Weinrib seems to think that there are three elements at work in every question of law: legal material, internal understanding, and external understanding.[81] But this claim is fallacious. The entire debate is not over *how to think about* legal materials. The debate is over *what counts* as legal material or, if you will, the content of law. It is to this aspect of his position that Weinrib turns a blind eye.

To see this point more clearly, let us return to Weinrib's discussion of the concept of a table. The question was "What makes a table a table?" Expressed in a more nominalist vein, the question is "What set of properties makes an object a table?" The social constructionist view of the matter[82] is that what makes an object a table is the aggregation of qualities that serve the function of tables. Weinrib rejects this approach in his claim that "[t]he set of properties that makes something a table, for instance, is found in all tables and constitutes the genericity of what it is to be a table."[83]

But Weinrib's rejection of this view goes beyond a rejection of functionalism: his fundamental objection to this approach to conceptualization is its "crucial presupposition . . . that a qualitative disjunction exists between the inquirer's thought and the object of inquiry."[84] And there is the presupposition that drives formalism. What his criticism reveals is the unarticulated presupposition that the "object" of thought has an existence outside of the subject of inquiry. In other words, there are "tables" in the world (both the real world and the world of thought) quite apart from anyone's using the object as a table (or anything else). The problem with all nonformalist accounts of understanding is that they attempt to impose "intelligibility . . . from the outside,"[85] that is, from outside the object.[86]

What does it mean to say that tables "exist" apart from some way of life in which tables are used? The very notion of a table depends upon the things we do with tables. Apart from the activities that give the concept of "table" its point, it seems that there is nothing to the notion. Weinrib's position on the conceptualization of so simple a notion as "table" reveals both the depth of presupposition in his formalism and the problematic nature of the position. The point of a con-

81. These distinctions drive concepts like transference of "the burden of intelligibility." *Id.*

82. This view is developed in the next section.

83. Weinrib, "Legal Formality," *supra* note 3, at 960.

84. *Id.* at 961.

85. *Id.*

86. In a very Hegelian expression of this view, Weinrib states that "[a]ccording to this view, the object is the target but need not be the embodiment of thought." *Id.* Further, "[L]aw is *constituted* by thought." *Id.* at 962. There is an obvious tension in Weinrib's account of conceptualization, for he sometimes wants to say that the object exists independently of thought while at others claiming that thought constitutes the object.

cept is simply unknowable apart from some activity or enterprise by which the concept is given content. The content of law is coextensive with and constitutive of the point of its notions. These both arise in the course of social life and are frequently contestable. It is this last, and most important, aspect of law that formalism seems to ignore.

As discussed earlier, Weinrib's aspiration is to provide a foundation for law that is conceptually distinct from the reach of other (mostly "external") disciplines (e.g., economics, critical theory, pragmatism). In short, as a form of critical reflection, immanent intelligibility is the preferred mode. If we are not satisfied with the self-evidence of Weinrib's claims for immanent intelligibility, the discussion might continue as some other ground is appealed to, and then another, and another, and another. Short of a claim of self-evidence,[87] nothing will stop the infinite regress of justification.

Unhappily, claims to self-evidence have too much the quality of faith and not enough of the attributes of argument. Arguments of this sort take on the character of an unending shift in the burden of proof. As each justification is offered, a further question is posed until the questioner is either satisfied or dismissed as a skeptic or some sort of vile creature. But this dismissal does not end the argument; it merely postpones it to another day.

The Social Construction of Form and Matter

The criticism just advanced will, in this section, be developed to show that the distinction between form and content can be understood in a way that is primordially social. The account will be successful if the distinction between form and content can both organize our thought about experience in ways that formalist accounts of knowledge deem important while avoiding the hermetic quality of the formalist rendering of the relationship between word and world. In taking this approach, it is hoped that the truth in formalism will be preserved; that in the process of thinking through the relationship of word to world,[88] the concerns and insights of the formalist account will not only be preserved but improved.

---

87. I take it Weinrib regards it as self-evident that it is always better to understand something in itself and not through something else. Hegel was equally enamored of self-evidence. See G. W. F. Hegel, *The Philosophy of Right* 3 (T. M. Knox trans., 1952). "The unsophisticated heart takes the simple line of adhering with trustful conviction to what is publicly accepted as true and then building on this firm foundation its conduct and its set position in life. Against this simple line of conduct there may be at once be raised the alleged difficulty of how it is possible, in an infinite variety of opinions, to distinguish and discover what is universally recognized and valid." But can we ever be satisfied with such an appeal? "[T]he classical model of rationality faces serious problems when it is consistently developed. The model requires that rationally acceptable claims be justified, and that the justification proceed from rationally acceptable principles in accordance with rationally acceptable rules. Each of these demands leads to an infinite regress unless we can find some self-evident principles and rules from which to begin, but these have not yet been found, and there is no reason to expect that they will be forthcoming." Harold I. Brown, *Rationality* 77 (1988).

88. I have taken this opposition from Michael Mulkay, *The Word and the World: Explorations in the Form of Sociological Analysis* (1985).

Let us return to Weinrib's discussion of what it is that makes a table a table. Weinrib argues that a table is a set of properties, but not just any set of properties. To be a table, a thing must be composed of the same elements that are "found in all tables [for these constitute] the genericity of what it is to be a table."[89] Can this be true? Think of tables: they are composed of many varied elements. Some are square, some are round, some have four legs, others three. Tables are made of many different kinds of things, for example, wood, plastic, or metal. With all these disparate elements and materials, which of these is it that, in Weinrib's words, marks "this" as a "table"?[90]

This is the wrong question. The intelligibility of something as a "this" and not a "that" depends not on the necessary integration of form and content. Rather, it depends upon the recognition of the role of form in the stream of social life.[91] The relationship of form to content is not, as Weinrib would have it, a *necessary* one. Forms tells us what any kind of object is. But the form is alive not in the mind but in the world.[92]

Consider the disparate elements of tables. These—that is, height, shape, material composition—we shall refer to as material elements.[93] What is it that brings these together under the rubric "table"? The answer is simple: the form of a table. But what is the form of a table? It is nothing more (nor less) than "[a]n answer to the question why we call a large variety of objects 'tables' and refuse the word to other objects."[94]

Why is it that *this* particular concatenation of things is referred to as "table"? Because it is objects having these (and other, similar) characteristics that we use to do the sorts of things we do with tables. Owing to certain features of our biology, it is usual to find tables being of roughly a certain height.[95] It is impor-

---

89. Weinrib, "Legal Formality," *supra* note 3, at 960.

90. Weinrib's question in this regard is "When we seek the intelligibility of something, we want to know *what* the something is. This search for 'whatness' presupposes that the something is a *this* and not a *that*, that it has, in other words, a determinate content." *Id.* at 958.

91. See Peter French, *The Scope of Morality* 83–84 (1979). For tables, this would include information about "how we came to have the need to distinguish types of furnishings in our homes, why we wanted to do so, and where it is important in our lives to do so; in addition, we would have to consider the physiological facts that necessitate that tables be a certain height, etc. The concept of a table emerged from such a sociohistory and the extension of "table" is governed by the concept (or intention) of that complex idea."

92. See Henry Focillon, *The Life of Forms in Art* 130 (E. Ladenson trans., 1989): "Forms transfigure the aptitudes and movements of the mind more than they specialize them. Forms receive accent from the mind, *but not configuration*. Forms are, as the case may be, intellect, imagination, memory, sensibility, instinct, character; they are, as the case may be, muscular vigor, thickness or thinness of the blood. But forms, as they work on these data, train and tutor them ceaselessly and uninterruptedly."

93. My term "material element" is synonymous with Weinrib's term "matter." I prefer "material element" to "content" because, in context, it is less cumbersome. The discussion that follows is informed by Julius Kovesi, *Moral Notions* (1967); Cavell, *supra* note 31, at 73–124; Wilfrid Sellars, *Philosophical Perspectives: History of Philosophy* 73–124 (1959).

94. Kovesi, *supra* note 93, at 4.

95. It is likewise true that because our legs bend at the knees, chairs are also made to be of a certain height.

tant to remember, however, that there is nothing necessary about our biology. If our bodies had a different constitution this would no doubt impact upon, but not absolutely determine, the formation of our concepts.[96]

These considerations suggest that the relationship between the formal and material elements of concepts is tied not to any process of thought as such but to human purposes. The things we do with tables, our reasons for having them, determine what counts as a table.[97] The relationship between these reasons, form, and matter can be represented thus:

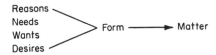

Human reasons or interests form what is, in effect, a point of view: a perspective from which material elements are collocated or brought together under one notional or conceptual category. There is a *point* to joining certain features together. It is that point or purpose that forges the link between formal and material elements. Without human needs there would be no notions or concepts. The connection between human reasons or, if you will, needs, wants, and desires (e.g., for tables and chairs) and the constitution of forms does not, contrary to Weinrib, constitute an unchanging relation between formal and material elements. As human needs, wants, desires, and reasons change, so too will our notions.

The reconstruction of the form/content relation offered here can be expanded further to show that it is sometimes the case that two situations with completely different material elements can be classed as being of the same form.[98] Consider the following two cases:

I reach across the dinner table to pick up the bowl of potatoes and with my elbow knock over the salt.

96. As Wittgenstein has remarked, "I am not saying: if such-and-such facts of nature were different people would have different concepts (in the sense of a hypothesis). But: if anyone believes that certain concepts are absolutely the correct ones, and that having different ones would mean not realizing something that we realize—then let him imagine certain very general facts of nature to be different from what we are used to, and the formation of concepts different from the usual ones will become intelligible to him." Ludwig Wittgenstein, *Philosophical Investigations* 230 (G. E. M. Anscombe trans., 3d ed. 1958). If the human body develops to the point where our legs no longer bend at the knee, then what will count as a table will change as well.

97. All that is required is that whatever material elements the proffered "table" has, those properties in relation must satisfy the social need for tables. Now one might object, "But can a chair not serve as a table? Can it not perform the function of a table and, thus, 'be' a table?" The very form of the question contains its own answer. Surely it is possible to treat a chair *as a* table; or a table *as a* chair. But, as Stanley Cavell reminds us, "[w]hat can serve *as a chair* is not a chair, and nothing would (be said to) serve as a chair if there were no (were nothing we called) (orthodox) chairs. We could say: It is part of the grammar of the word 'chair' that *this* is what we call 'to serve as a chair.'" Cavell, *supra* note 27, at 71.

98. The following example is taken from Kovesi, *supra* note 93, at 15–17.

While walking down the beach contemplating the relationship of metaphysics to reality, I am startled by a wave, jump back, and destroy a child's sand castle.

Other than the presence of a person in each scenario, there is virtually nothing that makes them the same. And yet they are the same, for each case constitutes an act of inadvertence. These two cases constitute, as it were, two of the many and "various ways in which we can perform inadvertent acts."[99] In seeing this, it is important to notice two things. The first is that inadvertency is not "extra element" over and above the "doing" of the acts in question. Inadvertency is what the doing of these acts amounts to.[100] The second thing to notice is that without this formal element, we should not be in a position to identify new cases of inadvertent acts. It is by virtue of the form of inadvertency that we are able to identify these two scenarios and others as examples of the same phenomenon. It is the form, and not the interpenetration of form and content, that enables us to see these different cases as instances of the same thing.[101]

Conclusion

Formalism's promise is to show that beneath the surface play of legal argument lies an immanent juridical structure, the nature of which must be disclosed for true understanding of law to be achieved. Grounded as it is in Aristotle's distinction between corrective and distributive justice, Weinrib's formalism succeeds to the degree that this distinction limits what can intelligibly be said from the juridical point of view. I have criticized Weinrib's argument for its failure both to demonstrate the necessity of Aristotle's distinction and, further, have suggested why Weinrib's claims for the primacy of immanent intelligibility cannot be sustained. Without the backup of necessity, the formalist's claims for coherence—and, thus, truth—are severely undermined. This is exacerbated by formalism's failure to take human interests into account in the theory of human understanding. For these reasons, and despite its many virtues, the formalist account of truth is ultimately unpersuasive.

99. *Id.* at 16.
100. *Id.*
101. Weinrib, of course, claims just the opposite: "Form is not separate from content but is the ensemble of characteristics that marks the content as determinate, and therefore marks the content as content." Weinrib, "Legal Formality," *supra* note 3, at 958.

3

Moral Realism and Truth in Law

> Surely if the history of philosophical reflection on the correspondence theory of truth has taught us anything, it is that there is ground for suspicion of the idea that we have some way of telling what can count as a fact, prior to and independent of asking what form of words might count as expressing truths, so a conception of facts could exert some leverage in the investigation of truth.
>
> John McDowell[1]

As noted in the introduction, realism—explaining truth by resort to something that transcends a particular enterprise—is a widely defended philosophical position. One finds the fullest convergence between realist philosophers and realist lawyers with respect to a certain picture of truth. The central question for realists is "What is it that makes our (moral or legal) beliefs true?"[2] For moral philosophers and lawyers of a realist orientation, the answer is the same: facts. Of course, once one claims there is some fact of the matter about a moral or legal proposition, then one must ask what it is that *makes* the proposition in question true or false. Realists of whatever stripe or discipline are united in the opinion that whatever renders a claim true, it is *not* a belief. Beliefs, realists argue, make nothing true (or false). This point is often made in the form of the assertion that the truth of propositions is "mind independent."

In this chapter, we examine the arguments of two contemporary defenders of the virtues of realism in law. We first consider the position of Michael Moore, who has championed the cause of realism in law from the perspective of ontology. In addition to Moore, David Brink has argued that the realist perspective in the philosophy of language illuminates the nature of legal disputes, in particular, questions of interpretation. Taken together, Moore and Brink present the best cases for the realist account of truth in law.

---

1. John McDowell, "Projection and Truth in Ethics," Lindley Lecture, University of Kansas, Department of Philosophy 11 (1988).

2. This is, perhaps, another way of asking the question "What are the truth conditions for propositions of law?"

Michael Moore's Ontological Realism

Michael Moore's metaphysical realism is the most vigorous modern defense of natural law theory. In what he terms "full-blooded realism,"[3] there are five elements: ontology, a theory of truth, a theory of logic, a theory of (sentence) meaning, and a theory about the meaning of words used in sentences.[4] Briefly stated, ontology is the theory of what there is in the world. The theory of truth, which is distinct from ontology, "examines the relation between what there is and the sentences we use to describe what there is."[5] Logic concerns bivalence; that is, the question whether propositions are always true or false.

Moore's metaphysical approach to sentence and word meaning is what concerns us most in his position. For Moore, a sentence is "true" when the proposition asserted by the sentence "corresponds" with the way the world is. A proposition is true to the degree it is consistent with the world (facts). To the degree it is not, the asserted proposition is false. In short, on Moore's account, a "realist sees sentences as corresponding to states of affairs in the world, her semantics will ignore all forms of deviant utterance that do not have to do with inaccurate representation of how things are."[6]

Moore is not only a participant in the realist/anti-realist debate, but its leading enthusiast. In "The Interpretive Turn in Modern Theory," Moore argues for the proposition that all contemporary efforts in legal theory are implicated in the realism/anti-realism debate, but only he is explicit about his commitment to its terms. Central to Moore's position is his argument that the truth of moral propositions is and must be directly implicated in legal reasoning. In short, Moore embraces the relational thesis—that the truth of a legal proposition depends, at least in part, on a true moral proposition.[7]

The relational thesis is best approached from a slightly tangential point of view, that of epistemology. As mentioned in the introduction, epistemology concerns itself with the question of what knowledge consists in (i.e., what it means for an agent to say "I know"). On Moore's realist theory, the truth of a legal proposition is "mind independent." That is to say, for Moore, legal truths exist apart from the beliefs of anyone. There is a fact of matter about law, which fact may be, but is not necessarily *to* be, discovered by us. Thus, for Moore, no theory of law can be complete without an epistemology.

---

3. Michael S. Moore, "The Interpretive Turn in Modern Theory: A Turn for the Worse?" 41 *Stan. L. Rev.* 871, 879 (1989) [hereafter "Interpretive Turn"] (describing the commitments of the full-blooded realist).

4. *Id.* at 875.

5. *Id.*

6. *Id.* at 879.

7. See Michael S. Moore, "Law as a Functional Kind," in *Natural Law Theory* 189 (Robert George ed., 1992) [hereinafter "Functional Kind"] ("As I shall use the phrase, a 'natural law theory' contains two distinct theses: (1) there are objective moral truths; and (2) the truth of any legal proposition necessarily depends, at least in part, on the truth of some corresponding moral proposition(s). The first I shall call the moral realist thesis, and the second, the relational thesis.").

Moore's epistemology is an epistemology of coherence. When it comes to beliefs, the question is what we are justified in believing. The test of coherence is Moore's test for the justification of belief. As he puts it: "[Justification] of any belief about anything is a matter of cohering that belief with everything else we believe."[8]

With this view of epistemology in mind, let us return to the relational thesis. The following paragraph sums up the commitments of Moore's metaphysical legal realist:

> To begin with, the legal realist as I shall define her is both a scientific and moral realist. That is, without regard to the law, she takes the metaphysically realist line on many entities or qualities such as electrons, intentions, justice, or kindness. Such an individual believes, first, that things like causal relations, intentions, and moral turpitude exist in a way not dependent on what we or anyone else thinks about them; second, that truth about such entities is a matter of correspondence between sentences and the way things are; third, that there is a right answer to all scientific queries and moral dilemmas; fourth, that the meaning of sentences about such entities is just the conditions under which such sentences are true; and fifth, that the meaning of words like "causation," "intention," and "culpability" is given by the nature of the things to which such words refer and not merely by conventional English usage.[9]

Moore is a "one-worlder";[10] that is, he believes that the moral and natural worlds are, in a real sense, the same.[11] There is no distinction between natural and moral entities. Here is where the metaphysics, truth, and coherence epistemology come together. For example, consider Moore's description of the realist lawyer's task in interpreting a statute:

> [The] legal realist will rely on her scientific and moral realism when applying these terms to particular cases. These metaphysical views will thus lead her to practice law in a quite distinct way. When statutes use such terms, she will understand judges to be directed to apply them in light of the best theories they can muster about the nature of the things to which the terms refer. This generates two very distinct features for the legal realist's theory of statutory interpretation. First, even when there are legal, linguistic or moral conven-

8. Michael S. Moore, "Precedent, Induction, and Ethical Generalization," in *Precedent in Law* 183, 198 (Laurence Goldstein ed., 1987).

9. Moore, "Interpretive Turn," *supra* note 3, at 882.

10. Michael S. Moore, "Moral Reality Revisited," 90 *Mich. L. Rev.* 2424, 2492 (1992) [hereinafter "Moral Reality"] ("I too am an empiricist 'one-worlder': if moral qualities exist, moral propositions are true, and moral beliefs are justified, it will be only in the sense of *exist, true,* and *justified* that science applies to the natural world.").

11. One reason Moore's arguments are so unconvincing is that as he embraces the mantle of empiricism, he fails to provide any role in his theory for the essence of empiricism, experiment. No one puts the point better than George Steiner. See George Steiner, *Real Presences* 75 (1989): "Two indispensable criteria must be satisfied by theory: verification or falsifiability by means of experiment and predictive application. There are in art and poetics no crucial experiments, no litmus-paper tests. There can be no verifiable or falsifiable deductions entailing predictable consequences in the very concrete sense in which a scientific theory carries predictive force. One must be crystal clear on this."

tions that purport to define such terms, even when such conventions clearly seem to cover some case, judges are not to base their interpretations on them. In the realist view, such conventions are but provisional theories or heuristics about the nature of the things referred to, to be put aside whenever a better theory about the true nature of the things demands that they do so. Second, the meaning of statutory terms will not run out—such statutes will not have a "penumbra" of uncertain application—even though legal, linguistic and moral conventions will have no clear application to many cases. Although conventions run out—novel cases may present situations quite unlike those covered by conventional definitions—reality doesn't run out. And it is reality, not convention, that fixes the meaning of terms like "contend," "cause," or "culpability."[12]

Moore's central contention, one that flows directly from his commitment to ontological metaphysical realism, is that the truth of a legal proposition flows from its correspondence with a mind-independent state of (moral) affairs.[13] As Moore himself states, it is not *we* who fix the meaning and reference of our terms; it is reality.[14] The promise of moral realism begins in the assertion that there is a fact of the matter about the truth status of our beliefs about law. Certain of our beliefs are true and certain of them false. If we accept Moore's account of truth as correspondence between a legal proposition and a mind-independent state of affairs, will that bring us any closer to deciding which of our beliefs are true and which false?

Consider disagreement over the truth of legal propositions. When it comes to legal propositions, even moral realists will disagree—they will have conflicting beliefs about the nature of moral reality. How do moral realists choose which beliefs to accept as true?[15] Does "moral reality" tell us which of our beliefs are true and which false? Again, it is important to remind ourselves that, for Moore, the truth of legal propositions is a matter "the way the world is." We find out the

---

12. Moore, "Interpretive Turn," *supra* note 3, at 882–83.

13. Even artifactual terms like "mower" have a mind-independent meaning. In "Law as a Functional Kind," Moore discusses the Seventh Circuit's opinion in *In re* Erickson, 815 F.2d 1091 (7th Cir. 1987). Moore endorses the court's finding that mowers have "a nature," which he describes in the following terms: "I call kinds like mowers functional kinds. Unlike nominal kinds, items making up a functional kind have a nature that they share that is richer than the 'nature' of merely sharing a common name in some language. Unlike natural kinds the nature that such items share is a function and not a structure. A stomach, for example, could have a silicon-based chemistry and be cubical in shape (rather than carbon-based and roundish) and still be a stomach because it performs the first-stage processing of nutrients distinctive of stomachs." Moore, "Functional Kind," *supra* note 7, at 208.

14. Moore, "Interpretive Turn," *supra* note 3, at 883.

15. As Jeremy Waldron points out in his critique of Moore's realism, there are questions of democratic legitimacy at issue here. See Jeremy Waldron, "The Irrelevance of Moral Objectivity," in *Natural Law Theory, supra* note 7, at 181: "The issue comes down to comparing like with like. If moral realism is true, then judges' beliefs clash with legislators' beliefs in moral matters. If realism is false, then judges' attitudes clash with legislators' attitudes. What we must not allow the realist defender of constitutional review to say is that it is a case of judge's beliefs clashing with legislators' attitudes. She is not entitled to be realist only about those whom she favours as decision-makers."

way the world is not by peering directly into moral reality, but by constructing theories about it. Theories are systems of beliefs. We believe a proposition to be true based upon how that proposition hangs together with everything else we take to be true (a succinct statement of Quinean holist epistemology). How do we choose which beliefs to regard as true and which not? Whence come the criteria for making such choices? Of course, they do not come from "the world" because that is the very thing under analysis.

Let us consider a specific example from Moore's work, his analysis of the meaning of "death":

> A realist theory asserts that the meaning of "death," for example, is not fixed by certain conventions. Rather, a realist theory asserts that "death" refers to a natural kind of event that occurs in the world and that it is not arbitrary that we possess some symbol to name this thing. (It may be arbitrary what symbol we assign to name this class of events, but it is not arbitrary that we have some symbol to name it). Our intentions when we use the word "death" will be to refer to this natural kind of event, whatever its true nature might turn out to be. We will guide our usage, in other words, not by some set of conventions we have agreed upon as to when someone will be said to be dead; rather, we will seek to apply "dead" only to people who are really dead, which we determine by applying the best scientific theory we can muster about what death really is.
>
> Further, on a realist theory of meaning fact will not outrun diction. Continuing with the example of "death": finding out that not all persons who have lost consciousness and who have stopped breathing, have also had their hearts stop, will not leave us "speechless" because we have run out of conventions dealing with such novelties. Rather, either "dead" or "not dead" will have a correct application to the situation, depending on whether the person is really dead or not. Whether a person is really dead or not will be ascertained by applying the best scientific theory we have about what death really is. Our present scientific theory may be inadequate to resolve the issue, but a realist will assert that there are relevant facts about whether the person is or is not dead even if we presently lack the means to find them. A realist, in other words, believes that there is more to what death is (and thus what "death" means) than is captured by our current conventions.
>
> Finally, a realist theory of meaning will not view a change in our conventions about when to apply a word as a change in its meaning. If we supplant "heart stoppage" with "revivability" as our indicator of "death," we will do so because we believe revivability to be a part of a better theory of what death is than heart stoppage. We will not have changed the meaning of "death" when we substitute one theory for another, because by "death" we intended to refer to the naturally occurring kind of thing, whatever the true nature of the event turned out to be. Our linguistic intentions are constant, on the realist theory, even if our scientific theories change considerably.[16]

The meaning of our words remains constant over time. The explanation for the constancy of meaning is the constancy of reality: to the degree speech fails to

---

16. Michael S. Moore, "A Natural Law Theory of Interpretation," 58 *S. Cal. L. Rev.* 277, 294 (1985) [hereinafter "Natural Law Theory"].

mirror reality, what we say will not be true. We make no contribution to the meaning of what we say. The facts about meaning are all out there, waiting for us to find them. If we do, we will be able to say meaningful things; if not, we are doomed to error.

Moore draws rhetorical strength for his position from a supposed distinction between realism and conventionalism.[17] Moore makes conventionalism the bogeyman in his story.[18] But the choice is not between the determinism of realism and the "idealism"[19] of conventionalism. A few examples will illustrate this thesis.

Consider the temperature of water.[20] We divide temperature into measures of degree, in whole numbers from 1 to 100 (degrees Celsius). Of course, we could have created any number of scales—perhaps an infinite number—so the choice of our present system is, in some (special?) sense of the word, "arbitrary." When we employ adjectives such as "hot," "cold," and "lukewarm," we are simplifying matters even further than the use of measurement by degrees. It is accurate, then, to say that the language of temperature is "conventional."

Suppose one says that "the bath water is hot." On a realist account of things, that statement is true if and only if there is some fact of the matter in virtue of which it is true. But there is no fact of the matter in virtue of which water is either hot or cold. We have chosen to take nature (water) and impose a conventional system[21] of designation upon it. Without our conventional systems of designation, water would be neither hot nor cold. And yet, variations in temperature "must exist and be perceptible to allow the contrast between *warm* and *hot* to *mean anything*."[22]

The words "warm" and "hot" do give us information about the world. And when those words are used correctly, the information we receive is true. What is the lesson to be drawn from this? It is the following: "*It is just as wrong to say*

17. See Moore, "Interpretive Turn," *supra* note 3, at 881: "The form of antirealism most appealing to lawyers is conventionalism. A conventionalist, like any antirealist, denies much of what the realist asserts in each of the five metaphysical theories mentioned earlier. In addition, social convention does the work for the conventionalist that convention-independent reality does for the realist."

18. See Moore, "Interpretive Turn," *supra* note 3, at 904: "Telling us we must choose and that some choices will *seem* better than others, without giving any reasons why we should choose one way or the other or why the 'seeming-better' should be taken to *be* better, does not engage us. Such suggestions are empty in the way that noncognitivist and existential ethics are always empty. For what it is worth, here in the realm of the noncognitivist, Rorty's world does not seem better to me. It seems a barren place in which all arguments are made only by pulling oneself out of deep existential nausea, itself possible only by bad-faith forgetfulness that all arguments are rhetorical substitutes for the bullets one either does not possess or is unwilling to use."

19. Moore has a distinct proclivity for referring to almost everyone who disagrees with him an "idealist." See Moore, "Moral Reality," *supra* note 10, at 2495.

20. Thus use of this example was suggested to me by John Ellis. See John Ellis, *Against Deconstruction* 46–50 (1989).

21. As the discussion of the adjectives "hot," "cold," and "warm" suggests, there is more than one group of terms to describe temperature.

22. Ellis, *supra* note 20, at 48–49.

that warmth is simply a fact of nature as it is to say that warmth is simply a fact about language; and the greatest error of all would be to assume that the falsity of the first of these alternatives required us to turn to the second."[23]

Of course, this is precisely the error Moore makes.[24] For Moore, there are only two conceptions of truth. On the realist account, propositions are true only if there is some fact of the matter in virtue of which they are true. To believe otherwise is to be an "idealist,"[25] one who believes that "true" is a label meaning nothing more than "we all agree." Moore's dichotomy between realism and anti-realism is utterly false. We could not say that water was warm if there were no water. Yet water does not come from nature either "hot" or "cold." The desire to see the correct use of these terms through the lens of the metaphysics of realism or anti-realism blinds Moore to the fact that his choice of terms is just too simplistic to make sense of something as straightforward as the vocabulary of temperature.[26]

These questions lead to the recognition that Moore's joinder of metaphysical moral realism with a coherence epistemology is an unhappy marriage. Uniting metaphysical realism to a coherence epistemology renders appeal to "the nature of things" empty. What Moore's theory fails to provide is any account of how "the nature of things" constrains in any way what we believe to be true. In short, for all its promise, Moore's metaphysical realism fails to demonstrate how "the world" provides a normative check on our talk about it. Unless Moore can show, as John McDowell puts it, how "a conception of facts could exert some leverage in the investigation of truth,"[27] it seems that the claim "the world makes the what we say true and false" is at best, a platitude.

23. *Id.* at 49. This sentiment is echoed and amplified by Hilary Putnam. See Hilary Putnam, *Realism with a Human Face* 28–29 (1990): "What I am saying, then, is that the elements of what we call 'language' or 'mind' *penetrate so deeply into what we call 'reality' that the very project of representing ourselves as being 'mappers' of something 'language-independent' is fatally compromised from the very start.* Like Relativism, but in a different way, Realism is an impossible attempt to view the world from Nowhere. In this situation it is a temptation to say, 'So we make the world,' or 'our language makes up the world,' or 'our culture makes up the world'; but this is just another form of the same mistake. If we succumb, once again we view the world—the only world we know—as a *product*. One kind of philosopher views it as a product from a raw material: Unconceptualized Reality. The other views it as a creation *ex nihilo. But the world isn't a product. It's just the world.* Where are we then? On the one hand—this is where I hope Rorty will sympathize with what I am saying—our image of the world cannot be 'justified' by anything but its success as judged by the interests and values which evolve and get modified at the same time and in interaction with our evolving image of the world itself. Just as the absolute 'convention/fact' dichotomy has to be abandoned, and for similar reasons. On the other hand, it is part of that image itself that the world is not the product of our will—or our dispositions to talk in certain ways, either."

24. Interestingly, we will see the flip side of this error in chapter 6, when we take up the view of Stanley Fish that all knowledge is interpretive in nature.

25. Moore goes so far as to label Putnam an idealist. See Moore, "Moral Reality Revisited," *supra* note 10, at 2495 (referring to Richard Rorty and Hilary Putnam as "sophisticated idealists").

26. This approach to "facts" is an important element in the pragmatism of Richard Rorty. See Rorty, "Texts and Lumps," in 1 *Philosophical Papers (Objectivity, Relativism, and Truth)* 81 (1991) ("Facts are hybrid entities; that is, the causes of the assertibility of sentences include both physical stimuli and our antecedent choice of response to such stimuli.").

27. McDowell, *supra* note 1, at 11.

But where does this leave us? Again, McDowell's words are instructive here: "We have no point of vantage on the question of what can be the case, that is, what can be a fact, external to the modes of thought and speech we know our way around in, with whatever understanding of what counts as better and worse execution of them our mastery can give us."[28]

Moore seems to want to say that current juridical and legislative practices are, in some way, defective or may be improved upon. Of course, the realist maintains that "the world" will be the measure of better and worse. As it turns out, Moore returns us to the very conventionalism he disdains. Even if we accept Moore's picture of current legal practice as a "theory" of the nature of things, Moore provides no reason for preferring some alternative picture of the world to the one we already have. Failing an alternative, Moore's theory seems more like a complaint than a genuine critique.

Realism and Normativity

Realism in law is least persuasive as an account of normativity in law. Such an account would, at least, explain what it means to say that a proposition of law is true; or, to put it differently, what making correct or incorrect legal judgments consists in. In short, justification—the activity of showing that a given proposition of law is true or false—is the central normative activity in law. I say that realism provides us with an unpersuasive account of normativity in law. Why?

The principal reason is that realism, at least from Moore's point of view, sees the participants in the practice of legal justification making no contribution to the constitution of truth in law. Realism's paradigm for truth is verisimilitude— harmony between facts asserted by a given proposition and some mind-independent state of affairs (truth conditions) that, should it obtain, makes the proposition in question "true."

Consider the act of the testator signing a will. What is the significance of the act of affixing a signature to this document? In the law, the proposition "This will is valid" (let us call this proposition *p*) is, *ceteris paribus*, true. How is this shown? This is a question that asks after the nature of juridical truth.

Assuming the existence of a statute of wills, one produces the relevant portion of the text of the statute, the section that details the validity requirements for wills. What is the connection between the statute of wills and *p*? In the law, the statutory text is the way one shows that *p* is true. The act of repairing to the text of the statute of wills has no normative significance outside legal practice. Without the status accorded the statutory text, the act of producing the text of the statute of wills would be an empty gesture. An explanation of legal justification must illuminate the normative significance of the text—the role it plays—in

---

28. McDowell, *supra* note 1, at 11. For a similar critique of Moore, see Brian Bix, *Law, Language, and Legal Determinacy* 149 (1993) ("Having meanings 'in the world' would only help us if there were some way for us to have cognition of, to grasp somehow, those meanings.").

the practice of legal justification. Moore's realist account does not do this. Thus, as an account of justification in law, it fails.

Moore sees legal justification as essentially causal in nature.[29] His question "Why do we have the beliefs we do?" tells us nothing about the normative character of law. Moore misses the normativity of law by treating all legal assertions as hypotheses. The realist account of law transforms an enterprise of justification into a quasi-scientific practice of hypothesis generation. Recall Moore's discussion of statutory interpretation.[30] The meaning of legal norms is not to be found in legal practice, but in a realm of facts to which we have no direct epistemic access. Legal terms are mere "provisional theories or heuristics about the nature of the things referred to, to be put aside whenever a better theory about the true nature of the things demands that they do so."[31] But assertions in law are not hypotheses about mind-independent states of affairs. Assertions in law are claims the truth of which are vindicated by intersubjective (not mind-independent) justificatory criteria (e.g., appeal to the text in the context of answering the question whether a will is valid). The forms of argument are the grammar of legal justification—the way lawyers show that propositions of law are true or false. Apart from these forms of argument, there is no legal truth.

Realism attempts to locate the authority for the meaning of legal norms in a realm removed from legal practice. This accomplishes nothing, save the introduction into law of an idling discourse (the empirical). If we want to know whether a given proposition of law is true, we must ask the participants in law how judgments of truth and falsity, correctness and incorrectness, are made. A perspicuous description of the way the truth and falsity of propositions of law is shown is the point of the inquiry; for this is what the normativity of law consists in.

David Brink and Natural Kind Semantics

In "Legal Theory, Legal Interpretation, and Judicial Review,"[32] David Brink advocates a central role in legal interpretation for considerations of human purpose. He states:

> It is important to remember that the primary objects of legal interpretation—statutes, constitutional provisions, and precedents—like most objects of interpretation, are human artifacts, the products of purposeful activity. In interpreting the products of purposeful activity, we must appeal to the purposes which prompted and guided the activity whose product we are trying to understand.[33]

---

29. This is what Moore means by the self-description "one-worlder." See Moore, "Moral Reality," *supra* note 10, at 2492.

30. See Moore, "Interpretive Turn," *supra* note 3, at 883.

31. *Id.*

32. David O. Brink, "Legal Theory, Legal Interpretation, and Judicial Review," 17 *Phil. & Pub. Affs.* 105 (1988).

33. *Id.* at 125.

The view that the meaning of human activities is best discerned from the point of view of the participants in the activity is one that is shared by philosophers from both the analytic and continental traditions.[34] Like others who argue for consideration of purpose in the interpretation of law, Brink recognizes that no account of the purposive nature of law as a human activity can be complete without considering problems of meaning. In jurisprudence, this recognition finds specific focus in the problem of legal indeterminacy. Given the "open texture" of legal norms, no theory of law can be adequate without some account of how problems of contextual indeterminacy are to be resolved. Indeed, without such an account, we cannot even make sense of the notion of "disagreement" in law.[35]

As Brink reads its history, contemporary jurisprudence has attempted to solve problems of indeterminacy with an inadequate tool: an empiricist semantic theory.[36] According to Brink, proponents of this theory make the following claims: "(1) the meaning of a word or phrase is the set of (identifying) properties or descriptions that speakers associate with it, and (2) the meaning of a word determines its reference."[37] Brink believes that traditional empiricist semantic theory[38] is flawed.[39] The nature of the flaw can be simply stated: empiricist semantic theory fails to draw a distinction between the meaning of a term and anyone's belief about its meaning.[40] By confusing meaning with belief, so Brink argues, legal theorists who embrace traditional semantic theory cannot account for the phenomenon of conceptual disagreement nor can they illuminate the connection between meaning and reference.[41]

---

34. See Hans-Georg Gadamer, *Truth and Method* (Garrett Barden & John Cumming trans., eds., 1975); Alasdair MacIntyre, "The Intelligibility of Action," in *Rationality, Relativism and the Human Sciences* 63–80 (Joseph Margolis et al. eds., 1986).

35. Brink, *supra* note 32, at 114.

36. *Id.* at 112. H. L. A. Hart is identified as a proponent of this view. *Id.* at 113.

37. *Id.*

38. Brink describes two versions of traditional semantic theory. He states, "An individualistic theory makes the meaning of a word depend upon the criteria which *the speaker* associates with the word, while a conventionalistic theory makes the meaning of a word depend upon the criteria with which the word is *conventionally* associated or with which it is associated by a *majority of speakers.*" *Id.*

39. As he describes it, I think he is right. But the strength of Brink's critique of the theory he identifies as "traditional" depends upon the degree to which it is shared by linguistic philosophers as a whole. I don't believe the theory Brink denominates "traditional" is the sort of theory advocated by, for example, Wittgenstein (Kripke's claims to the contrary notwithstanding). Therefore, I believe that the claims made against the theory Brink labels "traditional" leave untouched positions that challenge the claims he makes for a realist semantics. Brink admits as much in his statement that his "discussion of these semantic issues will, of necessity, ride roughshod over many interesting details." *Id.*

40. *Id.* at 117, 118, 121. Brink urges that legal theorists give up the claim of traditional semantic theory that meaning determines reference and follow a realist semantics whereby reference determines meaning. *Id.* at 117.

41. *Id.* at 113.

The inadequacies of traditional semantic theory can be avoided, so Brink argues, by a realist semantics. Following Saul Kripke[42] and Hilary Putnam,[43] Brink urges legal theorists to adopt a semantics of natural kinds,[44] whereby the meaning of general terms is determined not by anyone's beliefs about their meaning but by reference to properties in the world. As he puts it, "[N]atural kind terms . . . are general terms which refer to properties."[45]

Brink's realism is grounded in a metaethics of moral realism.[46] As he states, "Determination of the meaning and reference of legal standards will often require reliance on theoretical considerations [the metaethics of moral realism] about the real nature of the referents of language in the law."[47] This is potentially a powerful claim for, if true, it means that disputes over the meaning of general legal terms are irresolvable by traditional legal methods, which are clearly institutional.

Despite the initial appeal of the argument, it is far from clear that a realist semantics represents a viable alternative to conventional approaches to legal interpretation.[48] The meaning and reference of legal terms is not reducible to natural kinds because law is an institutional and not a scientific practice. Contrary to Brink's claims for the felicity of a natural kinds analysis, the meaning of general legal terms cannot be divorced from the beliefs of institutional participants in legal discourse nor can the meaning of general legal terms be discerned without reference to the beliefs and purposes reflected in legal institutions.

Not All General Terms Are Natural Kind Terms

Brink asserts that the realist semantics of Kripke and Putnam advance "claims for the semantics of both proper names and general terms, such as natural kind terms."[49] As Brink reads Kripke and Putnam, there is no *in principle* distinction between natural kinds and artificial kinds. As with scientific terms, the meaning and reference of legal terms "is given by the way the world is."[50] Like "atom," "neutrino," and "mass," "'[f]air' and 'cruel' are natural kind terms[;] . . . they

---

42. See Saul Kripke, *Naming and Necessity* (1980).

43. Hilary Putnam, "Meaning and Reference," in *Naming, Necessity, and Natural Kinds* 119–32 (Stephen Schwartz ed., 1977), and "The Meaning of 'Meaning,'" in *Mind, Language, and Reality* (1975).

44. Brink, *supra* note 32, at 118.

45. *Id.* at 120.

46. Brink's metaethical program does not figure directly in his arguments for the assimilation of general legal terms into a natural kinds analysis. The arguments in support of a metaethics of moral realism are advanced in David Brink, *Moral Realism and the Foundations of Ethics* (1989).

47. Brink, *supra* note 32, at 121.

48. *Id.* at 147–48.

49. *Id.* at 118. Brink also states that "Kripke and Putnam have defended these semantic claims for the semantics of general terms, such as natural kind terms." *Id.* at 120.

50. *Id.* at 123.

are general terms which refer to properties."[51] Therefore, the meaning of, say, constitutional terms is not "created," it is discovered.[52]

The meaning of a natural kind term is fixed in the following way: "The substance is defined as the kind instantiated by (almost all of) a given sample. . . . [T]he identity fixes a reference: it therefore is *a priori*."[53] As mentioned previously, Brink does not limit his realism to the domain of science or natural (as opposed to artificial) kinds. His semantic realism is presented in the form of a general argument for the meaning of all general terms.

To demonstrate the shortcomings of Brink's wide-ranging claims for realism, it is not necessary that one prove false the claim of Kripke and Putnam that there are natural kinds: it is only necessary to show that not *all* general terms refer in the way Kripke and Putnam claim that natural kind terms refer.[54]

Consider the meaning of the general legal term "negotiable instrument." This term is central to the conventions of drawing, assigning, and paying what are ordinarily referred to as "checks."[55] What counts as a check, the legal rights and obligations of the parties to a check, and the manner by which checks are processed for collection are all a matter of human institutional conventions. If there were no human beings, or no interest in a system of payment by means other than gold and silver, there would be no negotiable instruments.

Like the vast majority of general legal terms, "negotiable instrument" is an artifact, a creature of convention. The meaning of "negotiable instrument" is not "given by the way the world is";[56] there is no "real nature"[57] of a negotiable instrument. We do not "discover"[58] the meaning of "negotiable instrument" by discerning objects in the world having rigidly designated natural properties. It is only in and through the institutional conventions of commerce that "negotiable instrument" has its meaning. To know the meaning of this general legal term, one must consult the conventions for its use, for it is solely against that background that participants in legal discourse frame interpretive arguments. Those arguments are shaped through and through by institutional conventions that are constitutive of law.

Natural Kinds and Legislative Intent

I shall maintain my neutrality on the question of the possible existence of natural kinds, for that neutrality is convenient to my argument.

51. *Id.* at 120.
52. *Id.* at 123.
53. Kripke, *supra* note 42, at 136.
54. For a fuller demonstration of this claim, see T. E. Wilkerson, "Natural Kinds," 63 *Philosophy* 29 (1988).
55. The rules governing negotiable instruments are found in articles 3 and 4 of the Uniform Commercial Code (U.C.C.).
56. Brink, *supra* note 32, at 123.
57. *Id.* at 121.
58. *Id.* at 123.

One of Brink's central claims about interpretation is that the meaning and reference of legal terms is a function of the way the world is and is not dependent upon the beliefs of anyone.[59] When this claim is brought to bear on the question of how far, and to what extent, legislative purpose determines statutory meaning, the results are problematic.

According to traditional semantic theory, close attention must be paid to the intentions of constitutional or statutory framers[60] because "their intentions place constraints upon constitutional interpretation independently of the plausibility of the framer's moral or political beliefs."[61] But proponents of traditional semantic theory fail to distinguish between specific and abstract intent. An abstract intent takes the form of a policy or principle that is the impetus for particular legislation.[62] Specific intent reduces the extension of abstract intent to "certain actions and not others."[63]

Brink claims that specific intent is less important than proponents of traditional semantic theory take it to be.[64] The nub of his argument is that the meaning of statutory terms should not be tied to the intentions of their authors but is properly determined by our best current theory of the meaning of those terms.

Brink's example is a statute passed in 1945 imposing "strict standards of due care"[65] in the handling of toxic substances. If a court is today to decide a case under the statute involving a substance that, according to the best available theory in 1945, would not be considered toxic, is the court to decide the case on the basis of the best theory in 1945 or today's best theory? According to Brink, if one follows the traditional semantic theory, the court must decide the issue on the basis of the best theory in 1945.[66] On a realist semantics, the court's obligation is to decide the question of toxicity relative to our current best theory of the matter.

A realist semantics runs into trouble when we consider a different hypothetical. Consider a statute written in 1945 that prohibited all fishing within fifty miles of shore. Assume that at the time the statute was promulgated, Congress mistakenly believed that whales and dolphins were fish. In the preamble to the text of

---

59. *Id.* ("The meaning and reference of our terms is given by the way the world is"); *Id.* at 117 ("Beliefs do not determine reference.").

60. Brink explicitly rejects any "global" distinction between constitutional and statutory interpretation. See *id.* at 119 n.20.

61. *Id.* at 123.

62. *Id.* at 122. An example would be the U.C.C.'s purpose to simplify, clarify, and modernize the law governing commercial transactions. See U.C.C. § 1-102(2)(a).

63. To continue with the U.C.C., an example of a specific intention is the drafters' particular desire to repeal the common law that firm offers are not enforceable without consideration. See U.C.C. § 2-205 (firm offers need not be supported by consideration).

64. Brink, *supra* note 32, at 122 ("Proponents [of traditional semantic theory] . . . insist that the correct interpretation of any legal provision must be guided by, or at least not violate, the framers' (specific) intentions.").

65. *Id.* I presume Brink intends the reader to take the quoted phrase to mean strict liability as opposed to liability for negligence.

66. I must confess that the cogency of this claim escapes me, but I will not pursue the matter here.

the statute, Congress announced that the statute was passed to prevent the extinction of all forms of fish "including whales and dolphins." Our best current theory shows that whales and dolphins are not fish but mammals. Is it now the case that the clear meaning of the statute is to be ignored because Congress mistakenly classified whales and dolphins as fish?

The problem for a realist semantics is plain: ignoring Congress's "mistake" in classifying animals comes at the price of direct frustration of Congress's power to regulate "fishing." Obviously, Congress intended to include whales and dolphins within the purview of the statute and did so on the basis of a mistaken theory of classification. But if the court applies the statute to preclude the fishing of whales and dolphins, it can only do so on the basis of an inadequate semantic theory (the traditional theory). The meaning of "fish" is not determined "by the way the world is":[67] it is determined by the way Congress then thought the world was. In other words, it is the *belief* of Congress, not natural kind predicates, that determines the interpretive obligations of a court applying the statute.

The Realist Rejoinder

Brink maintains that his use of the word "real" "does not obviously require metaphysical realism."[68] As I will show directly, Brink equivocates in his use of "real." This equivocation produces a fundamental ambiguity in his argument. "Real" has two senses for Brink: (1) "true" or "correct" nature of "X" as determined by a theory of "X," and (2) real "in the world." In his original essay,[69] Brink advocates the second of these two senses of realism. In rejoinder to my argument, Brink seems clearly to be advocating the first sense of realism.

In his rebuttal, Brink describes the following three claims as "realist":

> [T]here are facts about social institutions, practices, and relations in the following senses: (i) those social phenomena are the *object of* people's conceptions and so antedate those conceptions; (ii) people's conceptions about those phenomena can be mistaken about the real nature of the phenomena; (iii) when people's conceptions of those phenomena are correct it is in virtue of correctly describing the nature of those institutions, practices, and relations.[70]

In reading this paragraph, one gets the impression that the second sense of "real" is intended.[71] In the next paragraph, Brink signals that he does not mean to make the bolder claim for realism at all. He says, "All these semantic claims presuppose is the kind of objectivity and fallibility in social domains secured by claims (i)–(iii) in the previous paragraph."[72] Following this caveat, Brink con-

---

67. Brink, *supra* note 32, at 123.

68. David O. Brink, "Semantics and Legal Interpretation (Further Thoughts)," 2 *Can J.L. Juris.* 181, 185 (1989).

69. Brink, *supra* note 32.

70. Brink, *supra* note 68, at 184.

71. I at least have that sense from the use of the phrase "real nature of the phenomena."

72. Brink, *supra* note 68, at 185.

firms our suspicion that "real" doesn't mean "real in the world" at all but something roughly equivalent to "what our best theory of 'X' is." Consider: "[T]he relevant sense of 'natural' in the claim that TDR [theory of direct reference] offers a semantics for natural kind terms is *not* 'natural scientific' or 'non-artifactual' but something like 'theoretical' or 'explanatory.'"[73] This definition (explication) of "real" shows Brink distancing himself from the second sense of "real."

Brink's use of the word "real" hides more than it reveals. If the meaning of "X" is coextensive with a theory of "X," then I fail to see what is added by the claim that "there is a real meaning of "X.'" If "real 'X'" simply means "the best theory of 'X,'" then why not drop the adjective altogether? If it does no work, then it just obscures the discussion. I think that much is clear.

Does "Real" Do Any Work?

As with the metaphysical moral realism of Michael Moore, appeals to "the way the world *really* is" do no work in Professor Brink's reformulation of his position. Perhaps the best evidence are Brink's own words. At no point does Professor Brink make any claims about the way the world *really* is. What he does offer is further elaboration of his theory of statutory interpretation. In response to my mammalian counterexample to his original claims for the theoretical power of semantic realism, Brink advances a purposive theory of interpretation. The key to the theory is in the distinction between abstract and concrete intent. As Brink puts the matter:

> [I]n the interpretive appeal to underlying purpose, we must often decide how best to characterize this purpose or intent and, in particular, that we must choose between the *abstract* intent or purpose (i.e. the kind of principle, policy, or value that the framers of the legal provision were trying to implement) and the *specific* intent or purpose (i.e. the particular activities that the framers expected the provision to regulate).[74]

I do not see that this distinction supports Brink's contention that his "semantic claims block the standard argument for legal indeterminacy and judicial discretion because they show that that standard argument rests on mistaken semantic assumptions."[75] What Brink needs to show is how "the way the world is" connects up with the judicial construction of "abstract intention." The reason this is so important is that any statute or line of cases is amenable to more than one purposive reconstruction. If purpose can be theoretically overdetermined, then appeals to realism must demonstrate how choice among competing purposive interpretations of legal materials is accomplished. For a realist this is no small task.

I have argued for two claims. The first is that Brink's claim that all general terms are natural kind terms cannot be sustained. Institutional practices such as

73. *Id.* (emphasis added).
74. *Id.* at 186.
75. *Id.* at 188.

law are replete with general terms the meaning of which can only be discerned by investigation of the beliefs and attitudes of participants in the practice.

My second claim is that a realist semantics is not itself free from difficulty when we are invited to adopt it as an exclusive semantic theory for legal interpretation. It is frequently the case that the meaning of a statute in a present context cannot be determined by direct consultation of the specific intentions of the drafters of a statute. But it is sometimes the case that to do otherwise would be to elide the distinction between legislation and adjudication. Disregard of the limitations of a realist semantics leads to just such undesirable outcomes.

Conclusion

In this chapter we have considered two approaches to a realist jurisprudence. Michael Moore urges that we take ontology seriously, to the point where we view justification in law as an exercise in theory construction about mind-independent moral entities and purposes. As argued, such an approach makes little sense of justification as we have come to know it in law. This is due no doubt to the fact that unlike science, law is not an empirical activity. Lawyers are not making sense of nature, they are characterizing the legal status of states of affairs. If Moore's account of the nature of legal justification had any suasive character, it would make sense of the distinction between a proposition's being "true" and its being "legally speaking true." Regrettably, Moore's realism cannot accommodate such a distinction.

David Brink's metaphysical moral realism is as robust as Moore's, albeit in a different way. In true realist spirit, Brink sets out to argue that "the way the world is" limits what we can say from the legal point of view. When pressed about the relationship between belief and truth, Brink is forced to concede that belief and not nature is the ground of truth in law. When lawyers interpret statutes, they are always interested in legislative aspiration and legislative belief. Yet there is a relationship between the way the world is and what legislators believe about the world. What Brink fails to realize is that it is law and not nature that determines what in that relationship is to count, and how it is to do so.

4

Legal Positivism

Laws are unavoidably indeterminate prescriptions of general adverbial obligations.

Michael Oakeshott[1]

Legal positivism is a theory about the nature of law and legal institutions. Apropos of the present study, positivism is also a theory about the truth conditions for propositions of law. The focus of this chapter will be on the work of the most important legal positivist of the twentieth century, H. L. A. Hart. In his most celebrated work, *The Concept of Law*,[2] Hart advances both an account of the idea of a legal system as well as a theory of adjudication. The present chapter focuses on Hart's theory of law, with particular emphasis on a central feature of his jurisprudence, the rule of recognition. Hart embraces a truth-conditional account of legal propositions. The rule of recognition is the source for the criteria for evaluating the truth status of propositions of law. For the present study, this is the most important aspect of Hart's jurisprudence.

Hart's Theory of the Legal System

We cannot understand Hart's legal positivism without understanding the question that animates it. That question—"What is law?"—is answered by Hart in the form of a theory of the nature of a legal "system."[3] For Hart, the legal system is a system of social rules. In this respect, legal rules are not unlike the rules of morality, etiquette, or the social club. Legal rules are social also in the sense that they originate from human social practices, such as legislation.

Unlike other sorts of social rules, however, legal rules have a systematic or "institutional" character. This character is reflected in the distinction between

1. Michael Oakeshott, "On History," in *On History and Other Essays* 144 (1983).
2. H. L. A. Hart, *The Concept of Law* (2d ed. 1994). The second edition of *The Concept of Law*, which was originally published in 1961, is no different from the first edition of the book, save for a postscript completed shortly before Hart's death in 1992. Where Hart's postscript is cited, an indication will be made.
3. See Hart, *supra* note 2, at 79–123. In putting the point this way I draw upon Richard H. Fallon Jr., "Reflections on Dworkin and the Two Faces of Law," 67 *Notre Dame L. Rev.* 553, 555 (1992).

two sorts of rules found in sophisticated legal systems, primary rules and second-ary rules.[4] Primary rules establish rights and duties within the legal system. Sec-ondary rules are rules to which officials have resort when they seek to identify, clarify, or change primary rules. Chief among secondary rules is the rule of rec-ognition, which specifies what is to count as a primary or secondary rule.[5]

Hart considers the rule of recognition a great advance for a legal system, so much so that he refers to it as the mark of advanced legal systems.[6] Why is the rule of recognition of such importance? Hart answers this way:

> Both private persons and officials are provided with authoritative criteria for identifying primary rules of obligation. The criteria so provided may, as we have seen, take one or more of a variety of forms: these include reference to an authoritative text; to legislative enactments; to customary practice; to general declarations of specified persons, or to past judicial decisions in particular cases.[7]

The relationship between the rule of recognition and primary and secondary rules is one of validity. The function of the rule of recognition is to provide both citi-zens and officials with the means for identifying valid law. Unlike primary and secondary rules, the rule of recognition is neither valid nor invalid. It owes its existence to the fact of social acceptance.[8]

One of the hallmarks of *The Concept of Law* is the degree to which it devel-ops and refines the basic positivist position that the validity of law depends upon its origination from an appropriate source.[9] John Austin, whose jurisprudence is the critical object of much of *The Concept of Law*, argued that law could best be thought of as a certain kind of command issuing from a sovereign; that is, orders backed by threat of sanction for noncompliance.[10] By clever example, Hart showed that this command theory failed to account for the important distinction between "being obliged" and "having an obligation." If we compare law to the order of a robber to turn over one's money, it makes perfect sense to say that the order obliges us to comply. But is there an obligation? Hart thinks not:

---

4. A legal system consists in the union of these two sorts of rules.

5. See Hart, *supra* note 2, at 94 (The rule of recognition "will specify some feature or fea-tures possession of which by a suggested rule is taken as a conclusive affirmative indication that it is a rule of the group to be supported by the social pressure it exerts.").

6. *Id.* at 91–99.

7. *Id.* at 100.

8. Hart states the relation between primary and secondary rules, and the rule of recognition, thus: "There are therefore two minimal conditions necessary and sufficient for the existence of the legal system. On the one hand those rules of behavior which are valid according to the system's ultimate criteria of validity must be generally obeyed, and, on the other hand, its rules of recogni-tion specifying the criteria of legal validity and its rules of change and adjudication must be effec-tively accepted as common public standards of official behavior by its officials." *Id.* at 116.

9. See *id.* at 269 (postscript): "According to my theory, the existence and content of the law can be identified by reference to the social sources of the law (e.g., legislation, judicial decisions, social customs) without reference to morality except where the law thus identified has itself incor-porated moral criteria for the identification of law."

10. See John Austin, *Lectures on Jurisprudence* 203 (1874) ("The essential difference which severs a positive law from a law not a positive law is this:—Every positive law (or every law simply or strictly so called) is set, directly or circuitously, by a sovereign individual or body.").

A orders B to hand over his money and threatens to shoot him if he does not comply. According to the theory of coercive orders this situation illustrates the notion of obligation or duty in general. Legal obligation is to be found in this situation writ large; A must be the sovereign habitually obeyed and the orders must be general, prescribing courses of conduct, not single actions. The plausibility of the claim that the gunman situation displays the meaning of obligation lies in the fact that it is certainly one in which we would say that B, if he obeyed, was 'obliged' to hand over his money.[11]

Obligation is not a psychological notion, as it must be on Austin's analysis.[12] In what, then, does obligation consist? In addition to the existence of rules, there must be a particular attitude shared by those who follow, apply, and violate the rules that give rise to obligations. This attitude manifests itself in certain sorts of normative behavior. "Rules are conceived and spoken of as imposing obligations when the general demand for conformity is insistent and the social pressure brought to bear on those who deviate or threaten to deviate is great."[13] What is important in all of this "is that the insistence on importance or *seriousness* of social pressure behind the rules is the primary factor determining whether they are thought of as giving rise to obligations."[14]

In these passages, Hart sows the seeds of one the most important aspects of his jurisprudence, the internal point of view. In Hart's view, we cannot have a complete understanding of the idea of obligation without attending to the attitude of those in a group who accept the (primary and secondary) rules. An observer who limits himself to description of internal, group regularities,

> is content merely to record the regularities of observable behavior in which conformity with the rules partly consists and those further regularities, in the form of the hostile reaction, reproofs, or punishments, with which deviation from the rules are met. . . .
>
> If, however, the observer really keeps austerely to this extreme external point of view and does not give any account of the manner in which members of the group who accept the rules view their own regular behavior, his description of their life cannot be in terms of rules at all, so not in terms of the rule-dependent notions of obligation or duty. Instead, it will be in terms of observable regularities of conduct, predictions, probabilities, and signs. For such an observer, deviations by a member of the group from normal conduct will be a sign that hostile reaction is likely to follow and nothing more. His view will be like the view of one who, having observed the working of a traffic signal in a busy street for some time, limits himself to saying that when the light turns red there is a high probability that the traffic will stop. He treats the light merely as a natural *sign that* people will behave in certain ways, as clouds are a *sign that* rain will come. In so doing he will miss out a whole dimension of the social life of those whom he is watching, since for them the red light is not merely a sign that others will stop: they look upon it as a *sig-*

11. Hart, *supra* note 2, at 82. For criticism of Hart's analysis of Austin's argument, see Jeffrie Murphy & Jules Coleman, *The Philosophy of Law* 265 (1984).

12. See *id.* at 83 (denying that obligation has anything to do with belief).

13. *Id.* at 86.

14. *Id.*

nal for them to stop, and so a reason to stop in conformity to rules which makes stopping when the light is red a standard of behavior and an obliga-tion. To mention this is to bring into the account the way in which the group regards its behavior. It is to refer to the internal aspect of rules seen from their internal point of view.[15]

Hart's project is descriptive[16] and hermeneutic[17] in nature. The meaning of legal obligation cannot be understood apart from the intersubjective activities of individuals who have occasion to refer to rules. Hart's insight was in noticing that the act of reference to the rule was *itself* a meaningful element in under-standing obligation. It is this intersubjective element that the command theory of law misses and the internal point of view illuminates.

The Rule of Recognition and the Sources of Law

The essence of legal positivism is "the search for a standard by which to distin-guish genuine from spurious pronouncements of law."[18] As we have noticed, Austin attempted to locate the standard between the genuine and the spurious in the commands of a sovereign backed by threat for noncompliance. Hart not only revealed the conceptual errors in Austin's approach, he substituted for the will of the sovereign the idea of law as a system of rules. This is Hart's central contribution to the positivist tradition in jurisprudence.

What does the rule of recognition do? The simple answer is that it provides criteria for the identification of positive law. How is this accomplished? Hart answers thus:

> By providing an authoritative mark it introduces, although in embryonic form, the idea of the legal system: for the rules are now not a discrete unconnected set but are, in a simple way, united. Further, in the simple operation of iden-tifying a given rule as possessing the required feature of being an item on an authoritative list of rules they have the germ of the idea of legal validity.[19]

Lest one think the rule of recognition provides a simple "test" for the iden-tification of law, Hart cautions that in a developed legal system,

> the rules of recognition are of course more complex; instead of identifying rules exclusively by reference to text or list they do so by reference to some general characteristic possessed by the primary rules. This may be the fact of

15. *Id.* at 89–90.

16. The passage of years did nothing to change Hart's characterization of his own work in this way. Compare Hart, *supra* note 2, at v ("[*The Concept of Law*] may also be regarded as an essay in descriptive sociology.") and postscript at 240 ("My account is descriptive.").

17. For discussion of the hermeneutic dimensions of *The Concept of Law*, see P. M. S. Hacker, "Hart's Philosophy of Law," in *Law, Morality and Society: Essays in Honour of H.L.A. Hart* 12–18 (P. M. S. Hacker & Joseph Raz eds., 1977).

18. Jules Coleman, Book Review, 66 Cal. L. Rev. 885, 887 (1978) (reviewing Ronald Dworkin's *Taking Rights Seriously* (1977)).

19. Hart, *supra* note 2, at 95.

their having been enacted by a specific body, or their long customary practice, or their relation to judicial decisions.[20]

In these passages, Hart expresses a central tenet of positivism, the "sources thesis." As Joseph Raz states, "The sources of a law are those facts by virtue of which [law] is valid and which identify its content."[21] The description of the sources thesis offered by Raz is more capacious than any found in Hart. Hart's concern is with the *validity* of law; how it is that one can say of a norm "this is law." Validity is a function of source or "pedigree."[22] However, as Roger Shiner notes, "It would only be in the rare case that the issue before a court would be resolved by a decision which *identified* a norm as a valid rule."[23]

Of course, Hart has been criticized severely for his claim that a rule of recognition is the means for distinguishing true from spurious claims about the content of positive law. Hart's most persistent critic, Ronald Dworkin, has argued that, in addition to rules which bear the correct pedigree, the law is composed of principles.[24] Despite much effort to beat back Dworkin's arguments against Hart's positivism, there is little doubt that Dworkin has succeeded in demonstrating that *at the level of sources*, there is more to law than that encompassed by Hart's rule of recognition.[25]

Of Sources and Meaning: Legal Positivism's One-Way Picture of Law

I shall not add to the critique of legal positivism at the level of the sources of law. My interest in positivism and its potential shortcomings has another motivation. The central element of the positivist emphasis on the rule of recognition is the idea of a social fact; that is, that the meaning of the law can be tied to the existence or nonexistence of some social fact (e.g., an act of the legislature).[26] Thus, for positivists, the truth of a proposition of law turns on social facts the existence of which *make* the proposition in question true.[27] Social facts are the truth conditions for propositions of law.

20. *Id*. at 95.
21. Joseph Raz, *The Authority of Law* 47–48 (1979).
22. E.g., a norm promulgated in the right way by a state legislature would be valid.
23. Roger Shiner, *Norm and Nature* 172 (1992).
24. See Ronald Dworkin, *Taking Rights Seriously* 14–45 (1977).
25. But see Rolf Sartorius, "Social Policy and Judicial Legislation," 8 *Am. Phil. Q.* 151 (1971) (arguing that Dworkin's argument against Hart commits Dworkin to the view that there exists a fundamental test for law).
26. See Hart, *supra* note 2, at 95 (The truth of a proposition of law is discerned "by reference to some general characteristic possessed by the primary rules. This may be the fact of their having been enacted by a specific body.").
27. Jules Coleman refines the relationship between the rule of recognition and truth in the following way: "The notion of a rule of recognition is ambiguous; it has both an epistemic and a semantic sense. In one sense, the rule of recognition is a standard that one can use to identify, validate or discover a community's law. In another sense, the rule of recognition specifies the

The positivist account of the truth of propositions is inadequate because social facts do not make propositions of law true. The truth of propositions of law is a matter of employing legal forms of argument, the use of which shows the truth of a given proposition of law. Positivism provides us with a "discovery" picture of the nature of legal truth. In this way, the positivist conceives of law as a matter of certain (social or institutional) facts, which can then be used in the same manner as scientific propositions (e.g., confirmation). But law is not as the positivist supposes (i.e., akin to science). The truth of a proposition of law is the product of an activity (justification) and is not a matter of correspondence between a proposition and a social fact.

These points may be made more concrete in the context of statutory construction. For this, let us turn to a well-known case considered earlier, that of *United Steel Workers of America v. Weber.*[28] Brian Weber, an employee of Kaiser Aluminum and Chemical Corporation sued his employer under Title VII of the Civil Rights Act, alleging that he had been the victim of unlawful discrimination. In an effort to adjust racial imbalances in its skilled worker population, Kaiser, a private employer, voluntarily adopted an affirmative action plan that provided craft training to blacks with less seniority than white workers. Because the plan involved employment and training, Weber alleged that it violated two key provisions of Title VII.[29] The essence of these two provisions was to prohibit "discrimination" on the basis of, among other things, race.

Section 703(d) of the act prohibits discrimination "against any individual because of his race, color, religion, sex, or national origin in admission to, or employment in, any program established to provide apprenticeship or other training."[30] Unfortunately, the key word in the statute—"discriminate"—is not defined in the act. By Weber's lights, the language of Section 703(d) prevented any and all forms of discrimination. But the majority of the Supreme Court of the United States disagreed with Weber, and for plausible reasons. The statutory history of the act, and these sections in particular, were at variance with the "literalist" reading urged by Weber.

---

conditions a norm must satisfy to constitute part of a community's law. . . . In my view legal positivism is committed to the rule of recognition in the semantic sense at least." Jules L. Coleman, "Negative and Positive Positivism," in *Markets, Morals and the Law* 5 (1988).

28. 443 U.S. 193 (1979).

29. Sections 703(a) and (d). Section 703(a) provides: "It shall be an unlawful employment practice for an employer—(1) to fail or refuse to hire or to discharge any individual, or otherwise to discriminate against any individual with respect to his compensation, terms, conditions, or privileges of employment, because of such individual's race, color, religion, sex, or national origin; or (2) to limit, segregate, or classify his employees or applicants for employment in any way which would deprive or tend to deprive any individual of employment opportunities or otherwise adversely affect his status as an employee, because of such individual's race, color, religion, sex, or national origin." Section 703 (d) provides: "It shall be an unlawful employment practice for any employer, labor organization, or joint labor-management committee controlling apprenticeship or other training or retraining, including on-the-job training programs to discriminate against any individual because of his race, color, religion, sex, or national origin in admission to, or employment in, any program established to provide apprenticeship or other training."

30. 78 Stat. 255–56 (1964).

Both the majority and dissenting opinions review the historical circumstances surrounding promulgation, debate, and passage of the act. The majority's argument is reflected in paragraphs like the following:

> Congress' primary concern in enacting the prohibition against racial discrimination in Title VII was with the plight of the Negro in our economy, and the prohibition against racial discrimination in employment was primarily addressed to the problem of opening opportunities for Negroes in occupations which have been traditionally closed to them. In view of the legislative history, the very statutory words intended as a spur or catalyst to cause "employers and unions to self-examine and to self-evaluate their employment practices and to endeavor to eliminate, so far as possible, the last vestiges of an unfortunate and ignominious page in this country's history," Albemarle Paper Co. v. Moody, 422 U.S. 405, 418, cannot be interpreted as an absolute prohibition against all private, voluntary, race-conscious affirmative action efforts to hasten the elimination of such vestiges.[31]

From the majority's analysis of the history of the act, it is clear that Congress had at least two expectations. First, that blacks would obtain jobs "which have a future"[32] in numbers sufficient to eradicate their economic deprivation. Second, that no employer would be forced to adopt an affirmative action plan. *Voluntary* affirmative action of the type employed by Kaiser would be permitted to correct racial imbalances. The natural inference is that "Congress chose not to forbid all voluntary race-conscious affirmative action."[33] With the statutory language duly massaged by history, the majority of the Court held "that Title VII's prohibition in §§ 703(a) and (d) against racial discrimination does not condemn all private, voluntary, race conscious affirmative action programs."[34]

Clear statutory language precludes the need to resort to history, for history—like parol evidence—is something one resorts to *only* when the text under consideration is ambiguous or otherwise unclear. At least that is how Justice Rehnquist saw the matter. But Justice Rehnquist was not afraid to match fact for fact with the majority. In fact, his dissent is correctly regarded as besting the majority at its own game, that of marshaling historical facts.[35] Yet, despite the overwhelming evidence that Congress's intent was to avoid government-mandated affirmative action programs, that was not the question raised by the *Weber* case. The Kaiser plan was a voluntary plan[36] by a private corporation. Thus, the historical evidence did not cut quite as deeply as either the majority or the dissent would like. Nevertheless, this left the dissent with its best argument, a textual one: the language of the statute prohibits discrimination. There being no compelling argument that the historical evidence points in a direction different from the language of the provisions under consideration, the dissent has the better of the argument.

31. 443 U.S. at 202–04.
32. *Id.* at 203 (quoting Senator Clark).
33. *Id.* at 206.
34. *Id.* at 208.
35. See *id.* at 231–53.
36. This characterization is tempered by the fact that the Kaiser plan was adopted in response to pressure from the Office of Federal Contract Compliance. See *id.* at 222.

Owing perhaps to the realization that its opinion founders on the history to which it had resort, the majority buoyed their position with what might be called a "modified intentionalist" stance.[37] It is clear from legislative history that Congress had two purposes in effecting the act. The first was to obtain more jobs for blacks. The second was achieving a "color-blind" society. Obviously, these two purposes were in conflict, and the majority offered no analysis of how it came to prefer one over the other.

Some scholars believe the weaknesses in the majority's opinion are avoided in the concurring opinion of Justice Blackmun.[38] Eschewing the grounds of text and history, Justice Blackmun rested his affirmation of the Kaiser plan on the grounds of doctrine and prudence. In a passage worth quoting at length, Justice Blackmun argues that Weber's reading of the statute

> places voluntary compliance with Title VII in profound jeopardy. The only way for the employer and the union to keep their footing on the "tightrope" it creates would be to eschew all forms of voluntary affirmative action. Even a whisper of emphasis on minority recruiting would be forbidden. Because Congress intended to encourage private efforts to come into compliance with Title VII, see *Alexander v. Gardner-Denver Co.*, 415 U.S. 336, 44, 94 S.Ct. 1011, 1017, 39 L.Ed.2d 147 (1974), Judge Wisdom [who wrote the court of appeals opinion] concluded that employers and unions who had committed "arguable violations" of Title VII should be free to make reasonable responses without fear of liability to whites. 563 F.2d, at 230. Preferential hiring along the lines of the Kaiser program is a reasonable response for the employer, whether or not a court, on these facts, could order the same step as a remedy. The company is able to avoid identifying victims of past discrimination, and so avoids claims for back pay that would inevitably follow a response limited to such victims. If past victims should be benefited by the program, however, the company mitigates its liability to those persons. Also, to the extent that Title VII liability is predicated on the "disparate effect" of an employer's past hiring practices, the program makes it less likely that such an effect can be demonstrated. Cf. *County of Los Angeles v. Davis*, 440 U.S. 625, 633–634, 99 S.Ct. 1379, 1384, 59 L.Ed.2d 642 (1979) (Hiring could moot a past Title VII claim). And the Court has recently held that work-force statistics resulting from private affirmative action were probative of benign intent in a "disparate treatment" case. *Furnco Construction Corp. v. Waters*, 438 U.S. 567, 579–580, 98 S.Ct. 2943, 2950–951, 57 L.Ed.2d 957 (1958).[39]

Certain forms of legal argument dominate the majority and dissenting opinions in *Weber*. Each opinion begins at the level of textual argument. The nub of textual argument is the meaning a legal text has to the common, professional reader. Historical argument proceeds by appeal to the then-present legislative context. What was Congress trying to do with this statute? What was its point or purpose? We saw that in *Weber* neither the textual nor the historical forms of

37. The phrase is William Eskridge's. See William N. Eskridge Jr., "Dynamic Statutory Interpretation," 135 *U. Pa. L. Rev.* 1479, 1491 (1987).
38. *Id.* at 1492–94.
39. 443 U.S. at 210–11.

argument yielded a compelling conclusion. Yes, the text of the statute does preclude "discrimination." But that term of art is not defined. When one looks to history for elucidation, one finds competing—if not conflicting—congressional purposes and aspirations. At the level of text and history, no clear direction is indicated.

Justice Blackmun's concurring opinion employs two different forms of legal argument: prudential and doctrinal. A prudential argument is one that measures the consequences of a decision. It asks after the effects of deciding a case one way rather than another. In his concurring opinion, Justice Blackmun argues that the effect of reading Title VII in the manner urged by the respondent, Weber, would be deleterious in the extreme, and he offers reasons for his conclusion it is on the whole better to side with the majority. The *measure* of good and bad effects employed by Blackmun comes not from a utilitarian calculus, but from precedent. Blackmun cleverly weaves prudential judgment with doctrinal argument to break the deadlock between text and history played out in the majority and dissenting opinions. To decide the case as Weber urges means departing from precedents sanctioning private affirmative actions plans. Additionally, reversing the lower court's decision would have negative effects in related matters such as "disparate effect" and "disparate treatment."[40] By fitting his prudential arguments within the fold of precedent, Blackmun breaks free of the intractable differences between the majority and the dissent, thereby enabling him to write an opinion that is far more persuasive than its competitors.

Let us return to our consideration of the positivist theory of law by reminding ourselves of what was at issue in *Weber*. The question posed by the case is whether the following proposition is true: "Title VII does not prohibit private employers and unions from agreeing on and implementing affirmative action programs that accord racial preferences for job training."[41] Of course, the Court held that the proposition is indeed true. But what does it mean to say this?

The legal positivist's answer to this question is that the proposition in question is true in virtue of some social fact. In cases of statutory interpretation, like *Weber*, the pertinent social fact is a legislative act (of Congress). According to legal positivism, the truth of the proposition at issue in *Weber* turns on the question whether certain conditions of social fact obtain. The disputed proposition of law is true if and only if Congress has not passed a law prohibiting private affirmative action plans of the sort employed by Kaiser. In short, and as Ronald Dworkin has noticed, for the legal positivist "propositions of law are propositions about laws."[42]

For the positivist, "truth" in law states a relation or correspondence between the disputed proposition and some state of affairs (social facts). The rule of recognition states criteria that, if they obtain, make the proposition at issue true. Thus, the proposition at issue in *Weber* is true if and only if there exists some

40. *See* 443 U.S. at 211.

41. The majority opinion states the proposition at issue in much the same way. See 443 U.S. at 209.

42. Ronald Dworkin, Introduction to *The Philosophy of Law* 6 (R. Dworkin ed., 1977).

social fact (e.g., an act of the legislature) in virtue of which it is true. Lawyers and judges are agreed on the criteria for satisfying the test for law set forth by the rule of recognition; the only question is whether those criteria are satisfied.

As this discussion of *Weber* illustrates, the proposition of law at issue there is not true in virtue of facts, social or otherwise. Like Austin, Hart adheres to the view that the legislative pronouncement is bounded, and that it is the task of the judge to discern where the boundary lies by locating the limit set by social facts. The truth of propositions of law turns on facts about what Congress or the legislature has done. But as the discussion of *Weber* shows us, there are no "facts" about what Congress has done that are the conditions for the truth of legal propositions. Yes, it *is* true that the proposition in question cannot be true unless the legislature has "done" something. But the point is that it is only through the use of forms of legal argument that we can even say what it is the legislature has done. The mistake legal positivists make is to believe that the meaning of the law lies in the acts of certain institutional players in the legal system. What the analysis of *Weber* shows is that the meaning of legislative action is a matter of forms of legal argument. Practice, not facts, is what the truth of legal propositions consists in.[43]

Propositions of law are not true in virtue of criteria specified by the rule of recognition. The forms of argument—the grammar of legal justification—are the means by which the truth of legal propositions is shown. There are no legal truths—no true propositions of law—outside these forms of argument. This is why the positivist's criterial test of legal truth misses the mark. Propositions of law are not *in virtue of* anything; not social facts, legislative facts, nor facts of past institutional decisions (e.g., prior judicial decisions).

Hart treats propositions of law as if they were hypotheses about institutional facts that, if verified, are then taken to be true. The forms of argument are not a bridge between a putative proposition of law and some state of affairs. When judges decide cases, they are not searching out facts about past legislative acts. Deciding cases is not the same thing as conducting an experiment. When a judge decides a case, she employs the forms of argument to justify her conclusion that the proposition in question is true or false. The forms, not social facts, are the measure of her judgment.

Forms of Argument and the Rule of Recognition

Might it be possible for a legal positivist to agree with the foregoing? Perhaps all I have managed to do is to show that legal positivism is the correct theory of law. Could I be said to have shown that the forms of argument are the rule of recognition itself, albeit a complex one?

For several reasons, I do not think this strategy is open to the legal positivist. The rule of recognition is itself a rule—indeed, a master rule—which states criteria for what counts as a primary rule of the legal system. As we have seen, the

---

43. See Gerald Postema, "'Protestant' Interpretation and Social Practices," 6 *Law & Phil.* 283, 318 (1987).

forms of argument are not a rule (or several rules). They are what makes following a legal rule possible. The forms of argument are the grammar of law. When one asserts that "the law of contracts provides a remedy for breach of the obligation of good faith," that assertion purports to state a true proposition of law. Lawyers employ forms of argument to show that this proposition is true as a matter of law.

According to legal positivism, the rule of recognition states criteria that must be satisfied if a proposition of law may be said to be a true proposition of law. Hart states as much in the following passage, in which he describes the central role of the rule of recognition in mature legal systems:

> Where . . . as in a mature legal system, we have a system of rules which includes a rule of recognition so that the status of a rule as a member of the system now depends on whether it satisfies certain criteria provided by the rule of recognition, this brings with it a new application of the word 'exist'. The statement that a rule exists may now no longer be what it was in the simple case of customary rules—an external statement of the *fact* that a certain mode of behaviour was generally accepted as a standard in practice. It may now be an internal statement applying an accepted but unstated rule of recognition and meaning (roughly) no more than 'valid given the system's criteria of validity.' In this respect, however, as in others a rule of recognition is unlike other rules of the system. The assertion that it exists can only be an external statement of fact. For whereas a subordinate rule of a system may be valid and in that sense 'exist' even if it is generally disregarded, the rule of recognition exists only as a complex, but normally concordant, practice of the courts, officials, and private persons in identifying the law *by reference to certain criteria*. Its existence is a matter of fact.[44]

Are the forms of argument criteria? Taken together, do the forms of argument amount to the same thing as the rule of recognition? Because the rule of recognition is a test of origins[45] or pedigree, the answer can only be in the negative:

> Very simply put, legal rules are all a part of the same legal system if they have the same pedigree—i.e., they can all be traced to the same rule of recognition or set of rules of recognition that define validity, for that system. This device also gives us an easy way to answer, at least for primary rules, the question of what it means to say that these rules *exist*. Some rule R exists as a rule in legal system S if its pedigree can be traced to the rule or rules of recognition defining legality for S. Thus: There exists (for example) a valid law prohibiting driving over 25 miles per hour in a residential area, *even if nobody ever obeys that law*, so long as the law was enacted in the proper law-creating and law-defining way.[46]

---

44. Hart, *supra* note 2, at 110 (second emphasis added).

45. Dworkin states the matter crisply in Dworkin *supra*, note 24, at 40 ("Most rules of law, according to Hart, are valid because some competent institution enacted them. Some were created by a legislature, in the form of statutory enactment. Others were created by judges who formulated them to decide particular cases, and thus established them as precedents for the future.").

46. Murphy & Coleman, *supra* note 11, at 37.

The account of the rule of recognition just offered cannot explain what is at stake in a case like *Weber*. The forms of argument there at issue—textual, historical, doctrinal, and prudential—cannot be traced to any source, let alone a single rule (of recognition). The origin of the forms of argument lies not in a particular decision of Congress or a legislature. They are our culturally endorsed forms of juridical appraisal. The forms of argument are not legislated into existence. Their continued use lies, in words employed by Dworkin in another context, "in a sense of appropriateness developed in the public and the profession over time."[47] It is by virtue of their use that they are "valid." It is *in* their use that propositions of law are characterized as true and false.

Conclusion

As a theory of the truth conditions for propositions of law, Hart's legal positivism is at one with the idea that reference is the key to meaning.[48] Of course, what a legal proposition refers to is some social fact (e.g., an act of a legislature) in virtue of which the proposition in question is true. In this chapter, I have taken no issue with the positivist claim that—at least in the case of legislation—there must be a text for there to be law. What I have challenged is the assertion that reference (to social facts) and not linguistic usage or practice—the forms of legal argument—is the key to legal meaning. As a theory of law, positivism is a theory of origins: it asserts that the truth of propositions of law lies in their having been promulgated *in the right way*. I have challenged this picture with a different one, that of truth as a matter of the grammar of legal justification. The truth of a proposition of law lies not in what the legislature has done but in how the legislative act is characterized. Use, not reference, is the key to meaning and, thus, truth.

47. Dworkin, *supra* note 24, at 40.

48. Of course, the argument that reference is the key to the meaning is a widely held view. See Stephen P. Schwartz, Introduction to *Naming, Necessity, and Natural Kinds* 13–41 (Stephen P. Schwartz ed., 1977) (contrasting older and newer theories of reference).

5

Law as Interpretation: The Jurisprudence of Ronald Dworkin

> There is a way of grasping a rule which is *not* an *interpretation*.
> Ludwig Wittgenstein[1]

Interpretive Universalism and Contemporary Legal Theory

Without a doubt, ours is the age of interpretation. From the natural sciences[2] to the social sciences,[3] the human sciences,[4] to the arts,[5] overwhelming evidence exists that interpretation is a central organizing theme of the late twentieth century.[6] In law, the importance of the "interpretive turn" can hardly be overestimated.[7] In addition to a plethora of symposia,[8] books,[9] and articles by leading

1. Ludwig Wittgenstein, *Philosophical Investigations* § 201 (G. E. M. Anscombe trans., 3d ed. 1958).

2. See Joseph Rouse, *Knowledge and Power: Toward a Political Philosophy of Science* (1987) (discussing the emerging influence of theories of interpretation on mainstream philosophy of science); Joseph Rouse, *The Interpretive Turn: Philosophy, Science, Culture* (David R. Hiley et al. eds., 1991) (including recent papers by Richard Rorty, Thomas Kuhn, and Hubert Dreyfus that detail the "interpretive turn" recently taken in the philosophy of the natural sciences).

3. See *Interpretive Social Science: A Second Look* (Paul Rabinow & William M. Sullivan eds., 1987) (including papers by Hans-Georg Gadamer, Charles Taylor, Clifford Geertz, and Jürgen Habermas that discuss the increased turn to interpretation in the social sciences).

4. The most articulate contemporary exponent of the hermeneutic perspective, Charles Taylor, describes the human condition in the following terms: "[W]e can therefore say that the human animal not only finds himself impelled from time to time to interpret himself and his goals, but that he is always already in some interpretation, constituted as human by this fact." Charles Taylor, "Self-Interpreting Animals," in *Human Agency and Language* 45, 75 (1985).

5. See Arthur C. Danto, *The Philosophical Disenfranchisement of Art* 39–46 (1986) (arguing that interpretation is a constitutive feature of any judgment that a work is a work of art).

6. See generally *The Linguistic Turn: Recent Essays in Philosophical Method* (Richard Rorty ed., 1967) (presenting a classic collection of essays that charts the rise of language as the central focus of philosophical attention in twentieth-century philosophy).

7. One legal scholar has observed that "[t]he notion that law is an interpretive practice, in which legal materials must be given meaning by purposive agents, has caught on with a vengeance." Richard H. Fallon Jr., "Reflections on Dworkin and the Two Faces of Law," 67 *Notre Dame L. Rev.* 553, 554 (1992). According to the editors of a recent collection of essays, interpretation of texts is a central focus of critical reflection on law: "Of course, legal events more often require the

scholars in all fields of substantive law,[10] the growth of interest in law on the part of academics in the humanistic disciplines[11] confirms that questions of textual meaning are the central, if not the organizing, concern of many sophisticated legal theorists.

There is something fundamentally wrong with the current interpretive orthodoxy.[12] The notion that every act of textual and verbal comprehension is a matter of some act or theory of interpretation is a deeply misconceived idea,[13] one born of a lack of attention to some obvious features of ordinary understanding, coupled with an inordinate emphasis upon, and faith in, the power of theory as the genesis of expressive intelligibility. As we shall see, by making interpretation central to legal thought, the proponents of interpretive universalism have created nothing short of a philosophical hall of mirrors.

In this chapter and the next, we explore the intricacies of interpretive universalism—the idea that all understanding is a matter of interpretation[14]—by examining the work of two exemplary proponents of its virtues, Ronald Dworkin and Stanley Fish. One would be hard-pressed, indeed, to find two other contemporary legal theorists who have done more to bring to the center of attention questions of meaning, truth, and textuality. Despite their several, sometimes bitterly

---

reading of texts such as wills, custody decrees, business contracts, and the like than scrutiny of administrative regulations, statutes, or constitutions. But what all such events do have in common is the necessity of interpretation, of giving meaning to the black ink on the white page. Though some argue that methods of interpretation may differ depending on whether a will or a constitution is being analyzed, few disagree that ascertaining the meaning of texts is a central reality of any legal system." *Interpreting Law and Literature: A Hermeneutic Reader* at ix (Sanford Levinson & Steven Mailloux eds., 1988).

8. See, e.g., Symposium, "Interpretation," 58 *S. Cal. L. Rev.* 1 (1985); Symposium, "Beyond Critique: Law, Culture, and the Politics of Form," 69 *Tex. L. Rev.* 1595 (1991).

9. See, e.g., *Legal Hermeneutics: History, Theory, and Practice* (Gregory Leyh ed., 1992); Richard A. Posner, *Law and Literature: A Misunderstood Relation* (1988).

10. See, e.g., Ronald Dworkin, "Law as Interpretation," 9 *Critical Inquiry* 179, 180–81 (1982) (characterizing a proposition of law as a combination of straightforward description and interpretive evaluations); Michael S. Moore, "The Interpretive Turn in Modern Theory: A Turn for the Worse?," 41 *Stan. L. Rev.* 871 (1989) (criticizing interpretivism for de-emphasizing the debate over legal realism).

11. See, e.g., Jean-François Lyotard & Jean-Loup Thébaud, *Just Gaming* (Wlad Godzich trans., 1985); Joel C. Weinsheimer, *Eighteenth-Century Hermeneutics: Philosophy of Interpretation in England from Locke to Burke* (1993).

12. Richard Rorty describes this orthodoxy as a "*thoroughly* pragmatic account of interpretation, one which no longer contrasts interpretation with use." Richard Rorty, "The Pragmatist's Progress," in *Interpretation and Overinterpretation* 100–01 (Stefan Collini ed., 1992).

13. See P. M. S. Hacker, "Language, Rules and Pseudo-Rules," 8 *Language & Comm.* 159, 168 (1988) ("[I]t is a grievous error to think that in understanding an utterance one always or even usually engages in interpretation.").

14. For an example of the pervasiveness of interpretive universalism in contemporary jurisprudence, see Frederick Schauer, *Playing by the Rules* 207 (1991) ("*[E]very* application of a rule is also an interpretation."). But see Richard Shusterman, *Pragmatist Aesthetics: Living Beauty, Rethinking Art* 120 (1991) (arguing against interpretive universalism but acknowledging that its influence is pervasive).

debated differences on interpretive and jurisprudential questions,[15] Dworkin and Fish are allied at the deepest level of philosophical conviction. As the arguments that follow demonstrate, interpretive universalism, and the manifold claims that issue from it, engender a seriously false and misleading picture of law.

Dworkin and Fish are not alone in having made interpretation a central focus of jurisprudential attention.[16] At the level of general jurisprudence, many theorists have advanced sophisticated accounts of legal interpretation.[17] From this vast literature, a central tenet emerges: Understanding a social practice (e.g., law) is a matter of imposing an interpretation on that practice.[18] Because interpretations or perspectives can and do differ, there may in principle be no way to choose between competing interpretations.[19] The slide to relativism is swift and sure, for there is no stopping the infinite regress of interpretation.[20] Every perspective begets another and so on and so on. In the end, it seems, all we have are our own perceptions.[21]

15. Examples of their earlier exchanges are found in Ronald Dworkin, "My Reply to Stanley Fish (and Walter Benn Michaels): Please Don't Talk About Objectivity Any More," in *The Politics of Interpretation* 287 (W. J. T. Mitchell ed., 1983); Stanley E. Fish, "Working on the Chain Gang: Interpretation in the Law and in Literary Criticism," 9 *Critical Inquiry* 201 (1982); Stanley E. Fish, "Wrong Again," 62 *Tex. L. Rev.* 299 (1983).

16. See, e.g., Symposium, "Interpretation," *supra* note 8. Of course, the source for the contemporary expression of the view that all understanding is interpretation is the master of hermeneutics, Martin Heidegger. See Martin Heidegger, *Being and Time* 188–95 (John Macquarrie & Edward Robinson trans., 1962). Of no less importance in this regard is the development of the hermeneutic tradition by Heidegger's student, Hans-Georg Gadamer. See Hans-Georg Gadamer, *Truth and Method* at xxxvi (Joel Weinsheimer & Donald G. Marshall rev. trans., 2d rev. ed. 1989).

17. A recent, interesting example of this phenomenon is Gunther Teubner, *Law as an Autopoietic System* (Zenon Bankowski ed., Anne Bankowska & Ruth Adler trans., 1993) (analyzing law as a self-reproducing system of communication).

18. See James F. Bohman et al., Introduction to *The Interpretive Turn*, *supra* note 2, at 1, 1–4 (emphasizing the importance of interpretation in the social sciences).

19. Some regard the effort to choose among interpretations as futile: "[T]hose of us who are classified as nihilists have drunk deeply at the well of those branches of modern thought most skeptical of concepts like truth, neutrality, or disinterestedness, insofar as all of these terms retain a strong barrier between the knowing subject and the object of knowledge. Many of us, instead, view what is professed to be known as itself constituted by the subject that claims to know. 'Truth' may continue to be a word within modernist culture, but only as a synonym for culturally shared conventions." Sanford Levinson, *Constitutional Faith* 175 (1988).

20. See Michael Williams, *Unnatural Doubts: Epistemological Realism and the Basis of Scepticism* 61 (1991) ("Trying to justify a given proposition by citing a further proposition as evidence gets us nowhere. . . . [T]hat proposition will itself need to be justified, as will anything we cite as evidence for it, and so on.").

21. This notion is, of course, familiar to us from Friedrich Nietzsche: "'Everything is subjective,' you say; but even this is interpretation. The 'subject' is not something given, it is something added and invented and projected beyond what there is.—Finally, is it necessary to posit an interpreter behind the interpretation? Even this is invention, hypothesis. In so far as the word 'knowledge' has any meaning, the world is knowable; but it is *interpretable* otherwise, it has no meaning behind it, but countless meanings.—'Perspectivism.' It is our needs that interpret the world; our drives and their For and Against. Every drive is a kind of lust to rule; each one has its perspective that it would like to compel all the other drives to accept as a norm." Friedrich Nietzsche, *The Will to Power* 267 (Walter Kaufmann ed., Walter Kaufmann & R. J. Hollingdale trans., 1968).

One impulse giving rise to the idea that interpretation is our primary mode of cognition is, of course, the antifoundationalist spirit:[22] the aspiration to throw off all accounts of knowledge as resting upon an edifice and to replace them with perspectives or points of view. Inspired by the idea that we cannot study "the phenomenon itself" apart from a language of description, the possibility of objectivity in judgment is sacrificed in favor of a perspectival epistemology.[23]

Critics of foundationalism have been supremely successful in their efforts to call into question the central tenets of the foundationalist enterprise.[24] However, in their effort to escape the grip of foundationalism, interpretive universalists may have displaced foundationalism[25] only to reduplicate it.[26] In other words, one foundation—call it 'Cartesianism'—has been replaced by another, that of the interpretive perspective.[27] Unfortunately, interpretive universalists have managed

22. By "antifoundationalist" I mean "eschewing all appeals to ontological or epistemological or ethical absolutes." John McGowan, *Postmodernism and Its Critics* at ix (1991). For a broader discussion of antifoundationalism and its place in current discussions of postmodernism, see Dennis Patterson, "Postmodernism/Feminism/Law," 77 *Cornell L. Rev.* 254, 269–79 (1992).

23. But see John McDowell, "Projection and Truth in Ethics," Lindley Lecture, University of Kansas, Department of Philosophy 11 (1988) (noting that speaking "within a language does not engender the demise of objectivity").

24. Some of the best efforts include Laurence BonJour, *The Structure of Empirical Knowledge* (1985); Richard Rorty, *Philosophy and the Mirror of Nature* (1979); Charles Taylor, "Interpretation and the Sciences of Man," in *Philosophy and the Human Sciences* 15 (1985). Philosophers are not united in rejecting foundationalism. See, e.g., William P. Alston, *Epistemic Justification* (1989) (arguing that foundationalism is a live option with fewer problems than coherentism); Robert Audi, *Belief, Justification, and Knowledge* (1988) (defending a modest foundationalism); Paul K. Moser, *Empirical Justification* (1985) (arguing for an epistemic intuitionist version of foundationalism).

25. Richard Shusterman provides a helpful description of both interpretive universalism and its folly: "[T]he universalists are right to reject . . . foundational understanding, but wrong to conclude from this that all understanding is interpretation. Their mistake, a grave but simple one, is to equate the non-foundational with the interpretive. In other words, what the universalists are successfully arguing is that all understanding is non-foundational; that it is always corrigible, perspectival, and somehow prejudiced or prestructured; that no meaningful experience is passively neutral and disinterestedly non-selective. But since, in the traditional foundationalist framework, interpretation is contrasted and designated *the* form of non-foundational understanding, the inferior foster home of all corrigible, perspectival perception, it is easy to confuse the view that no understanding is foundational with the view that all understanding is interpretive. Yet this confusion of [interpretive] universalism betrays an unseemly residual bond to the foundationalist framework, in the assumption that what is not foundational must be interpretive." Shusterman, *supra* note 14, at 120.

26. This needs to be explained. I am not saying that antifoundationalist accounts of knowledge are merely disguised foundationalist accounts. I am saying that just as some foundationalists assume that knowledge must rest on an indubitable foundation, antifoundationalists simply assume that understanding a phenomenon is a matter of interpreting it. Thus, the antifoundationalist "solution" to the shortcomings of foundationalist epistemology stems from the substitution of one premise for another. This is an unsatisfying way to solve a philosophical problem.

27. Descartes argued that we could not have knowledge without an indubitable foundation for it. See René Descartes, *Meditations on First Philosophy* 12 (John Cottingham trans., 1986) (1641). Similarly, interpretive universalists maintain that our understanding of the world can proceed only on the basis of an interpretation and that without interpretation there is no understanding.

only to replace one orthodoxy with another, thereby falling into the same trap as the foundationalists they are so eager to criticize.[28]

This brings us to the premier proponents of interpretive universalism in law, Ronald Dworkin and Stanley Fish. Now, many theorists—including Dworkin and Fish themselves—see little convergence in their respective substantive jurisprudential views.[29] Dworkin, the arch-defender of liberal virtues, contrasts sharply with the irreverent, playful, and free-wheeling character of Fish. Yet, the differences between Dworkin and Fish are merely superficial. On the question of legal normativity,[30] Dworkin and Fish embrace precisely the same form of explanation.[31] In short, the thesis of this chapter and the next is that Dworkin and Fish are united at the deepest level of philosophical conviction.

Dworkin and Fish each reduce legal understanding to an act of apprehension. Understanding law is not a practice or ability; rather, legal truth is the product of a connection between language and a sublime explanatory device. I argue that this account of the nature of legal understanding is profoundly misleading. It turns the ordinary into the mysterious, and it fails to account for the fact that understanding and interpretation are distinct activities. To reduce one to the other obfuscates the role of language in the exercise of legal justification and, more importantly, the relationship of language to the world.

From the beginning, Ronald Dworkin's project has been driven by a central philosophical concern, that of specifying the truth conditions for propositions of law. Dworkin's jurisprudence is the most sustained attempt in the literature to make the case for the relational thesis—that is, the idea that the truth of propositions of law is dependent upon the truth of moral propositions.[32] While I concentrate on Dworkin's mature expression of his view—the idea that law is an interpretive practice—it is important to understand that throughout the development of his view, Dworkin's attention has never wavered from his position on how one can specify the truth conditions for propositions of law: by identifying principles that best explain the purposes and structure of the legal system.

---

28. Consider this representative example of interpretive theory from the field of cultural anthropology: "[F]acts are made, fabricated, constructed, . . . observations are not independent of theory, . . . the ethnologist and his informants are collaborators in a work of interpretation, the informants proposing to the ethnologist, following an entirely special rhetoric of presentation, the "explanations" they invent as a function of their notion of their expectations and at the cost of a truly theoretical effort, one implying the assumption of an extraordinary stance induced by the interrogatory situation itself." Pierre Bourdieu, Afterword to Paul Rabinow, *Reflections on Fieldwork in Morocco* 164–65 (1977).

29. See *supra* note 15 and accompanying text.

30. By "normativity" I mean that which explains our judgments of correctness and error. See *infra* note 122.

31. That is, each sees the truth of propositions of law as true *in virtue of* some practice-transcendent state of affairs. For Dworkin, it is moral principles and for Fish agreement within an interpretive community.

32. Michael Moore, whose position we explored in chapter 3, has a similar project. See Michael S. Moore, "Moral Reality Revisited," 90 *Mich. L. Rev.* 2424, 2426 (1992) (noting that Dworkin is known for "his linkage of the truth of legal propositions to idealized constructions of moral conventions"). Moore has made an effort to reach the same end from the perspective of moral

Ronald Dworkin and Constructive Interpretation

From Positivism to Law as Interpretation

Dworkin's theory of law was born in his criticism of legal positivism. In an early article on judicial discretion, Dworkin countered the positivist claim that the content of law is exhausted by its rules with the argument that, in addition to rules, the law is composed of principles and policies.[33] With this observation, Dworkin established his as a new voice in Anglo-American analytic jurisprudence.[34] Twelve years later, in 1975, Dworkin published his first expression of a complete theory of law. In "Hard Cases,"[35] Dworkin advanced what he referred to as the "rights thesis"—that even in hard cases, one party has the right to win the lawsuit as a matter of principle.[36] Furthering his earlier attack on legal positivism, Dworkin argued "that even when no settled rule disposes of the case, one party may nevertheless have a right to win."[37]

The most significant aspect of "Hard Cases"—what marked it as a remarkable departure from prior theories of law—was the manner in which Dworkin put law together with political theory in a way that could only ennoble the activity of deciding cases. In detailing the interplay between political theory and adjudication, Dworkin described the obligation of a judge in deciding a constitutional case in the following words:

> He must develop a theory of the constitution, in the shape of a complex set of principles and policies that justify that scheme of government. . . . He must develop that theory by referring alternatively to political philosophy and institutional detail. He must generate possible theories justifying different aspects of the scheme and test the theories against the broader institution. When the discriminating power of that test is exhausted, he must elaborate the contested concepts that the successful theory employs.[38]

In Dworkin's view, hard cases force the critically reflective jurist (and lawyer) to develop a theory of political institutions and to employ it by identifying moral principles that "can supply a justification for a particular decision."[39] This justification is achieved "only if the principle cited can be shown to be consistent with earlier decisions not recanted, and with decisions that the institution is prepared to make."[40] Justification in hard cases begins by identifying those principles that

---

realism. See *id.* at 2425 (arguing that legal propositions depend upon "the truth of some corresponding moral proposition(s)").

33. Ronald Dworkin, "Judicial Discretion," 60 *J. Phil.* 624, 634 (1963).

34. See Fallon, *supra* note 7, at 553–54 (describing Dworkin's groundbreaking attempt to establish a "third theory of law," separate from the existing positivist and natural law theories).

35. Ronald Dworkin, "Hard Cases," 88 *Harv. L. Rev.* 1057 (1975).

36. Dworkin later incorporated a revised version of that article into Ronald Dworkin, *Taking Rights Seriously* 81–130 (1977).

37. *Id.* at 81.

38. *Id.* at 107.

39. *Id.* at 88.

40. *Id.*

provide an abstract justification for the institutional scheme as a whole.[41] Thus, the movement of thought is downward, passing through institutional detail to a scheme of abstract and concrete rights, and then to the identification of a principle that is in keeping with the best understanding of the institution taken as a whole and is dispositive of the issue posed by the hard case at hand.[42]

Dworkin has never wavered from this picture of legal justification. A hiatus of more than a decade from "Hard Cases" to *Law's Empire*[43] served not to alter but only to broaden and deepen his capacious view of legal justification. Resort to the grand sweep of political theory and principle would no longer be limited to the occasion of the hard case. In its mature expression in *Law's Empire*, Dworkin's theory of law places political theory at the center of judicial decision making. He states the general thesis thus: "Law as integrity, then, requires a judge to test his interpretation of *any part* of the great network of political structures and decisions of his community by asking whether it could form part of a coherent theory justifying the network as a whole."[44] Dworkin then applies this theory to reading statutes: "Integrity and fairness will constrain justice and wisdom . . . in a variety of ways. Integrity requires him to construct, for each statute he is asked to enforce, some justification that fits and flows through that statute and is, if possible, consistent with other legislation in force."[45]

He also applies the theory to constructing precedent, using an example from tort law:

> A successful interpretation must not only fit *but also justify* the practice it interprets. The judicial decisions [in typical tort cases] force some people to compensate others for losses suffered because their otherwise lawful activities conflicted, and since these decisions are made after the event, they are justified only if it is reasonable to suppose that people held in damages should have acted in some other way or should have accepted responsibility for the damage they caused. *So the decisions can be justified only by deploying some general scheme of moral responsibility the members of a community might properly be deemed to have*, about not injuring others or about taking financial responsibility for their acts.[46]

If anything stands out in Dworkin's picture of justification, it is his consistent return to the idea that legal justification, properly understood, can never be confined to the realm of what lawyers ordinarily think of as legal reasoning.[47] The positivist picture of law as a body of rules was shown to be incomplete because it failed to include principles.[48] The words of a statute, which alone articu-

---

41. See *id.* at 123.

42. See *id.* at 123–30.

43. Ronald Dworkin, *Law's Empire* (1986).

44. *Id.* at 245 (emphasis added).

45. *Id.* at 338.

46. *Id.* at 285 (emphasis added).

47. See, e.g., *id.* at 43–44 (contending that legal justification does not result from the traditional method of consulting a body of fixed rules and then applying the rules to particular facts).

48. See Dworkin, *supra* note 43, at 627. There has been much debate over whether Dworkin's critique of positivism is anything other than a helpful, as opposed to a damning, criticism. See,

late a mandate of the legislature, can never be a sufficient justification for a judicial decision, for those words must be consistent with "some justification that fits and flows through that statute."[49] In construing precedent, it is not enough to invoke the normal requirements of articulate consistency and the like, for precedent must be validated by a scheme of principle that, morally speaking, puts doctrine "in the best light."[50]

At the heart of Dworkin's picture of justification lies the idea that to be justified, law must be validated by something beyond the confines of text, precedent, legislative purpose, and history. In short, no matter how well the judge goes about her decisional task (as conventionally understood), her decision is not justified if it cannot be shown to be consistent with the demands of moral principle. Prior to its validation through the justificatory process Dworkin describes, the judicial decision is, in effect, only a placeholder—a "proto-justification"—that awaits validation by resort to an external, moral measure.[51]

Shortly after the publication of "Hard Cases," Dworkin characterized his differences with positivism over the meaning of "truth." His words in the following passage also bear out the reading of his view given above: that justification in law must come from beyond the law. He said:

> Lawyers use propositions of law to describe or declare certain relationships, particularly relationships of rights and duties, within the institution of law, and when they disagree about these relationships they argue about the truth of such propositions. They argue, for example, about whether the law, properly understood, provides that someone has a right to be compensated for economic damage he suffers because of an injury to someone else. Lawyers find difficulty, however, in setting out in any general way what such propositions mean, or, *what comes to the same thing, the conditions under which they are true or false.*[52]

---

e.g., Jules L. Coleman, "Ronald Dworkin's *Taking Rights Seriously*," 66 *Cal. L. Rev.* 885, 892 (1978) (book review) (stating that "the positivist might accept Dworkin's argument that principles figure in judicial decisions but deny" that positivism would define rules as narrowly as Dworkin claims it would); Rolf Sartorius, "Social Policy and Judicial Legislation," 8 *Am. Phil. Q.* 151, 153 (1971) (arguing that principles can easily be incorporated into the idea of a rule of recognition).

49. Dworkin, *supra* note 43, at 338.

50. *Id.* at 67.

51. Others have noticed that this element of Dworkin's theory is not as clear as it might be. For example, Ernest Weinrib argues: "[Dworkin] characterizes interpretation as the striving to make an object the best it can be. Dworkin's thesis is that the internal point of view necessitates, through interpretation, reference to 'the best.' Even if reference to 'the best' is required by the internal point of view, however, is Dworkin's conception of the best itself internal to law? The matter can be put as follows: Is an interpretation best because it is internal or is it internal because it is best? Although Dworkin does not, to my knowledge, explicitly raise this issue, the answer he would give is crucial. If internality is controlling, Dworkin would be depending on an unarticulated notion of form. If on the other hand, goodness is controlling, Dworkin's theory would not be fully internal. Dworkin seems to want to have it both ways and to be simultaneously inside and outside." Ernest J. Weinrib, "Legal Formalism: On the Immanent Rationality of Law," 97 *Yale L.J.* 949, 1014 n.132 (1988).

52. R. M. Dworkin, Introduction to *The Philosophy of Law* 1, 5 (R. M. Dworkin ed., 1977) (emphasis added).

In answer to the question "What does it mean to say that a proposition of law is true?" Dworkin replies that a proposition of law is true only to the extent it can be justified by resort to a political theory that identifies a principle that puts legal practice in its best light.[53] In other words, a proposition of law is true because the best political justification *makes it so*. Of course, a judge may not be in a position to know whether or not the political theory she advances in support of her decision is the best political theory, all things considered. But this, Dworkin maintains, cannot warrant denying the existence, in principle, of one political justification standing above all others.[54]

Dworkin's characterization of the nature of disagreements over truth conditions highlights, albeit in a different way, his differences with legal positivism:

> Since there is no agreement about the conditions which, if true, establish the truth of [controversial] propositions, they cannot be assigned any straightforward sense, and must therefore be understood in some special way, if at all.
>
> In this way a central and critical issue in the philosophy of law is also a central and critical issue in the philosophy of meaning. . . .
>
> There can be no effective reply to the positivist's anti-realist theory of meaning in law, however, unless an alternative theory of propositions of law is produced. That theory must assign a sense to controversial propositions of law comparable to the sense that controversial propositions in science, history, literature, and academic awards are supposed, by those who use them, to have. It must at least show how disagreement about such propositions may seem genuine to lawyers and not, as the anti-realist position would insist, illusory.[55]

In these paragraphs, Dworkin signals his agenda for the next decade. Having demonstrated the paucity of positivism's picture of legal practice, and having forged a link between political theory and legal justification, Dworkin sets the trajectory for the next major development in his thought—the turn to interpretation as the constitutive feature of legal practice. It is to that development that I now turn.

---

53. See Dworkin, *supra* note 43, at 225 ("According to law as integrity, propositions of law are true if they figure in or follow from the principles of justice, fairness, and procedural due process that provide the best constructive interpretation of the community's legal practice."); see also Ken Kress, "The Interpretive Turn," 97 *Ethics* 834, 835 (1987) ("For Dworkin, legal propositions are true if they follow from that coherent scheme of principles which best justifies and explains the legal institutional facts (e.g., constitutions, statutes, and precedents).").

54. Dworkin, for example, argues: "Some readers may object that, if no procedure exists, even in principle, for demonstrating what legal rights the parties have in hard cases, it follows that they have none. That objection presupposes a controversial thesis of general philosophy, which is that no proposition can be true unless it can, at least in principle, be demonstrated to be true. There is no reason to accept that thesis as part of a general theory of truth, and good reason to reject its specific application to propositions about legal rights." Dworkin, *supra* note 36, at 81.

55. Dworkin, *supra* note 52, at 8–9.

The Interpretive Turn

In *Law's Empire*, Dworkin moves beyond the positivist doctrine that law is a matter of authoritative sources[56] to argue for the proposition that legal reasoning is an exercise in what he terms "constructive interpretation."[57] Law, Dworkin now informs us, is an interpretive practice,[58] but one of a special sort. Dworkin's interpretive or "hermeneutic"[59] account of law is illustrated by an analysis of an imaginary social practice of "courtesy."[60] We are asked to imagine a community whose members have a set of rules that requires certain forms of conduct in specified circumstances (e.g., a rule requiring the removal of one's hat in the presence of a nobleman). In the beginning, the members simply follow the rules of courtesy in an unreflective manner. They gradually develop reflective proclivities and begin to see their practice as serving some point or purpose—the rules exist for a reason (or combination of reasons). Once the members see that there is a point to what they do, they discover that they do not always agree on what courtesy requires in a given context. In short, the members disagree over the point of the practice. This, Dworkin maintains, is the point at which interpretation leads to the transformation of social practice.

Before turning to the specifics of how the practice of courtesy changes, let us examine more closely the particulars of the practice in the "preinterpretive stage,"[61] the point before which there is reflection on the point of the practice. Dworkin tells us that the community's members "follow a set of rules, which

---

56. See H. L. A. Hart, *The Concept of Law* 182 (1961) (stating that the law can be ascertained by reference to sources such as constitutions, legislative acts, and judicial precedents).

57. Dworkin, *supra* note 43, at vii. Dworkin's assertion that law is a practice of constructive interpretation and not a thing found (e.g., a rule) serves to distance him from positivism all the more. Before *Law's Empire*, it might have been said of Dworkin that he shared the positivist conception of law as "a thing found" and only disagreed about the extent of the items found (rules *and principles as well*). Now that Dworkin takes the view that all legal reasoning is a matter of "constructive interpretation," *id.* at 52, he breaks totally with the idea that law is *in any sense* found and not made. As Dworkin describes the course of his own thought, "In *Taking Rights Seriously* I offered arguments against legal positivism that emphasized the phenomenology of adjudication: I said that judges characteristically feel an obligation to give what I call 'gravitational force' to past decisions, and that this felt obligation contradicts the positivist's doctrine of judicial discretion. The present book, particularly in Chapter 4, emphasizes the interpretive rather than the phenomenological defects of positivism, but these are, at bottom, the same failures. I have also argued for many years against the positivist's claim that there cannot be 'right' answers to controversial legal questions, but only 'different' answers; I have insisted that in most hard cases there are right answers to be hunted by reason and imagination. Some critics have thought I meant that in these cases one answer could be *proved* right to the satisfaction of everyone, even though I insisted from the start that this is not what I meant, that the question whether we can have reason to think an answer right is different from the question whether it can be demonstrated to be right." *Id.* at viii–ix.

58. See *id.* at vii ("[L]egal reasoning is an exercise in constructive interpretation."); *id.* at 87 ("Law is an interpretive concept."); cf. *id.* at 52 ("[C]onstructive interpretation is a matter of imposing purpose on an object or practice.").

59. Dworkin discusses hermeneutic philosophy in *Law's Empire*, *supra* note 43, at 419 n.2.

60. *Id.* at 47–49.

61. *Id.* at 65.

they call 'rules of courtesy.'"[62] The rules are quite specific (as the "nobleman hat rule" illustrates), and compliance appears unreflective, almost mechanical. In a curious turn of phrase, Dworkin describes the members' conduct at this unreflective stage of the practice as having "the character of taboo."[63] He characterizes the members' attitude toward the rules this way: "[T]he rules are just there and are neither questioned nor varied."[64]

The movement from taboo to the interpretive attitude does not occur all at once, but it is pervasive. As Dworkin puts it, "Everyone develops a complex 'interpretive' attitude toward the rules of courtesy."[65] At that point everyone sees that courtesy serves some point or purpose. Further, they see that the requirements of courtesy—the specific forms of behavior called for by the practice—are not what the members of the group had always taken these requirements to be.[66] This move to interpretation causes the members to reshape their notions of what the rules of courtesy ought to be and what those rules require. The effects of the interpretive attitude are thorough and systematic, for "[o]nce this interpretive attitude takes hold, the institution of courtesy ceases to be mechanical; it is no longer unstudied deference to a runic order."[67]

Once the members of the community of courtesy are freed from the bonds of mechanical, unreflective compliance with the tradition-bound order of the past, they discover not only that the practice of courtesy has a point beyond the rules of practice; they discover also that they have deep disagreements with each other about just what that point is, and thus about what courtesy requires.[68] In short, the members of the community have awakened to two logically distinct aspects of their situation. First, they agree that the practice of courtesy serves some point; second, they disagree about what that point is. It is now up to all members of the community, *qua* participants in the practice of courtesy, to advance their own conception of the practice—what, for them, would put the practice "in its best light."[69]

In providing an account of courtesy or any other social practice, one relies on "a theory of interpretation."[70] In this approach, understanding the acts of another is a matter of one's having a theory about those acts.[71] But the interpretation of

---

62. *Id*. at 47.
63. *Id*.
64. *Id*.
65. *Id*.
66. *Id*.
67. *Id*.
68. *Id*. at 66–67.
69. *Id*. at 47.
70. *Id*. at 49. Dworkin describes this process as "an interpretation of the higher-order practice of using interpretive concepts." *Id*.
71. Dworkin shares this view with Posner: "The process of understanding is . . . a matter of understanding people, practices (such as living in houses), and the physical environment (the consequences of fire)—forms of understanding that depend on sharing the same basic life experiences. Alternatively, it is an imaginative process enabled by this sharing. We understand a message by putting ourselves in the speaker's shoes. . . . [T]he congruence between the speaker's intentions and our imaginative reconstruction—the success of the latter—is what enables communication to

social practices should not be seen as something special, for "people interpret in many different contexts, and we should begin by seeking some sense of how these contexts differ. *The most familiar occasion of interpretation—so familiar that we hardly recognize it as such—is conversation.* We interpret the sounds or marks another person makes in order to decide what he has said."[72]

Conversational interpretation—deciphering the sounds of another—is not, however, the appropriate model for the practice of law, which is "not conversational but *constructive*."[73] The aim of law as an exercise in constructive interpretation is not "to decipher the authors' purposes or intentions in writing a particular novel or maintaining a particular social tradition, just as we aim in conversation to grasp a friend's intentions in speaking as he does."[74] Constructive interpretation requires the adoption of a "protestant"[75] attitude toward the

---

succeed. The role of imagination in understanding is one reason you can decode the sentence." Richard Posner, *The Problems of Jurisprudence* 101 (1991) (citation omitted). In a footnote to this paragraph, Posner states, "This is not to say that the listener must be able to re-create in his mind an image in the speaker's mind." *Id.* at 101 n.1. The sentence is then followed by an example that, we are told, is "based on Wittgenstein—see *The Blue and Brown Books* 3 [1958]." *Id.* What is ironic about the footnote is Posner's belief that in the quoted paragraph he is saying something *consistent* with Wittgenstein. In fact, he provides an account of understanding that is a perfect example of the sort of pseudo-explanation of meaning Wittgenstein rails against in the book cited by Posner. See Ludwig Wittgenstein, *The Blue and Brown Books* 3–7, 32–36 (1958) (arguing that difficulty in interpreting a sign does not necessarily mean the sign itself is uncertain or that meaning is merely a product of interpretation). Posner's account of understanding is troubled for at least two reasons. First, understanding a sentence is not a matter of "congruence between intentions." What possible sense could be made of the idea of two intentions being "congruent"? If you order minestrone soup for lunch, and the waiter brings it, what work does the picture of "congruency" do? Second, intentions do not establish meanings. If you utter the sentence "I would like minestrone soup" but intended to order chicken noodle soup, the meaning of your request is clear. Furthermore, your intention is completely irrelevant to the meaning of what you said.

72. Dworkin, *supra* note 36, at 50 (emphasis added). In unpacking understanding in terms of interpretation or theory, Dworkin follows recent work in the philosophy of language, in particular that of Donald Davidson. See Donald Davidson, "Thought and Talk," in *Inquiries into Truth and Interpretation* 157 (1984) ("[A] creature cannot have thoughts unless it is an interpreter of the speech of another."). The following description of the implications of Davidson's theory-driven account of linguistic understanding applies equally well to Dworkin. In both domains (law as well as language) (intersubjective) understanding—for Dworkin and Davidson—is a matter of theory building: "If all human behaviour requires redescription in order to be grasped as human action (with its freight of intentions, beliefs, and desires), then that segment of behaviour which involves the utterance of sounds also requires redescription in order to be understood as a linguistic utterance with a specific meaning. The more primitive behavioural evidence requires organization by linguistic and semantic concepts; and once again the notion of organizing evidence seems to demand the use of the terms 'theorizing' and 'theory'. This is why Davidson [and for that matter Dworkin] feels justified in regarding everyday references to linguistic meaning (e.g., in reporting what someone said) as a mode of theory-building—or, as he puts it: 'Everyday linguistic and semantic concepts are part of an intuitive theory for organizing more primitive data. . . . If our ordinary concepts suggest a confused theory, we should look for a better theory, not give up theorizing.'" Stephen Mulhall, *On Being in the World: Wittgenstein and Heidegger on Seeing Aspects* 102 (1990) (quoting Davidson, *supra* at 143).

73. Dworkin, *supra* note 43, at 52.

74. *Id.* at 51–52.

75. Dworkin describes the protestant attitude thus: "What is law? Now I offer a different kind

practice, the implication of which is the obligation of "imposing purpose on an object or practice [e.g., the practice of courtesy] in order to make of it the best possible example of the form or genre to which it is taken to belong."[76]

This last element—the element of *value* present in the duty to produce the *best*—is of the utmost importance to understanding the normative character of protestant interpretation. In constructing the meaning of a practice, the interpreter proposes that others see the practice in a certain way.[77] It is in the advancement of a "mode of seeing" the practice that the individual participant *qua* individual "proposes value for the practice by describing some scheme of interests or goals or principles the practice can be taken to serve or exemplify."[78] The argument is not that this proposed value is there *in* the practice and is discovered through interpretation. As Dworkin states, the meaning is "imposed" *on* the practice *by* the interpreter.[79] This process of imposing value is not limited to the arena of constructive interpretation but is ubiquitous in interpretive activity:

> We would then say that all interpretation strives to make an object the best it can be, as an instance of some assumed enterprise, and that interpretation takes different forms in different contexts only because different enterprises engage different standards of value or success. Artistic interpretation differs from scientific interpretation, we would say, only because we judge success in works of art by standards different from those we use to judge explanations of physical phenomena.[80]

Of course, it is inevitable that different members of a practice (e.g., the practice of courtesy) will disagree as to the point of their shared enterprise. One may

---

of answer. Law is not exhausted by any catalogue of rules or principles, each with its own dominion over some discrete theater of behavior. Nor by any roster of officials and their powers each over part of our lives. Law's empire is defined by attitude, not territory or power or process. . . . It is an interpretive, self-reflective attitude addressed to politics in the broadest sense. It is a protestant attitude that makes each citizen responsible for imagining what his society's public commitments to principle are, and what these commitments require in new circumstances. . . . Law's attitude is constructive: it aims, in the interpretive spirit, to lay principle over practice to show the best route to a better future, keeping the right faith with the past." *Id.* at 413. Ultimately, the act of putting the practice "in its best light" is something individuals (including judges) do. Interpretation is not intersubjective for Dworkin, but deeply personal.

76. *Id.* at 52.

77. Dworkin explains: "I mean that an interpretation is by nature the report of a purpose; it proposes a way of seeing what is interpreted—a social practice or tradition as much as a painting—as if this were the product of a decision to pursue one set of themes or visions or purposes, one 'point,' rather than another." Dworkin, *supra* note 43, at 58–59.

78. *Id.* at 52.

79. See *id.* at 52. The imposition of a purpose on a practice by an interpreter is in sharp contrast to Hart's positivism, as well as to the hermeneutic tradition of thought, which locates normativity intersubjectively. See P. M. S. Hacker, "Hart's Philosophy of Law," in *Law, Morality and Society: Essays in Honour of H. L. A. Hart* 5, 9 (P. M. S. Hacker & J. Raz eds., 1977) ("One of the salient themes of hermeneutics is that description of distinctively human phenomena must involve understanding the situation described as it is apprehended by the agent whose behaviour is to be explained and understood.").

80. Dworkin, *supra* note 43, at 53.

see the respect of social rank as the key to understanding the repertoire of behaviors that make up the practice of courtesy, while another sees facilitation of social exchange as the principle of established practice. In the end, it is up to each individual to make of the practice what she will. In reflecting on courtesy, Dworkin posits: "[Each] citizen, we might say, is trying to discover his own intention in maintaining and participating in that practice—not in the sense of retrieving his mental state when he last took his cap off to a lady but in the sense of finding a purposeful account of his behavior he is comfortable in ascribing to himself."[81] In finding a value for the practice, the individual's ultimate turn is inward. Dworkin's provocative metaphor for this process is "interpretation as a conversation with oneself, as joint author and critic."[82] Thus, it is the duty of each participant in any practice to distinguish between trying to decide what other members of his community think the practice requires and trying to decide for himself what it really requires.[83] How does all of this relate to law? Let us turn now to that connection.

Interpretation and Law

The practice of constructive interpretation is composed of three stages:

1. The preinterpretive stage: the point at which "the rules and standards taken to provide the tentative content of the practice are identified."[84]
2. The interpretive stage: the point "at which the interpreter settles on some general justification for the main elements of the practice identified at the preinterpretive stage."[85]
3. The postinterpretive or reforming stage: the point at which the individual interpreter "adjusts his sense of what the practice 'really' requires so as better to serve the justification he accepts at the interpretive stage."[86]

One of the most interesting aspects of Dworkin's account of law as a constructive, interpretive practice is his analysis of the relationship between intersubjectivity and the normativity of law. For Dworkin, the normativity of law ultimately reposes in the soul of the individual interpreter.[87] To uncover the relationship between intersubjectivity and normativity, we must focus on the specifics of Dworkin's account of the movement from agreement on details in the preinterpretive stage to the ultimate justification of claims about what the practice "really" requires at the postinterpretive stage.

81. *Id.* at 58.
82. *Id.*
83. *Id.* at 65.
84. *Id.* at 65–66. As Dworkin states, the word "preinterpretive" is "in quotes because some kind of interpretation is necessary even at this stage." *Id.* at 66.
85. *Id.*
86. *Id.*
87. See *id.* at 413 ("Law's empire is defined by [the interpretive] attitude, not territory or power or process.").

While in the preinterpretive stage, each interpreter holds a fairly uniform idea about the basic details of the practice. As she enters the interpretive stage, the interpreter "proposes value for the practice by describing [a] scheme of interests or goals or principles the practice can be taken to serve or express or exemplify."[88] Her proposal will "consist of an argument why a practice of that general shape is worth pursuing, if it is."[89] Some values are screened out by the requirement that the proposed value "fit enough for the interpreter to be able to see himself as interpreting that practice, not inventing a new one."[90] The screen at this stage will not filter out all proposals. In fact, several divergent perspectives can meet the test of fit quite well. How is a choice made from among competitors? The answer comes in the third and final stage.

When we reach the postinterpretive stage, the agreement reached in earlier stages as to elements of detail has no normative force.[91] Once the interpretive attitude takes hold, interpreters do not advance descriptions (however contestable) of the practice; rather, what emerges are "conflicting views about what the practice as presently constituted really is and what, as a result, it really requires of participants."[92] It is individual interpretations that determine what the practice "really requires"[93] and not any aspect of the practice itself. It is this aspect of the theory that conjures up the label "protestant," for like Luther's disciples, Dworkin's interpreters have to come to their own personal understanding of what the practice really requires.[94] And this, Dworkin argues, can come about only by peering into one's soul to discern what "the best justification" of the practice requires in any given case.[95] Thus, each interpreter's personal understanding of

---

88. *Id.* at 52.

89. *Id.* at 66.

90. *Id.*

91. See Gerald J. Postema, "'Protestant' Interpretation and Social Practices," 6 *Law & Phil.* 283, 292 (1987) ("[I]f the interpretive attitude has taken hold in a practice, consensus requirements collected at the preinterpretive stage have no final authoritative status."); see also Richard H. Fallon Jr., A "Constructivist Coherence Theory of Constitutional Interpretation," 100 *Harv. L. Rev.* 1189, 1234 n.206 (1987) ("Dworkin assumes that an interpretive conception of legal practice, within which everyone reaches her own interpretation of what legal practice requires, must postulate a 'preinterpretive stage' in which 'the rules and standards taken to provide the tentative content of the practice are identified.'").

92. Postema, *supra* note 91, at 293.

93. Dworkin, *supra* note 43, at 64. Again, one wonders what work the adverb "really" does in Dworkin's argument.

94. Gerald Postema details this point quite well: "There is nothing in Dworkin's meta-theory of interpretation . . . that requires attention to the interpretive activities of fellow participants. Herein lies the strong 'protestantism' of Dworkin's theory. Not only is each participant encouraged to take up the interpretive enterprise . . . but each individual participant also has access to the truth, as it were, about what the practice is and requires, through private interpretation of the practice-text. While Dworkin seems to recognize that the practice is common, he counsels participants to live as if each had a private understanding of his own." Postema, *supra* note 91, at 296–97; see also Fallon, *supra* note 91, at 560 ("On my reading, Dworkin's conception of interpretive protestantism implies that judges characteristically are not and should not be concerned with the rival interpretations that others will predictably develop.").

95. Dworkin, *supra* note 43, at 66.

the normative content of a rule is not at all dependent upon an intersubjective consensus.

We can now summarize the salient points of Dworkin's interpretive theory and identify its implications for his theory of law.[96] Understanding a social practice (e.g., law) is a matter of one's having an interpretation of the practice. The act of interpretation is the way participants in the practice answer the question "What does this practice 'really' require?" Dworkin's bold claim is that this question cannot be answered by appeal to intersubjective agreement.[97] Rather, the individual, not the community, decides what the practice really requires.

Critique

There are at least three levels at which Dworkin's account of law as an interpretive practice is problematic. The first and most basic of these is with respect to the claim that all understanding—be it of law, social practices, or the words of another person—is a matter of interpretation. This is an implausible description of the activity of legal justification. In the next section, I show that interpretation is logically a second-order activity: it cannot get off the ground except against the background of an existing practice. The second point of criticism is that the need for interpretation is not, as Dworkin maintains, an ever-present aspect of legal practice. Interpretation in law involves a decision about how, from among several candidates, one chooses whether to extend a rule one way rather than another. Interpretation becomes necessary only when some real doubt exists about how to apply a rule. Interpretation is the act of appraising various candidates for how to "go on" with the rule. Lastly, I contend that Dworkin's account of law as an interpretive practice is descriptively inadequate. In short, legal interpretation simply does not proceed in the way Dworkin describes it.

Understanding as Interpretation

For Dworkin, understanding law is akin to understanding language. As we have noticed, Dworkin sees interpretation as a pervasive feature of many aspects of human existence. He believes it to be of central importance to jurisprudence. Dworkin explains that because "law is an interpretive concept, any jurisprudence worth having must be built on some view of what interpretation is."[98] As we shall see, Dworkin makes far too much of the work of interpretation.

Before turning to the role of interpretation in law, we need to look closely at Dworkin's general claim that understanding in law (or any other social practice)

---

96. Dworkin himself states one of the principal implications: "[I]f law is an interpretive concept, any jurisprudence worth having must be built on some view of what an interpretation is, and the analysis of interpretation I construct and defend in this chapter is the foundation of the rest of the book." *Id.* at 50. Thus, the success of the theory of law is totally dependent on the success of the theory of interpretation.

97. *Id.* at 62–64.

98. Dworkin, *supra* note 43, at 50.

is a matter of interpretation. Perhaps it is best to begin by reminding ourselves of the putative work of interpretation. To do this, recall the following statement by Dworkin: "We interpret the sounds or marks another person makes in order to decide what he has said."[99] What role does Dworkin assign to interpretation in his account of one person understanding the written or spoken words of another? In the sentence just quoted, it is fair to say that interpretation mediates between the sounds or signs emanating from the mouth or pen of another and the act of meaning apprehension on the part of the listener or reader. Interpretation, as Dworkin says, is something we do. And why do we do it? What results from it? We do it "in order to decide what [another person] has said."[100]

Presumably, if we interpret another correctly, we have grasped the meaning of his words. If not, then we have interpreted him incorrectly. Whether correct or not, the act of interpretation is interposed between the utterance and our grasp of its meaning. Interpretation is an act of mediation: Done correctly, it results in the apprehension of meaning. Done poorly, comprehension eludes us.

Dworkin's claims to the contrary notwithstanding, understanding an utterance is not a matter of deriving its meaning through an act or operation of mind.[101] The criterion for understanding an utterance is not engagement of a process; rather, it is acting appropriately in response to the utterance.[102] For example, one evinces understanding of the request "Please pass the salt" by passing the salt or by explaining why it is impossible to do so. Understanding is made manifest in the *act* of passing the salt, and the act is a criterion for having understood the utterance.[103] Understanding is acting properly in response to the request. If the request is vague or otherwise opaque, interpretation of the request may be necessary, otherwise not.

This last point suggests a certain logical problem endemic to accounts such as Dworkin's, which assign a primordial role to interpretation in normative activities. As mentioned, interpretation is best thought of as an activity we engage in when our understanding of an utterance is somehow in question (e.g., a request to pass the salt when the salt is directly in front of the person making the request). Interpretation is an activity of clarification: we take the utterance in question and appraise competing construals or interpretations of it in an effort to clarify its meaning.[104]

---

99. *Id.*

100. *Id.*

101. See Hacker, *supra* note 13, at 168 (arguing in the spirit of Wittgenstein that understanding is best explained as an ability).

102. *Id.* at 167–68 ("Understanding sentences of a language is a skill that is manifest in using sentences correctly in appropriate circumstances, *in reacting appropriately to their use*, and in explaining (if asked) what they mean." (emphasis added)).

103. See Ludwig Wittgenstein, *On Certainty* § 29 (G. E. M. Anscombe & G. H. von Wright eds., Denis Paul & G. E. M. Anscombe trans., 1972) ("Practice in the use of the rule also shews what is a mistake in its employment.").

104. See Hacker, *supra* note 13, at 168 (arguing that interpretation is explanation and that explanation is usually required only when a statement contains "[o]bscurities, ambiguities, or complexities").

If all understanding were interpretation, then each interpretation would itself stand in need of interpretation, and so on, infinitely regressing to infinity.[105] This logical problem, one long ago recognized,[106] suggests that there is something deeply wrong with assigning to interpretation a mediating role between utterances and the understanding of them. The only way out of this vicious regress is to recognize that the normativity of rule-guided behavior (e.g., law) lies not in the act of the individual (e.g., interpretation) but in a practice. Of course, Dworkin argues that law is a practice, and in this he is surely correct. He has simply misstated the role of interpretation in that practice.

Interpretation and Justification

In addition to the logical problem just discussed, there is an additional difficulty with Dworkin's assignment of a primordial role to interpretation. Dworkin's motivation in this regard is his belief that only through interpretation consistent with the demands of law as integrity will we know what the law "really requires."[107] In other words, only through interpretation will we *really* know when propositions of law may be said to be true.

Recall that Dworkin identifies three distinct stages of legal interpretation: the preinterpretive, the interpretive, and the postinterpretive.[108] By casting interpretation in this way, Dworkin invites an obvious question: Does every legal judgment require one to go through all three stages of interpretation? Another way of asking this question is in terms of easy and hard cases. One might ask the question the way Dworkin's imaginary critic does: Is the method Dworkin develops reserved for hard cases only?[109] Dworkin takes up this question in the following passage, which is worth quoting in its entirety:

> We have been attending mainly to hard cases, when lawyers disagree whether some crucial proposition of law is true or false. But questions of law are sometimes very easy for lawyers and even for nonlawyers. It "goes without saying" that the speed limit in Connecticut is 55 miles an hour and that people in Britain have a legal duty to pay for food they order in a restaurant. At least

105. A recent discussion of this problem in the context of rule-following is Charles Taylor, "To Follow a Rule," in *Rules and Conventions* 167 (Mette Hjort ed., 1992).

106. Wittgenstein mentions the problem in the following discussion: "This was our paradox: no course of action could be determined by a rule, because every course of action can be made out to accord with the rule. The answer was: if everything can be made out to accord with the rule, then it can also be made out to conflict with it. And so there would be neither accord nor conflict here. It can be seen that there is a misunderstanding here from the mere fact that in the course of our argument we give one interpretation after another; as if each contented us at least for a moment, until we thought of yet another standing behind it. What this shews is that there is a way of grasping a rule which is *not* an *interpretation*, but which is exhibited in what we call 'obeying a rule' and 'going against it' in actual cases. Hence there is an inclination to say: every action according to the rule is an interpretation. But we ought to restrict the term 'interpretation' to the substitution of one expression of the rule for another." Wittgenstein, *supra* note 1, at § 201.

107. Dworkin, *supra* note 43, at 64.

108. See *id.* at 65–66.

109. See Dworkin, *supra* note 43, at 354.

this goes without saying except in very unusual circumstances. A critic might be tempted to say that the complex account we have developed of judicial reasoning under law as integrity is a method for hard cases only. He might add that it would be absurd to apply the method to easy cases—no judge needs to consider questions of fit and political morality to decide whether someone must pay his telephone bill—and then declare that in addition to his theory of hard cases, Hercules needs a theory about when cases are hard, so he can know when his complex method for hard cases is appropriate and when not. The critic will then announce a serious problem: it can be a hard question whether the case at hand is a hard case or an easy case, and Hercules cannot decide by using his technique for hard cases without begging the question.

This is a pseudoproblem. Hercules does not need one method for hard cases and another for easy ones. His method is equally at work in easy cases, but since the answers to the questions it puts are then obvious, or at least seem to be so, we are not aware that any theory is at work at all. We think the question whether someone may legally drive faster than the stipulated speed limit is an easy one because we assume at once that no account of the legal record that denied that paradigm would be competent. But someone whose convictions about justice and fairness were very different from ours might not find that question so easy; even if he ended by agreeing with our answer, he would insist that we were wrong to be so confident. This explains why questions considered easy during one period become hard before they again become easy questions—with the opposite answers.[110]

Again, the question of motivation can provide insight into Dworkin's efforts to ground legal justification in interpretation. In *Law's Empire*, Dworkin is extremely critical of legal positivism.[111] His chief complaint is that for positivism, "the law" is exhausted by conventional or institutional methods and materials. For a positivist (of the Hartian variety), "propositions of law are true . . . in virtue of social conventions that represent the community's acceptance of a scheme of rules empowering such people or groups to create valid law."[112] Thus, for the positivist the proposition "The speed limit in California is fifty-five" is true "because the people of California have accepted, and continue to accept, the scheme of authority deployed in the state and national constitutions."[113] In short, Dworkin states that for Hart "the truth of propositions of law is in some important way dependent upon conventional patterns of recognizing law."[114]

Dworkin's project is to persuade us that the positivist view of law—that law is a matter of social conventions—is somehow defective.[115] In the passage from Dworkin just quoted, he argues that there is no methodological difference be-

---

110. *Id.* at 353–54.

111. In *Law's Empire*, positivism is identified as "conventionalism." *Id.* at 34.

112. *Id.*

113. *Id.*

114. *Id.* at 35.

115. For a powerful response to Dworkin's critique of positivism as conventionalism, see Jules L. Coleman, "Negative and Positive Positivism," in *Markets, Morals and the Law* 3, 12–20 (1988) (arguing that Dworkin's objections to positivism do not refute positivism's capacity to accept the existence of controversial legal standards as compatible with the conventional nature of law).

tween easy and hard cases. Of course, the distinction between hard and easy cases fits well with the conventionalist notion that easy cases are easy because the conventions of justification are settled.[116] That is, easy questions require no extensive analysis (interpretational or otherwise) because existing conventions readily answer the question posed (e.g., "Is the speed limit in California fifty-five miles per hour?"). The conventionalist argument is that this question is easy because the meaning of the statute is clear.[117] Because the meaning of the statute is clear, the question is easily answered. This is precisely the point Dworkin seeks to deny.

Again, the question is not whether there are hard or easy cases. All agree—Dworkin included—that there are both hard and easy cases. Differences arise over what constitutes a hard or an easy case or, to put it differently, what it is about law that makes a "hard case" hard and an "easy case" easy.

The conventionalist's answer is roughly that easy cases are easy because there exist established institutional criteria for what counts as a justification for a claim that a given proposition of law is true.[118] Hard cases are those where the conventions of justification yield no clear answer, or perhaps more than one answer.[119] The speed limit proposition poses an easy case because in law the existence of a clear and relevant statute on point is dispositive of the question. To the question "What justifies your assertion that the speed limit in California is fifty-five miles per hour?" the answer is "Why the statute, of course."[120]

Dworkin denies the answer that comes so easily to both the conventionalist and the common lawyer. He has to, of course, for to do otherwise would mean that he cannot distance himself from the conventionalism he is so eager to discredit. But as a consequence, he is forced into an implausible account of easy cases. Dworkin tells us that "Hercules does not need one method for hard cases and another for easy cases. His method is equally at work in easy cases, but since the answers to the questions it puts are then obvious, or at least seem to be so, we are not aware that any theory is at work at all."[121]

116. Dworkin anticipated this conventionalist (i.e., positivist) response. See Dworkin, *supra* note 43, at 265–66.

117. One might say that the meaning of the sentence is clear because the meaning of the sentence is fixed by a horizon of meaning: "The meaning of a sentence, if it is a meaningful sentence, can be completely determined by reference to some appropriate fixed horizon of meaning, and the oscillations of hermeneutical theory are then short-circuited. The meaning is given directly because the relevant horizon is immanent in the language that we already speak." Robert J. Ackermann, *Wittgenstein's City* 18–19 (1988).

118. See Neil MacCormick & Ota Weinberger, *An Institutional Theory of Law* 9–16 (1986) (discussing the evolution of institutional norms as a basis for codified and common law); Dennis M. Patterson, "Law's Pragmatism: Law as Practice & Narrative," 76 *Va. L. Rev.* 937, 983 (1990) ("The easy case is the one which can be decided by reference to a rule, the extension of which clearly covers the case and against the application of which no good reason can be advanced.").

119. See Patterson, *supra* note 118, at 986 (describing hard cases as those in which there are two plausible answers to the legal questions involved but no way definitively to determine which is better).

120. Dworkin seeks to displace the conventionalist justification of appeal to the language of the appropriate statute with the further question "And what justifies *that*?" See Dworkin, *supra* note 43, at 354.

121. *Id.*

Dworkin here seems to be saying that whenever a judge decides a case, there is always some "theory" at work. We see the theory in hard cases, but it is apparently out of sight in easy cases. Other than the need to discredit conventionalist accounts of legal justification, there is no need to introduce the idea of a "theory" (recognized or unrecognized) to explain the truth of legal propositions. We do not need a theory to understand legal rules any more than we need a theory to understand the rules of baseball, violin performance, or addition. The standards for correct and incorrect assertions are not "hidden from view," nor does one need a theory to know whether the speed limit is fifty-five miles per hour or not.

What Dworkin provides is a false picture of *normativity*. Normativity identifies the ways in which we appraise assertions of correctness and incorrectness, truth and falsity. In short, an account of normativity identifies what making correct and incorrect judgment consists in.[122] In both easy and hard cases, Dworkin maintains that a "theory" is always at work.[123] Thus, normativity is explained by Dworkin as being a matter of one's having a theory. We need theories to understand the speech of another and to make judgments about the truth and falsity of legal propositions (e.g., the proposition that the speed limit in California is fifty-five miles per hour). Easy cases differ from hard cases only in that we see theory at work in hard cases and are unaware of its presence in easy cases.[124]

---

122. See G. P. Baker & P. M. S. Hacker, *Language, Sense & Nonsense* 257–58 (1984). According to Baker and Hacker, "[n]ormative behaviour, viewed externally, in ignorance of the norms which *inform* it, may seem altogether unintelligible. A story is told of a Chinese mandarin passing through the foreign legations' compound in Peking. Seeing two of the European staff playing an energetic game of tennis, he stopped to watch. Bemused, he turned to a player and said, 'If it is, for some obscure reason, necessary to hit this little ball back and forth thus, would it not be possible to get the servants to do it?' An alien observing a Roman transferring ownership in a slave by casting a piece of copper into a balance while gripping the slave and pronouncing an appropriate formula may well think that some bizarre form of magic is afoot. Having one's body smeared with oil, one's head weighed down with 10 lb. of metal, one's hand filled with a metallic ball and rod, all to the roars of acclaim of thousands, is altogether unintelligible to someone ignorant of the history, conventions and meaning of coronation ceremonies. But one need not invoke such relatively arcane practices to realize that much of our daily behaviour, including our speech, is bizarre and unintelligible save when seen from a normative point of view.

Explanation of normative phenomena may take many forms, depending upon what feature is perplexing. In general, explanation of a normative act consists in rendering the act intelligible by clarifying its *meaning*, elucidating its *goal* and the *reasons* for performing it. Why did A write his name on that piece of paper?—Because he was signing a cheque. Why was he signing a cheque?—In order to buy an insurance policy. Why did he wish to buy an insurance policy?—Because he recently became a parent and therefore had reason to make provision for his family. And so on. A normative explanation may identify an act in normative terms (identify writing one's name *as* a signing of a cheque). It may explain the normative (conventional) consequences of the act (payment for an insurance policy). It may characterize an act as conformity to a mandatory norm, or as the exercise of a normative power having normative consequences. In general, normative explanations render acts intelligible not by subsumption under causal laws, but by elucidations of their normative meaning, and the goals and purposes that may be pursued, given the possibility of the act having such-and-such a meaning." *Id.* at 257–58 (footnotes omitted).

123. See Dworkin, *supra* note 43, at 354 (According to Dworkin, Hercules has one method for both hard and easy cases).

124. In a recent essay, Dworkin reaffirms this position: "Lawyers reason about what the law in new or controversial cases is by constructing what they take to be the best justification for past

Dworkin's conception of law as fundamentally an interpretive, theory-driven enterprise fails to account for the everyday activities of lawyers. Much of the lawyer's work involves no sort of "interpretation" or "theory" whatsoever. If this is true—if so much of legal practice is not a matter of just these sorts of activities—then Dworkin's claim that his argument comes from "the internal, participants' point of view"[125] is severely undercut.

Consider the client who visits his lawyer with a document labeled "Equipment Lease."[126] He tells her the following:

> I am leasing my bulldozer worth $48,000 to Perkins. As you can see, the lease calls for forty-eight equal monthly payments of $1,000. At the end of the lease, Perkins has the option of buying the bulldozer for $1 or returning

---

rules and practices, and then trying to extrapolate that justification forward into those new cases. In that way they interpret and re-interpret their institution's past, formulating, re-formulating, testing and probing rival justifications. They disagree with one another when and because they adopt somewhat different justifications for the same history, or extrapolate much the same justification differently. The process is not self-conscious or explicit in every case: 'Easy' cases are those in which any plausible interpretation of the past would dictate the same decision now, and the new decision therefore seems unreflective and near automatic. But every appellate judge, at least, faces hard cases, in which the process of justification and extrapolation becomes more self-conscious and explicit, closer to the fully reflective and explicit form it takes in, say, classroom argument, which is only another, differently structured and motivated, forum in which the same practices unfolds [*sic*]. (In *Law's Empire*, I try to defend the views about adjudication summarized in this paragraph)." Ronald Dworkin, "Pragmatism, Right Answers, and True Banality," in *Pragmatism in Law and Society* 359, 386 n.25 (Michael Brint & William Weaver eds., 1991).

125. Dworkin, *supra* note 43, at 14; see also *id.* at 65–68, 87–88. Despite his long-standing claim that his account of law derives from "the internal, participants' point of view," *id.* at 14, Dworkin's arguments always ultimately rest on moral philosophy and not law. Dworkin's most recent book continues in this vein. See Jeffrey Rosen, "A Womb with a View," *New Republic*, June 14, 1993, at 35 (reviewing Ronald Dworkin, *Life's Dominion* (1993)). Rosen states: "*Life's Dominion*, like Dworkin's previous work, is all but bereft of references to constitutional history and structure. Dworkin promises to reason from the 'inside out,' beginning with practical problems such as abortion and euthanasia, and then asking what philosophical issues are necessary to resolve them. But there is no real need, in 'inside out' reasoning, for close readings of constitutional text, history and structure: Dworkin has altogether abstracted away the need to consult a written, historically rooted document. He calls his theories, in a revealing and unfortunate metaphor, 'bespoke, made for the occasion, Savile Row not Seventh Avenue.' In fact, Dworkin acknowledges one modest restraint on judges: actual legal practice. Any interpretation of the Constitution, he says in a distinction developed more carefully in *Law's Empire* (1986), should be subjected to two tests: the test of justice and the test of 'fit.' And the most just interpretation, which is the interpretation that 'best reflects people's moral rights and duties,' should always be preferred, unless it is 'wholly inconsistent' with actual legal practice. When push comes to shove, however, legal practice does not seem to constrain Dworkin in any meaningful way. There is not a single point in his book where Dworkin is willing to forgo the 'best, most accurate understanding of liberty and equal citizenship,' even when it is patently inconsistent with legal practice, such as Dworkin's suggestion that government has a constitutional duty to fund abortions for poor women." *Id.* at 36.

126. This example is offered not as any sort of paradigm or exemplar of legal reasoning as such. The example is offered as a counter to Dworkin's claim that all understanding is interpretation. The point of the example is that there is nothing in what a competent lawyer does here which might be characterized as "interpretation." Thus, the example is a counterexample to Dworkin's sweeping claims for the fundamental character of interpretation.

it to me. I like this deal. I maintain ownership of the bulldozer and receive a monthly payment to boot. Perkins is happy because he gets to write off the lease payments and can buy the bulldozer at the end of the lease for little money.

Here, it seems that no interpretation is in order. The client brought a document that bears some of the features of a chattel lease but, in fact, is not a lease at all.[127] The rights created by the document are the transfer of an ownership interest in a chattel and the retention of a lien in the form of a security interest. When a lawyer evaluates what her client has done in crafting his agreement, she spells out for the client the implications of his agreement in the context of commercial law, specifically Article 9 of the Uniform Commercial Code.[128] No "theory" need be advanced. In fact, no theory (or interpretation) of any kind is called for.[129] What is required is knowledge of the appropriate legal concepts (e.g., "sale," "security interest," "lease," and the like). Knowing the law means, among other things, knowing the legal consequences of what the client has done.[130]

In this situation, one might say the lawyer has certain knowledge. But what sort of knowledge is it? Is it, as Dworkin would say, "interpretive" knowledge?[131] What is it that the lawyer knows? The answer is plain to see: she knows the law. But what does it mean to say "she knows the law"? Is her knowledge reducible to the observation that she can predict how courts will treat the deal her client has struck?[132] Is her knowledge coextensive with the reactions other lawyers will have to this transaction? Or is it simply enough to say that if called upon to justify her claim that the transaction was a sale with the retention of a security inter-

---

127. The lease is not a "true lease" but is, rather, the sale of a chattel with the retention of a security interest. See U.C.C. § 1-201(37) (1991).

128. See *id.* § 9-102(1) (stating the application of Article 9 to any transaction that is designed to create a security interest in personal property).

129. The lawyer does not interpret the language of the statute in question any more than we interpret the sounds of another person when they say something. In the following passage Baker and Hacker recognize that we do not "interpret" everyday communications: "Typically, we view our conduct in appropriate ways *under the aspect of normativity*. We do not *interpret* it thus, we see it so. Our application of normative predicates to the behaviour we view thus does not typically rest on any *inference*. When a chess player makes an appropriate move, I do not *interpret* it as a move (as if it might have been just a muscular 'tic' causing him to move his queen two squares), I take it as one. When someone says 'What is the time?', I take him as having asked me the time, not as having made a noise which now needs interpreting (viz. maybe it was Chinese, or just a meaningless sound)." Baker & Hacker, *supra* note 122, at 261.

130. In other words, we show the client that her everyday understanding of "ownership" is not sustained in the technical context of secured transactions. This is not a matter of choice: we do not "choose" to see this act (signing this document) as one thing rather than another. We do not "impose" a meaning on the text to make it the best it can be (that would simply be malpractice). We hopefully see it *for what it is*! The *meaning* of this act is constituted by the conceptual discourse of commercial law. Thus, the linguistic practice that constitutes Article 9—and not some private interpretation of it—will dictate the meaning of the document.

131. See Dworkin, *supra* note 43, at 49–53 (describing the process of knowing something as an act of choosing a certain interpretation of that thing).

132. Of course, this is the view of law one gets on a certain reading of American legal realism. The classic text presenting this view remains Karl N. Llewellyn, *The Bramble Bush* (1951).

est and not a lease, the lawyer could show the truth of her claim?[133] This way of accounting for legal knowledge provides no opportunity for interpretation to take hold. The reason interpretation never takes hold (and theory is never required) is that there is no occasion for it—the need for interpretation simply does not arise.[134]

This critique has significant implications for Dworkin's accounts of meaning and knowledge. As we saw above, interpretations alone do not generate knowledge. The only way for any semiotic activity to get off the ground is for people to use words in the same way; that is, to have a practice. Once a practice is established, meaning is something one finds in the practice—the intersubjective coordination of verbal usage.[135] Appeal to individual interpretation in a theory of meaning or a theory of knowledge is thus a nonstarter, for such an activity never connects with others at the level of practice.[136] And once linguistic coordination is established, resort to the private intentions, interpretations, or theories of individual participants in the practice is, at least for purposes of finding meaning, rendered superfluous.[137]

Rethinking Interpretation

I have argued against the idea that interpretation is the essence of legal practice. Toward this end, I have advanced two arguments. The first was a logical argument to the effect that the reduction of understanding to interpretation generates an infinite regress of justification, as each interpretation itself stands in need of interpretation. The second point of criticism was to show that the truth of legal propositions is not a matter of any sort of "theory." Easy cases are easy precisely because the conventional means of justification often (but not always)

---

133. Her justification would consist primarily in appeal to the text of a statute. See U.C.C. § 1-201(37) (1991) (defining a security interest and the retention of title in sales). Were anything further required, she might explain the underlying problems that led to the distinction in law between a true lease and a lease intended for security. See Barkley Clark, The Law of Secured Transactions Under the Uniform Commercial Code § 1.05, 1-26 to 1-43 (2d ed. 1988) (describing the difficulty of distinguishing a "true" lease from an installment sale described as a lease).

134. Further, it will not do to say that lawyers' modes of understanding are just "lawyerly interpretations." See Andrei Marmor, *Interpretation and Legal Theory* 151 (1992) (observing that acting according to a rule indicates an understanding of the rule but does not involve interpretation).

135. We need to be reminded that "the natural phenomenon that is normal human life is itself already shaped by meaning and understanding." John McDowell, "Meaning and Intentionality in Wittgenstein's Later Philosophy," in 17 *Midwest Studies in Philosophy: The Wittgenstein Legacy* 40, 51 (Peter A. French et al. eds., 1992).

136. Cf. Nancey Murphy, "Scientific Realism and Postmodern Philosophy," 41 *Brit. J. Phil. Sci.* 291, 295 (1990) (asserting that "language and the search for knowledge are *communal* achievements" (emphasis added)).

137. For an excellent discussion of problems of meaning, mind, and normativity, see P. M. S. Hacker, *Wittgenstein: Meaning and Mind* (1990) (providing a full-length treatment of Wittgenstein's thought on the problems of meaning and mind).

provide clear answers to legal questions (e.g., "Is the speed limit in California fifty-five miles per hour?"). Having argued against interpretation as a *foundational* aspect of legal practice, the time has now come to describe the proper role of interpretation in law.

Let us begin by reminding ourselves that in Dworkin's account of the matter, interpretation ends with the interpreter choosing a value (principle) that she thinks puts the practice of law in its best light.[138] This way of characterizing the role of interpretation renders the individual judge's moral and/or political philosophy morally superior to other (e.g., legal) modes of justification.[139] As will be shown, Dworkin's argument for the jurisprudential superiority of the judge's political philosophy cannot be sustained.

Imagine a statute that "prohibits the employment of an alien for any purpose.[140] Does this statute answer the question "May a winery in California hire migrant workers who are aliens to pick its annual crop of grapes?" Of course it does. And how is that? The statute answers our question because the statute tells us what an "alien" is, and we know that hiring people to pick grapes is a form of employment. How do we know these things? The answer is simple: We have read the statute, and we understand English.

In making a case that the law on a particular issue is thus and so, one appeals to the text as a way of justifying one's assertion of the truth of a position of law.[141] In making such an argument, a lawyer does not appeal to the meaning of the words in the statute; she assumes it.[142] Typically, she does not argue about word meanings; instead, she calls the court's attention to texts that support her client's position. Were this not the case, her argument would not be merely implausible, it would be impossible.

More importantly, appeal to the text as a mode of justifying one's claim of legal truth is possible only because textual argument is a recognized mode of legal justification.[143] Appeal to the text only makes sense in a practice where the text

---

138. See Dworkin, *supra* note 43, at 52–53.

139. *Id.* at 285.

140. Just such a statute was involved in *Church of the Holy Trinity v. United States*, 143 U.S. 457 (1892). The relevant provision of the statute reads: "Be it enacted by the Senate and House of Representatives of the United States of America in Congress assembled, That from and after the passage of this act it shall be unlawful for any person, company, partnership, or corporation, in any manner whatsoever, to prepay the transportation, or in any way assist or encourage the importation or migration of any alien or aliens, any foreigner or foreigners, into the United States, its Territories, or the District of Columbia, under contract or agreement, parol or special, express or implied, made previous to the importation or migration of such alien or aliens, foreigner or foreigners, to perform labor or service of any kind in the United States, its Territories, or the District of Columbia." Alien Contract Labor Law of Feb. 26, 1885, ch. 164, § 3, 23 Stat. 332 (1885) (emphasis omitted).

141. For an account of textual argument in constitutional law, see Fallon, *supra* note 91, at 1237–51 (addressing how different methods of constitutional interpretation fit together and weigh against each other) and chapter 7 of the present work.

142. The lawyer is not appealing to the words as such but to what they mean.

143. See Philip Bobbitt, *Constitutional Fate* 25–38 (1982) (stating that textual argument is possible only because of the status we accord the text in legal practice).

is accorded justificatory power. Without that presupposition, appeal to the text would be nothing more than an empty, perhaps unintelligible, gesture.[144]

The meaning of the statute does not "come from" its words. The statute has a meaning because it is written in a language.[145] The law is intelligible—it tells us what is prohibited—because the meaning of the words is clear. This clarity is not an achievement of the interpreter but of the drafter of the statute. The person(s) who wrote the statute had facility in the language. It is owing to this facility that the statute is amenable to clear answers in a variety of different circumstances.

Just because the statute is clear in one case does not mean it will be so in all. It is one thing if the "alien" in question is an undocumented worker being exploited by a grape-grower. It is quite another matter, however, if the "alien" in question is an English cleric. But what is it about the law that makes this distinction one that makes a difference in answering the question posed?

The answer is the practice of statutory interpretation. One aspect of that practice is the move to legislative purpose as one way of answering the question "What is the law on this question?" Within the practice of statutory interpretation, appeal to the historical intent of the legislature is one way of justifying a claim that the law requires an outcome different from that indicated by the text. Of course, it is also part of this practice that, in the absence of such a purpose, statutory language controls the question.[146]

If we look only at these two modes of justifying legal claims—for example, a claim that the law does not prohibit employing an English cleric to meet the spiritual needs of a New York congregation—we see little of the protestant character Dworkin claims for law. The assertion that a statute does or does not prohibit a given act is not made true by appeal to "law's grounds" as Dworkin defines the term.[147] In cases of statutory interpretation—for example, instances of conflict among forms of legal argument—the work of interpretation is in making the case that one form ultimately controls the question at hand. How this is done, by what criteria the choice is made, and whether those criteria may themselves be the subject of debate are all pertinent and open questions. What is not

---

144. Again, it is the practice of law, not the text itself, that accords justificatory power to the text.

145. This is not to say that in cases of statutory interpretation the text is always clear and, thus, dispositive. Rather, the point is that many legal questions can be settled by resort to an authoritative text. To deny this truism, as Dworkin does, is tendentious. See Richard A. Posner, "Statutory Interpretation—In the Classroom and in the Courtroom," 50 *U. Chi. L. Rev.* 800, 808 (1983) ("Of course the words of a statute are always relevant, often decisive, and usually the most important evidence of what the statute was meant to accomplish.").

146. Even progressive constructivists concede that in our legal practice, the text often controls the tenor of the moves that can be made. See, e.g., William N. Eskridge Jr., "Dynamic Statutory Interpretation," 135 *U. Pa. L. Rev.* 1479, 1483 (1987) (developing a theory of dynamic statutory interpretation in which the text is "critical" because it is "the formal focus of interpretation and a constraint on the range of interpretive options available").

147. See Dworkin, *supra* note 43, at 5 (arguing that disputes over "law's grounds" implicate theoretical debates over the meaning and interpretation of the statutory text).

in question is the very thing Dworkin denies—that this activity is conducted in concert with others. Charles Taylor describes the process this way:

> What if someone does not "see" the adequacy of our interpretation, does not accept our reading? We try to show him how it makes sense of the original nonsense or partial sense. But for him to follow us he must read the original language as we do, he must recognize these expressions as puzzling in a certain way, and hence be looking for a solution to our problem. If he does not, what can we do? The answer, it would seem, can only be more of the same. We have to show him through the reading of other expressions why this expression must be read in the way we propose. But success here requires that he follow us in these other readings, and so on, it would seem, potentially forever. We cannot escape an ultimate appeal to a common understanding of the expressions, of the "language" involved.[148]

But what of Dworkin's claim that legal practice, as an exercise in constructive interpretation, requires each citizen (including judges) to impose a "purpose on a . . . practice in order to make of it the best possible example of the form or genre to which it is taken to belong?"[149] Recall Dworkin's metaphor for the activity of a judge in the third or postinterpretive stage of constructive interpretation. He characterizes that moment as "a conversation with oneself, as joint author and critic."[150] For Dworkin, *understanding* the practice of law appears to be something lawyers do in concert with each other. Interpreting the practice— that is, discovering what the law "really requires"[151]—is something only the individual can do. There are, then, two distinct levels to Dworkin's conception of legal practice. The first level is the public process of understanding. The basic elements of the practice are gathered together and the participants come to some preliminary agreement on a justification for the practice. The second level, which is coextensive with the third stage of constructive interpretation, is a thoroughly private affair, one where one acts not in concert with others but in private meditation on the true grounds of law.[152]

What is wrong with this picture of the interpretive aspects of the practice of law? For the same reason that following a rule is intersubjective in nature,[153] interpretation must be as well. The very idea of interpretation as a normative activity demands that the process of interpretation be a practice and not a private conversation with oneself. If we are speaking to ourselves, how can we ever know that it is the law we are interpreting and not something else? When we *think* we are interpreting, how do we know it is the law we are interpreting and not some

148. Taylor, *supra* note 24, at 17.

149. Dworkin, *supra* note 43, at 52.

150. *Id.* at 58.

151. *Id.* at 64.

152. Like the interpreter in the practice of courtesy, the interpreter in law must find an account of the practice "not in the sense of retrieving [a prior] mental state . . . but in the sense of finding a purposeful account of his behavior he is comfortable in ascribing to himself." *Id.* at 58; see also Postema, *supra* note 91, at 297 ("While Dworkin seems to recognize that the practice is common, he counsels participants to live as if each had a private understanding of his own.").

153. See note 122, *supra*.

other text? In short, how can we know whether we are actually interpreting the law and not merely *thinking* we are interpreting the law?[154]

Because interpretation is an activity of mind conducted in concert with others, Dworkin's conception of law as a private, interpretive conversation with oneself has neither normative nor descriptive appeal. This is not surprising. For instance, when a lawyer or judge interprets a statute, the interpretation is evaluated in accordance with criteria to which the lawyer or judge appeals in urging the interpretation.[155] When we interpret, we attempt to get others to see the law as we do; we try to persuade them that our reading meets legal measures of adequacy and perspicuity.[156] The fact that we do not always agree in our judgments, and sometimes see things differently, does not mean that we have no standards. It means only that there is more than one plausible way to resolve difficult questions of rule application.

The central claim in Dworkin's jurisprudence is that law is an interpretive activity.[157] As we have seen, that claim is the corollary of a general approach to the nature of human understanding—that all understanding is interpretation.[158] Dworkin's description of law must persuade both at the descriptive and normative levels. Doubt as to the accuracy and cogency of the account has been raised at both levels. It is not accurate because it attempts to turn the ordinary into the marvelous (understanding into interpretation), and it is philosophically defective because it cannot break out of the infinite regress of justification. We now turn our attention to the arguments of another proponent of interpretive universalism, Stanley Fish.

154. See Wittgenstein, *supra* note 1, § 202 ("And to *think* one is obeying a rule is not to obey a rule.")

155. See Baker & Hacker, *supra* note 122, at 266 ("We fix what is to *count* as following a given rule, and hence what it is to conform to it. Hence a rule can contain no more than we collectively decide, in our normative practices, to put into it.")

156. Again, the central insight of post-Quinean philosophy of science is that it is *the community* that, in light of its practices, decides (largely on pragmatic grounds) what it takes to make a persuasive argument. See Murphy, *supra* note 136, at 295 (explaining that the community decides when to alter the Quinean network of beliefs). Even Karl Popper, the last great thinker in the positivist tradition in the philosophy of science, introduces a conventionalist element into the epistemology of falsification when he grants that, metaphysical realism to the contrary notwithstanding, it is *the community* of scientists that decides when falsification occurs and when it does not. In short, even for Popper, a conventionalist element enters into the most basic features of scientific practice. See generally Karl R. Popper, *The Logic of Scientific Discovery* (Harper & Row 2d ed. 1968) (1934) (determining that the basis for scientific objectivity and falsification is repeated testing with reproducible outcomes).

157. Additionally, jurisprudence for Dworkin is itself an interpretive activity, its object being the interpretive activity of law. See Dworkin, *supra* note 43, at 49 ("[A] theory of interpretation is an interpretation of the higher-order practice of using interpretive concepts.").

158. *Id.* at 50

6

Law as an Interpretive Community: The Case of Stanley Fish

I hold, the text, while always there, is always an interpreted object.
Stanley Fish[1]

The Text in the Reader

Like Ronald Dworkin, Stanley Fish has exhibited consistent attention to a single theme. Above all else, Fish is committed to the proposition that meaning lies with the reader and not with the text. Fish's thought contains a counterpart to Dworkin's relational thesis. For Fish, the truth of propositions of law depends on the interpretive assumptions of the reader. When this idea is translated into a jurisprudential theory, it engenders interesting and surprising consequences. Instead of the law being something about which one can make objective judgments,[2] the truth of a legal judgment is a function of the interpretive assumptions of the reader of the text (e.g., a judge). Thus, on Fish's account, the truth of a proposition of law is a function of the interpretive assumptions of the various readers of the legal text. Objectivity, then, means having the same interpretive assumptions as those in agreement with one's preferred interpretation of the legal text.

Before turning his skills to law, Stanley Fish enjoyed (and continues to enjoy) a considerable reputation as a literary critic.[3] In the late sixties and seventies, Fish was identified with a school of literary criticism known as reader-response theory.[4] Whether in reaction to the then-reigning school of formalism, or simply in an

---

1. Stanley Fish, *Doing What Comes Naturally: Change, Rhetoric, and the Practice of Theory in Literary and Legal Studies* 563 n.31 (1989).

2. For an excellent, recent discussion of the philosophical issues involved in truth and objectivity, see Crispin Wright, *Truth and Objectivity* (1992) (recasting the contemporary realism/anti-realism debate). See also Brian Leiter, "Objectivity and the Problems of Jurisprudence," 72 *Tex. L. Rev.* 187 (1993) (reviewing Kent Greenawalt, *Law and Objectivity* (1992)).

3. See John M. Ellis, *Against Deconstruction* 116 (1989); Elizabeth Freund, *The Return of the Reader: Reader-Response Criticism* 9–10 (1987) (both discussing Fish's works as a literary critic).

4. Freund, *supra* note 3, at 90–92.

effort to strike out in a new direction, Fish's efforts on behalf of reader-response theory were directed at enhancing the role of the reader in the production of textual meaning.[5] For Fish, the objectivity of the text was "a dangerous illusion."[6] In reader-response theory, not only was the reader freed from the shackles of the text, meaning was as well; for henceforth meaning would reside not in the text but in the reader. As Fish put it: "The meaning of an utterance, I repeat, is its experience—all of it—and that experience is immediately compromised the moment you say something about it."[7]

Not surprisingly, Fish's effort to make individual readers the source for meaning came under heavy attack from several quarters.[8] In response to the criticism, Fish moderated his claims for the dominant role of the reader not by bringing back the text but by adding more readers to the enterprise of the production of meaning. By 1980, meaning was no longer an experience in the reader but had become group property: "[M]eanings are the property neither of fixed and stable texts nor of free and independent readers but of interpretive communities that are responsible both for the shape of a reader's activities and for the texts those activities produce."[9]

Thus we encounter the idea with which Fish has become inextricably linked, that of the "interpretive community."[10] The text has meaning only by virtue of the fact that a group of persons shares a strategy for reading. It is only by virtue

---

5. As a leading scholar of the English Renaissance, Fish's earlier work focused primarily on seventeenth-century English poetry. See generally Stanley Fish, *Surprised by Sin: The Role of the Reader in* Paradise Lost (1967); Stanley Fish, *Self-Consuming Artifacts: The Experience of Seventeenth-Century Literature* (1972).

6. Stanley Fish, *Is There a Text in This Class?: The Authority of Interpretive Communities* 43 (1980).

7. *Id.* at 65.

8. See, e.g., Ellis, *supra* note 3, at 121 (pointing out that Fish's reader-response theory ignores communal assumptions and ensures that the author's understanding of the text will be unrelated to the reader's).

9. Fish, *supra* note 6, at 322.

10. In what is perhaps the most insightful article ever written about Fish, Pierre Schlag describes how Fish's theory of interpretive communities lets him have it all: "For the relatively autonomous self, Fish offers the best of all possible worlds. What's more, Fish allows the self to claim that it is right when it insists on acting or deciding in an intuitionistic pragmatic sort of way. The self can say, 'Yes, I know your theory of [. . .] requires that I should do such and such, but you see I am not a theorist; I am a self and I know things in an intuitionistic non-theoretical practical way which your theory could not possibly understand. So go away—go do your theory (which is just a form of practice anyway) and let me go on with my business.' The concept of interpretive communities is attractive for the simple reason that it leaves the self as the final adjudicator of its own acts without responsibility for the choice. The self cannot choose its interpretive constructs. It is always already within them. But at the same time (and quite conveniently) very little can be known about these interpretive constructs so the self need not feel closeted by an overly determined objectivity. The concept of interpretive communities offers the self *a formal closure* against the claims of theory, reason and history. But at the same time, the concept is *substantively empty*, so that the self can project into 'interpretive communities' just about anything it wants." Pierre Schlag, "*Fish v. Zapp*: The Case of the Relatively Autonomous Self," 76 *Geo. L.J.* 37, 45 (1987) (citation omitted) (brackets in original).

of this overlap in personal reading strategy[11] that "the facts of literary study—texts, authors, periods, genres—become available."[12]

Fish's Account of Linguistic Meaning:
The Reader and the Text

Through its various reformulations, Fish's basic approach to questions of meaning has remained essentially unchanged.[13] Above all else, Fish is committed to the view that we make sense of the world by moving within grids of intelligibility, which we lay upon the world in order to make sense of it.[14] On the surface,

---

11. See Fish, *supra* note 6, at 169 (showing how critics with similar interpretive strategies will arrive at similar interpretations of a text). The following description of *Dworkin's* theory of law as interpretation fits *Fish* as well: "That which appears common in the practice is merely the overlap of extensions of the (more or less explicit) interpretive theories of individual participants." Gerald Postema, "'Protestant' Interpretation and Social Practices" 6 *Law. & Phil.* 283, 300 (1987).

12. Fish, *supra* note 6, at 355.

13. But see Ellis, *supra* note 3, at 121 n.6 (suggesting that Fish has recently committed himself to views incompatible with essential doctrines of reader-response criticism). Ellis explains: "Stanley Fish . . . has long since committed himself to the initial assertions of reader-response criticism and . . . continues to do so but, by changing his position a number of times, has struggled with the kinds of unacceptable consequences of those assertions that I have set out in this chapter. But his latest reformulation [*Is There a Text in This Class?*], which is offered as if no more than a refinement, amounts in fact to his abandoning its essentials completely. His most recent version, then, involves the postulation of interpretive communities, with assumptions and conventions that guide interpretation; this, in his view, allows communication to take place and so rescues him from the consequences of earlier formulations. Now it is, of course, true that a text means nothing without conventions shared by the speakers of the language concerned, but to acknowledge this *fully* would, as Fish sees, abolish his reader-response position: if readers are guided by the rules of language, they do not have the freedom envisaged by reader-response theory, and so the text together with its relation to the linguistic system can be the place to which disputes are appealed after all, contrary to the statement by Fish that I cited. In order to continue to cling to his reader-response position, then, Fish continues to deny that it is sharing a language and 'knowing the meanings of individual words and the rules for combining them' that is involved in communication but, instead, a 'way of thinking, a form of life.' But this direct denial that the shared rules of language makes [*sic*] communication possible is surely bizarre, and the distinction he makes here is certainly untenable. Oddly enough, Fish's language here recalls Wittgenstein's, but in using it Wittgenstein was pointing out precisely that a language with its rules, conventions, and agreements *is* a way of thinking and form of life!" *Id.* (quoting Fish, *supra* note 6, at 303) (citation omitted).

14. In one review of *Doing What Comes Naturally*, a reader noted that "Fish, it seems, is still arguing that the reader's cognitive activities supply everything, that we 'write' the texts we read when, to many, this debate seems to have run its course." Michael Benton, Book Review, 30 *Brit. J. Aesthetics* 386, 387 (1990). Lest my discussion here be misunderstood in this regard, I should state explicitly that Fish's view was and is hopelessly contradictory: On the one hand, the reader produces the meaning of the text; on the other, the reader's choices are constrained by the community of interpretation. This contradiction has been at the heart of Fish's project since its inception: "On the one hand [Fish's] theory posits a reader whose mind is the conscious, competent and responsible agent of meaning production, but on the other it proclaims him to be the product of a determinate and pre-existing structure of norms. Controlled by the systems of competence he has internalized, the reader can produce only those meanings (or bewilderments) he is programmed (by his competence or by the author of his text) to produce. This doubleness circles back to the

this view has a certain plausibility. One reason for this is that ideas similar to Fish's are already very much a part of the background of contemporary "sophisticated" thought and reflection. For example, Thomas Kuhn is often thought of as the person who first advanced the idea that scientists produce their knowledge by virtue of a "paradigm," a conceptual framework within which physical reality is rendered intelligible.[15] All understanding occurs within a framework, people have different frameworks or paradigms, and no "superframework" for settling disagreements between paradigms exists. Hence, paradigms are by their nature "incommensurable."[16]

Seen against the background of the soft relativism of Kuhn, Fish's perspective appears almost indistinguishable. Fish himself encourages the comparison:

> Kuhn challenges this story [the orthodox history of science as progress] by introducing the notion of a paradigm, a set of tacit assumptions and beliefs within which research goes on, assumptions which rather than deriving from the observation of facts are determinative of the facts that could possibly be observed. It follows, then, that when observations made within different paradigms conflict, there is no principled (i.e., nonrhetorical) way to adjudicate the dispute.[17]

This passage gives perfect expression to the popular understanding of Kuhn's achievement.[18] There can never be absolute knowledge of the external world, for "the experienced world" is a product not only of data but of theory.[19] This picture of the relationship between subject and object presumes that the world is somewhere "out there" beyond consciousness, and while consciousness may have some impression of it, consciousness will never know the world as it exists in itself.[20] Our knowledge of the external world, then, is relative to a given framework or paradigm, one that we can neither throw off nor improve upon because the very idea of "improvement" (e.g., getting closer to reality) presumes a relationship to the world we can never have.

---

question of the authority underwriting literary meanings, and to yet another version of the recoil from the impasse of reading." Freund, *supra* note 3, at 96–97.

15. See Gary Gutting, Introduction to *Paradigms and Revolutions: Appraisals and Applications of Thomas Kuhn's Philosophy of Science* 1, 1 (Gary Gutting ed., 1980). The inspiration for the idea of a paradigm is Ludwik Fleck's notion of the "thought-collective" (*Denkkollektiv*). See Thomas S. Kuhn, Foreword to Ludwik Fleck, *Genesis and Development of a Scientific Fact* at viii–ix (Thaddeus J. Trenn et al. eds., Fred Bradley et al. trans., Univ. of Chicago 1979) (1935) (describing Fleck's impact on Kuhn's work).

16. Thomas S. Kuhn, *The Structure of Scientific Revolutions* 148–50 (2d ed. 1970).

17. Fish, *supra* note 1, at 487.

18. For a more sober assessment, see Paul Hoyningen-Huene, *Reconstructing Scientific Revolutions: Thomas S. Kuhn's Philosophy of Science* (Alexander T. Levine trans., 1993).

19. For a brilliant discussion of Kuhn and the positivist position in the history and philosophy of science, see Peter Galison, "History, Philosophy, and the Central Metaphor," 2 *Sci. Context* 197, 203–07 (1988) (arguing that Kuhn is best seen from within the positivist tradition in the philosophy of science).

20. The classic argument in this regard is found in Immanuel Kant, *Critique of Pure Reason* 266–75 (Norman K. Smith ed. & trans., Macmillan 1929).

Given such assumptions, how does Fish account for meaning? We know that the text itself does not produce meaning because the text is just another piece of "the world"—an inert object with no inherent meaning. If the world does not produce meaning, then there is only one other available source for meaning: the reader. Freed from the constraints of the text, readers are set free. In fact, the "meaning of the text" is no less than "the meanings produced by innumerable readers."[21] Because the reader is the source of meaning and the text exerts no power or limit over him, the text cannot limit what it is the reader can do *with* the text. The text, *qua* inert object, has no meaning. The reader gives the text a meaning by *doing something* with or to the text.[22]

Notwithstanding his apparent relativism with respect to the act of reading and meaning production, Fish has a quite unequivocal picture of reading as an activity of consciousness. Reading is an activity that always takes place *within an interpretive framework*. In other words, understanding is interpretation (of the text) from the perspective of some interpretive framework: "I hold, the text, while always there, is always an interpreted object; and when the conditions of interpretation change, the text is not merely recharacterized but changed too."[23]

On Fish's view, of course, the reader produces the meaning of the text. However, the mechanisms by which the reader produces meaning come not from the reader but from the interpretive framework chosen by the reader.[24] It is as if all readers have within their possession a variety of interpretive templates that, when the spirit moves them, they "lay over" texts to produce meanings.[25] When two readers use different templates on the "same" text, they inevitably "produce" different texts. The reason, of course, is simple: Because the text cannot act to constrain which template is selected, the reader is "free" to choose a template at random or for a given purpose. Owing to the fact that no "master template," no "template of templates," exists, nothing that could count as "constraint" can ever enter into this picture of meaning production. Interpretation *is* the only game in town.

How, then, does Fish answer the question at the heart of our inquiry: "What does it mean to say that a proposition of law is true?" We get a good sense of Fish's answer in his essay "Don't Know Much about the Middle Ages: Posner on

---

21. Fish, *supra* note 1, at 75.

22. This point highlights what one might say is Fish's "rhetorical foundationalism." Fish says that he is not against foundations; he merely objects to a certain way of thinking about them: "The thesis of anti-foundationalism is *not that there are no foundations*, but that whatever is taken to be foundational has to be established in the course or [*sic*] argument and debate and does not exist to the side of argument and debate. This thesis includes itself within its own scope, not in any self-contradictory sense, but in the sense that it too must make its way in the face of counter-examples and purportedly 'irrefutable' evidence." *Id.* at 582 n.28 (emphasis added).

23. *Id.* at 563 n.31.

24. According to Fish, even the choice of the interpretive framework is made from within the reader's existing interpretive framework. See *id.* at 394–96.

25. This is what Fish means when he says things like "meaning is 'in' the reader." See Fish, *supra* note 6, at 21–67 (arguing that language's meaning is derived from the reader's experience—language is not a repository of extractable meanings).

Law and Literature."[26] Here, Fish directs his critical gaze at some remarks of Judge Richard Posner on the parol evidence rule. Judge Posner states:

> If a document states that it is the complete integration of the parties' contract, and the price stated in the document is $100 per pound, the parol evidence rule will prevent the seller from later offering testimony that in the negotiations leading up to the contract the parties agreed that the price would be $100 per pound only for the first ten pounds, after which it would be $120 a pound. The document is not ambiguous.[27]

To this textbook statement of the parol evidence rule, Fish objects thus:

> Posner misses the point. The document is neither ambiguous nor unambiguous in and of itself. The document isn't *anything* in and of itself, but acquires a shape and a significance only within the assumed background circumstances of its possible use, and it is those circumstances—which cannot be *in* the document, but are the light in which "it" appears and becomes what "it," for a time at least, is—that determine whether or not it is ambiguous and determine too the kind of straightforwardness it is (again for a time) taken to possess.[28]

There is much in this paragraph over which we might puzzle. What draws immediate attention, however, is the fact that Fish, himself a sometime professor of contract law, completely misses Posner's main point.[29] Fish's singular focus on the question of ambiguity misses the point that the parol evidence rule is designed to prevent a party from upsetting a written agreement by resort to an earlier (written or oral) agreement of the parties.[30] Posner stipulates that the parties agree on price. In virtue of that stipulation, Posner is completely justified in claiming that the parol evidence rule precludes the admission of evidence to show that the parties' actual agreement was 120 dollars.

Fish focuses attention on a different matter. He attacks what he takes to be Posner's claim that the meaning of the sign "$100" is unambiguous "in and of itself."[31] Fish counters with a point Posner would not dispute: In the particular

---

26. Fish, *supra* note 1, at 294.

27. Richard A. Posner, "Law and Literature: A Relation Reargued," 72 *Va. L. Rev.* 1351, 1371 (1986).

28. Fish, *supra* note 1, at 301.

29. It is interesting to note that with all his talk of "communities of interpretation" Fish fails to criticize Posner at the level of the relevant community—lawyers. If Fish were true to at least this strand of his argument, one possible—but incorrect—criticism would be that Posner's reading of the parol evidence rule is inconsistent with the understanding of most lawyers. But Fish does not take this tack. Instead, he chooses to criticize Posner's view from a completely abstract level—the level of the theory of meaning.

30. See E. Allan Farnsworth, *Contracts* § 7.2, at 466 (2d ed. 1990) ("It may help to avoid confusion if the rule is thought of as applicable to prior negotiations rather than to parol evidence."); see also Arthur L. Corbin, "The Interpretation of Words and the Parol Evidence Rule," 50 *Cornell L.Q.* 161, 189 (1965) (explaining the modern conception of the parol evidence rule as a substantive rather than an interpretive doctrine of contract law).

31. Fish, *supra* note 1, at 301. Notice that Posner *never said* the document was unambiguous *in and of itself.* He simply said the document was not ambiguous. Posner, *supra* note 27, at 1371. He never offered his reasons why he thought it was neither ambiguous nor unambiguous. Fish merely assumes the interpretation that best suits his own purposes and argues accordingly.

circumstances of this transaction, there might be a trade usage[32] to the effect that "it goes without saying that there is an escalation of 20 percent after the first ten pounds."[33] Thus, the meaning of the sign "$100" cannot be known apart from some particular context of use (in this case a trade usage).

Fish's point in this connection seems to be identical to that of Wittgenstein: the meaning of a word is a function of how that word is used in various activities.[34] This surface similarity with Wittgenstein should not obscure Fish's deeper philosophical agenda, one quite alien to Wittgenstein's thought.[35] For Fish, it is not enough to say that a word has meaning by virtue of the ways in which it is used (action); Fish's claim is much stronger than that. The meaning of "$100" is not simply a consequence of the sign being used in certain ways; the meaning of the sign is "the product of interpretive assumptions [that] . . . will always be a function of something prior to it."[36] The meanings of our words rest on "tacit assumptions"[37] that give the signs the meanings they have.

Now why might this difference with Wittgenstein be important? If, as Fish states, "[a]ll shapes are interpretively produced,"[38] then it is inevitable that one will be led to make the following wide-ranging claim for the priority of interpretation:

> The point is a simple one: All shapes are interpretively produced, and since the conditions of interpretation are themselves unstable—the possibility of seeing something in a "new light," and therefore of seeing a *new* something, is ever and unpredictably present—the shapes that seem perspicuous to us now may not seem so or may seem differently so tomorrow. This applies not only to the shape of statutes, poems, and signs in airplane lavatories, but to the disciplines and forms of life within which statutes, poems, and signs become available to us.[39]

Fish sees the meaning of everything—from poems, to rules, to lavatory signs— as always and everywhere "up for grabs." In this way, he turns Wittgenstein's insight on its head. True, it is "we" who breathe life—meaning—into dead signs. But these conventional understandings are *not* interpretations. The moves we make in everyday language are neither negotiated nor interpreted at every turn. There is nothing (least of all interpretation) between us and the world; there is only our interaction with the world. Our conventional understandings are not interpretations, implicit or otherwise. Rather, "[o]ur conventional understanding of the world *is* just the way we are in the world."[40]

---

32. "Trade usage" is defined in the Uniform Commercial Code as "any practice or method of dealing having such regularity of observance in a place, vocation or trade as to justify an expectation that it will be observed with respect to the transaction in question." U.C.C. § 1-205(2) (1991).

33. Fish, *supra* note 1, at 301.

34. See Ludwig Wittgenstein, *Philosophical Investigations* § 43 (G. E. M. Anscombe trans., 3d ed. 1958) ("[T]he meaning of a word is its use in a language.").

35. See Ellis, *supra* note 3, at 121 n.6.

36. Fish, *supra* note 1, at 301.

37. *Id.* at 302.

38. *Id.*

39. *Id.*

40. James Tully, "Wittgenstein and Political Philosophy," 17 *Pol. Theory* 172, 197 (1989).

Fish *contra* Dworkin

We can gain a better sense of Fish's theory of linguistic meaning and its relationship to his view of law and legal practice by considering the particulars of his critique of Dworkin's jurisprudence. The essence of Fish's challenge to Dworkin is philosophical; the locus of the challenge is the theory of linguistic meaning. There are two aspects to Fish's argument. At the critical level, Fish finds fault with Dworkin's views on two counts. First, Fish disputes Dworkin's efforts to distinguish the theory of law as integrity from the theories of conventionalism and pragmatism. Second, Fish argues that Dworkin fails to demonstrate that his program of law as integrity has meaningful content. The second aspect of Fish's critique is his own theory of the nature of linguistic meaning. Fish has an account of meaning that, if correct, both trumps the Dworkinian theory and provides an alternative account of the nature of legal argument. We first consider the critical claims.

Fish's target is the Dworkin of *Law's Empire*, in which Dworkin defends his theory of "law as integrity." Dworkin develops the theory by contrasting it with two leading theories of law, conventionalism and pragmatism.[41] A conventionalist account of law, as Dworkin describes it, "restricts the law of a community to the explicit [or implicit] extension of its legal conventions like legislation and precedent."[42] For the legal pragmatist, there are no first principles; the judge's obligation is to do the best thing, all things considered. Thus in the pragmatic account, "legal rights are only the servants of the best future: they are instruments we construct for that purpose and have no independent force or ground.[43]

Against conventionalism and pragmatism, Dworkin opposes law as integrity, which has the following features:

1. It "accepts law and legal rights wholeheartedly."[44]
2. Law's constraints benefit society "by securing a *kind* of equality among citizens that makes their community more genuine and improves its moral justification for exercising the political power it does."[45]
3. Rights and responsibilities "flow from" past political decisions "when they follow from the principles of personal and political morality [that] the explicit decisions presuppose by way of justification."[46]

---

41. Ronald Dworkin, *Law's Empire* 94–95 (1986) (stating that legal pragmatism is a skeptical conception of law that rejects the notion that society gains from the use of precedent); *id.* at 115–16 (asserting that conventionalism is an interpretive conception of law which holds that judges must respect the established legal conventions of their community). Conventionalism is best exemplified by legal positivism and pragmatism by economic analyses of law. See John Stick, "Literary Imperialism: Assessing the Results of Dworkin's Interpretive Turn in *Law's Empire*," 34 *UCLA L. Rev.* 371, 401, 418 n.125 (1986) (reviewing Ronald Dworkin, *Law's Empire*) (defining conventionalism as an "interpretive version of positivism" and noting that Dworkin's pragmatism has similarities to some writers in law and economics).

42. Dworkin, *supra* note 41, at 124.

43. *Id.* at 160.

44. *Id.* at 95.

45. *Id.* at 96 (emphasis added)

46. *Id.*

Fish contests Dworkin's effort to distinguish his theory from conventionalism and pragmatism. He poses three objections:

1. Dworkin's critique of conventionalism and pragmatism is "irrelevant because neither is a program according to which a judge might generate his practice."[47]
2. Dworkin's theory of law as integrity cannot claim to represent "an additional or extra step in adjudication—a 'distinct virtue' . . .—which can be invoked as a constraint against the appeal of lesser virtues and as a check against the pressures of the political and the personal."[48]
3. "[I]f 'law as integrity' is anything, it is either the name of what we already do . . . or a rhetorical/political strategy by means of which we give a certain necessary coloring to what we've already done."[49]

For Fish, conventionalism (and pragmatism) cannot be possible forms of judicial action. For someone to actually "do" conventionalism, "it would have to be the case that language . . . can set limits on its own interpretation."[50] For Dworkin, Fish maintains, conventionalism asserts that certain words contained in canonical statutes "contain explicit directions that serve to guide the activities of legal actors."[51] The attraction that conventionalism holds is its seeming power to constrain or put limits on the place of the interpretive power of judges and administrators. To the conventionalist picture Fish objects: "[O]f course, th[e] entire picture of things, and the possibility of *being* a conventionalist, depends on the assumption that explicit or literal meanings do in fact exist, and it is my contention that they do not."[52]

The conventionalist, as described by Dworkin, sees the source of constraint on the subjectivity of the judge in the extant conventions of legal practice. It is these conventions that limit the range of meanings a judge may impose on the law. Fish counters that these meanings only become perspicuous against a background of interpretive assumptions, in the absence of which reading and understanding would be impossible. "A meaning that seems to leap off the page, propelled by its own self-sufficiency, is a meaning that flows from interpretive assumptions so deeply embedded that they have become invisible."[53] For Fish, "[t]he moral is clear: someone who stands on a literal or explicit meaning in facts stands on an interpretation, albeit an interpretation so firmly in place that it is impossible (at least for the time being) not to take as literal and unassailable the meanings it subtends."[54]

Fish does not disagree with Dworkin that judges are *in fact* constrained in what they can do by way of legal interpretation. The disagreement is over the

---

47. Fish, *supra* note 1, at 357.
48. *Id.*
49. *Id.*
50. *Id.*
51. *Id.* at 357–58.
52. *Id.* at 358.
53. *Id.*
54. *Id.* at 359.

source of that constraint.[55] In his critique of conventionalism, Dworkin strives to distinguish law as integrity by showing how its idea of constraint differs from that of conventionalism.[56] In the course of making this distinction, Dworkin sets up what Fish sees as a false dichotomy. There is no distinction because there is nothing like conventionalism as described by Dworkin. The Dworkinian conventionalist is a figment of Dworkin's imagination. There is no distinction because no one subscribes to the conventionalist position Dworkin describes.[57]

Let us turn now to Fish's comments on Dworkin's critique of legal pragmatism.[58] Pragmatists eschew any effort to make a decision consistent with the past.[59] The pragmatist, as described by Dworkin, makes a decision about what is "best" in a given case not on the basis of history but simply on the basis of theory (specifically *political* theory) alone.[60] Fish objects that the "very ability to formulate a decision in terms that would be recognizably legal depends on one's having internalized the norms, categorical distinctions, and evidentiary criteria that make up one's understanding of what the law is."[61] Fish's point is that the pragmatist does not first develop an understanding and then apply it to legal materials. The materials and the recognition of them as *legal* materials is all of a piece. The legal actor's thinking is, Fish states, "irremediably historical, consistent with the past in the sense that it flows from the past."[62]

Fish's complaint against Dworkin is that Dworkin's arguments against conventionalism and pragmatism are, as Fish terms them, "academic," because neither of them are positions one could take in practice. Likewise, law as integrity is a position one could not fail to put into practice. Fish explains:

> The reasoning is simple: if pragmatism is not an option for practice because the history it supposedly ignores is an ingredient of any judge's understanding, then law as integrity, which enjoins us to maintain a continuity with history, enjoins us to something we are already doing. This is a conclusion that Dworkin would certainly resist since it is his basic thesis that law as integrity is a "distinct political virtue," a thesis that is first developed in the context of a distinction between conversational and constructive (or creative) interpretation.[63]

55. See *id*. at 365–68 (arguing that judges are constrained by their awareness that they are acting as judges, in contrast to Dworkin's view that judicial constraints come from the adoption of a particular decision-making methodology).

56. See Dworkin, *supra* note 41, at 96 (distinguishing law as integrity from conventionalism by the fact that the former secures a "kind of equality among citizens that makes their community more genuine").

57. See Fish, *supra* note 1, at 360 (concluding that because Dworkin's strict conventionalism is "a practical impossibility, . . . there is no point in arguing against it").

58. Again, it is important to keep in mind that law and economics is Dworkin's prime example of legal pragmatism.

59. See Dworkin, *supra* note 41, at 95 (asserting that legal pragmatism "denies that a community secures any genuine benefit by requiring that judges' adjudicative decisions be checked by any supposed right of litigants to consistency with other political decisions made in the past").

60. See *id*. (positing that under legal pragmatism "judges do and should make whatever decisions seem to them best for the community's future").

61. Fish, *supra* note 1, at 360.

62. *Id*.

63. *Id*. at 361 (citation omitted).

We now turn to Fish's second critique, his attack on Dworkin's own program of law as integrity. Because law as integrity is a program of constructive interpretation, the point of the enterprise is for the interpreter to impose a "purpose on an object or practice in order to make of it the best possible example of the form or genre to which it is taken to belong."[64] Fish contends that much in Dworkin's account depends on how Dworkin unpacks the claim that we need to make the interpretive object the "best" it can be."[65] Fish sees this as a two-step process. First, the interpreter determines the shape (or meaning) the object apparently has, and then, second, he wrestles it into another shape according to some prior sense of what it would be *best* for it to mean.[66]

The problem with this account of interpretation is that it commits Dworkin to the two positions from which he is so eager to free himself: strict conventionalism and freewheeling pragmatism. Positing that an object has an identity apart from some interpretation of it (step one) commits Dworkin to the conventionalist account of plain meaning. The second step, a thoroughly pragmatist one, devolves into subjectivism, for it assigns to the interpreter the power of *imposing* a purpose on the object. Indeed, as Fish says, "if we take the word 'imposing' seriously, this is not an account of interpretation at all, but an instance of what Dworkin has elsewhere stigmatized as 'changing' or 'altering.'"[67] Either the object or practice is *already* the best it can be and, thus, does not need the interpreter to do anything (in which case Dworkin is a positivist), or by making it the best it can be, the interpreter rides roughshod over the object and refashions it according to her own lights (in which case Dworkin is a subjectivist).

Could Dworkin not reply that he is being misunderstood and that the purpose imposed by the interpreter is not the interpreter's own but one that belongs to a "coherent theory"[68] or abiding "set of principles,"[69] that, while they may not be explicit, are in a sense implicit or "presuppose[d] by way of justification"?[70] Because an interpreter is creative without being willful, he can claim to be guided by something independent of himself and yet not slavishly constrained, because he is guided by something he must construct.

Indeed, this is a more capacious account than Dworkin's own. But Fish is equally critical of it in his third objection to law as integrity. Fish claims that the picture rests upon a distinction between legal practice as a set of discrete acts and legal practice as a continually unfolding story about principles such as justice, fairness, and equality. The distinction is a false one insofar as it purports to represent genuine conceptual alternatives, for it is not possible (except in a positivist world of isolated brute phenomena) to conceive of a legal act apart from just that story and those principles. In other words, to understand legal practice *at all*, one must first be inside an interpretation. As Fish puts it:

64. Dworkin, *supra* note 41, at 52.
65. Fish, *supra* note 1, at 361.
66. *Id.* at 361–62.
67. *Id.* at 362.
68. Dworkin, *supra* note 41, at 245.
69. *Id.* at 243.
70. *Id.* at 96.

> It is not that the novice student sees the practice detached from the principles underlying it; he doesn't see "the practice" at all but something else (perhaps some other practice if its assumptions are strongly enough the content of his perception). Conversely, the initiated student who has thoroughly internalized the distinctions, categories, and notions of relevance and irrelevance that comprise "thinking like a lawyer," cannot see anything *but* the practice (nor can he remember what it was like to not see it) and along with it, because it is inseparable from the practice, he sees the set of principles of whose unfolding the practice is the story.[71]

In the end, Dworkin is committed to the necessity of something special or "extra" in the constructive interpretation of law—"a distinct level of interpretive striving which distinguishes the truly responsible interpreter," as Fish states it.[72] In other words, Dworkin is committed to the necessity of two types of reasons—personal ones and institutional ones.[73] Fish attacks this distinction. He asks how a judge comes to "think it unjust to require compensation for any emotional injury."[74] For Fish, institutional opinion is nothing but a personal opinion shared by a group of people who comprise the institution. Thus, there are no such things as "personal preferences," if by that phrase one means preferences formed apart from contexts of principle.[75] A preference is something one cannot have independent of some institution or enterprise within which the preference could emerge as an option. The institution or enterprise is itself inconceivable independent of some general purpose or value—some principle—its activities express. It follows then that it is a mistake to oppose preference to principle.[76] The proper opposition, Fish argues, is between preferences that are appropriate to a given enterprise and those that are not. The conflict is never between preference and principle but between preferences that represent different principles. Dworkin's entreaty to judges to "accept integrity" is rejected as superfluous.[77] What judges do all the time is to act in a manner they regard as exhibiting integrity. This is what they do by virtue of their being judges and lawyers. Thus, it is pointless to entreat them to do it.

A Red Herring?

One reason for the staying power of Fish's views in legal circles is the fact that critics always try to fault Fish's position on its own terms. For example, take Owen Fiss's argument that unless judicial interpretation is constrained by "disciplining

71. Fish, *supra* note 1, at 363–64.
72. *Id*. at 365.
73. *Id*.
74. *Id*. at 365–66 (quoting Dworkin, *Law's Empire, supra* note 41, at 177).
75. *Id*. at 366.
76. As Fish puts it, "We begin to see that the fear of personal preferences is an empty one, and I would go so far as to say that there are no such things as 'personal preferences' if by that phrase one means preferences formed apart from contexts of principle." *Id*.
77. *Id*. at 368.

rules," adjudication will quickly turn into politics and be rendered illegitimate.[78] Fish has a ready reply to this worry:

> If the [disciplining] rules are to function as Fiss would have them function—to "constrain the interpreter"—they themselves must be available or "readable" independently of interpretation; that is, they must directly declare their own significance to any observer, no matter what his perspective. Otherwise, they would "constrain" individual interpreters differently, and you would be right back in the original dilemma of a variously interpretable text and in an interpretively free reader. To put the matter another way, if the rules tell you what to do with texts, they cannot themselves be texts, but must be—in the strong sense assumed by an older historiography—documents. Unfortunately, rules *are* texts. They are in need of interpretation and cannot themselves serve as constraints on interpretation.[79]

The force of Fish's critique of Fiss is derived from Fish's presuppositions about meaning. From Fish's point of view, the reason Fiss's call for objectivity must be in vain is simple. The idea of disciplining rules is invoked to restrict the interpretive activity of judges. This move can only fail, because like the objects to which they are directed (authoritative texts), disciplining rules are *themselves* texts and, as such, require interpretation. Because, on Fish's account of meaning, the text cannot constrain anyone or anything (e.g., another text), Fiss's position never gets off the ground. It falters the moment it is advanced.

It is easy to see why Fiss's argument fails to persuade: he embraces the same picture of meaning as Fish. Like Fish, Fiss sees only two options: Either the reader is constrained by the text (disciplining rules), or everything is permitted. The only way for Fiss to avoid Fish's critique is to demonstrate that Fish's picture of meaning is incoherent. Fiss never does so, and for that reason his arguments never succeed. Once we know why Fish's account of meaning fails, we can begin to see how Fiss's concerns might succeed.

Why does meaning come from the reader? As we have seen, Fish's answer is that the text fails to exercise any constraint on the reader's activities of meaning production (interpretation).[80] Because understanding is always within a framework—and different understandings are a matter of different interpretive templates—the reader is "free" because the text cannot dictate which interpretive grid the reader is to select. If one's only options are text and reader, and the reader produces meaning through choice of interpretive template, then it is a foregone conclusion that the reader controls the meaning of the text. The key to intersubjective discourse about a text, then, is to get together with other folks who have the same interpretive template. When you do, you are then part of an interpretive community.

Despite its apparent plausibility, Fish's theory of interpretation fails to persuade for the same reason as Dworkin's, although the failure occurs in a somewhat different way. Like Dworkin, Fish believes that our fundamental mode of

---

78. See Owen M. Fiss, "Objectivity and Interpretation," 34 *Stan. L. Rev.* 739, 762–63 (1982).
79. Fish, *supra* note 1, at 121 (citation omitted).
80. See *supra* text accompanying notes 21–22.

being-in-the-world is interpretive. To be is to be the bearer of an interpretive grid. One comes to have a world by virtue of one's possession of an interpretive template laid against the external world, and the external world is then rendered intelligible. But this strategy cannot get off the ground, for as we saw in connection with the earlier discussion of law as an exercise in constructive interpretation,[81] interpretations by themselves do not accomplish anything.[82] When one asks of the directional arrow on a road sign "What does this arrow mean?" it is of no help to say "Let us interpret it thus." The fact is (and Fish would not disagree) that the sign may be interpreted in a thousand different ways, none of which stands apart from the rest. Thus, there is no impetus and no normative requirement to take the sign one way or another. From this fact, Fish makes the move to saying that if nothing is required, then everything (by way of interpretation) is permitted. This is his fatal mistake.[83]

From the fact that nothing is required with respect to choice among interpretive alternatives one should infer *not* that everything is permitted, but that something more—something *in addition* to the categories "text" and "interpreter"—is required. That "something more" is action.[84] Go back to the simple example of the arrow indicating direction. On Fish's account of meaning, "understanding" the meaning of the arrow is a matter of imposing some interpretive strategy on it that enables the interpreter to do at least two things: (1) see the arrow as a meaningful object, and (2) take the tip as the indicator of direction. If someone else—another interpreter—has an interpretive grid that takes the tail as indicating direction, Fish is committed to seeing that reading as equally justified.[85] Both readers, he would have to say, are always inside some interpretation. Their interpretations differ, hence their meanings differ.

81. See chapter 5.

82. See Wittgenstein, *supra* note 34, § 198 ("Interpretations by themselves do not determine meaning.").

83. Fish is not alone in courting this danger: "It would obviously be nice to believe that *my* Constitution is the true one and, therefore, that my opponents' versions are fraudulent, but that is precisely the belief that becomes steadily harder to maintain. They are simply *different* Constitutions. There are as many plausible readings of the United States Constitution as there are versions of *Hamlet*, even though each interpreter, like each director, might genuinely believe that he or she has stumbled onto the one best answer to the conundrums of the texts." Sanford Levinson, "Law as Literature," 60 *Tex. L. Rev.* 373, 391 (1982). A critic of Levinson's argument captures well the nature of the mistakes repeated by Fish: "[Levinson] falsely assumes . . . that our ability to decipher a text—whether that text be a legal document or some other text need not concern us here—depends on our ability to grasp what he calls 'some presumed inner essence' that reposes *in* the 'text being interpreted.' Judging quite correctly that no such inner essence exists, Levinson leaps to several illogical conclusions: that legal and other texts are therefore marked by a radical indeterminacy, that there is no real truth in interpretation and 'anything is permitted,' and that what eventually gets construed as the correct interpretation in any given instance is a function merely of the institutional fiat or 'coerciveness' of the interpreter." Gerald Graff, "'Keep off the Grass,' 'Drop Dead,' and Other Indeterminacies: A Response to Sanford Levinson," 60 *Tex. L. Rev.* 405, 406 (1982). (footnotes omitted).

84. For an extremely clear and persuasive discussion of the failures of the arguments by critical legal scholars in support of claims of legal indeterminacy, see Lawrence B. Solum, "On the Indeterminacy Crisis: Critiquing Critical Dogma," 54 *U. Chi. L. Rev.* 462 (1987).

85. This is confirmed in Fish's reading of Riggs v. Palmer, 22 N.E. 188 (N.Y. 1889). See *infra* text accompanying notes 91–108.

What Fish's account leaves out is the role of action in the constitution of meaning. Meanings do not spring from interpretations but from action—ways of *using* signs (linguistic and otherwise).[86] Meaning arises not from an interpretation but from regular use.[87] And this use, it is important to point out, is a *publicly accessible* use. In order for there to be meaning, the practice or action that gives rise to meaning must be a public process, one accessible in principle to everyone.[88] Fish's account of meaning as interpretation fails because, like Dworkin, Fish does not give due account to the role of intersubjectivity in the constitution of meaning.[89] Just like Dworkin's interpreters in the third or postinterpretive stage of interpretation, Fish's interpreters are windowless monads; the only thing they have in common with other monads is the fact that each possesses (not shares) the same interpretive template.[90]

Real Interpretation

Refuting Fish's claim that all understanding is a matter of interpretation requires more than the observation that action, not interpretation, is the key to under-

86. See G. P. Baker & P. M. S. Hacker, *Scepticism, Rules and Language* 88 (1984). Baker and Hacker explain how using rules in different ways is related to meaning in the following passage: "Following a rule is a *Praxis*, a regular activity. One's understanding of a (rule-governed) expression is ultimately exhibited in its *application*, in *action*. For the mastery of the technique of using an expression in accord with a rule is a skill or capacity. Capacities in general, *a fortiori* normative capacities, are manifest in behaviour. Normative capacities involve the *use* of rules, in teaching, explaining, justifying, and correcting. It is the technique of employing a rule as a standard of correctness which determines what counts as doing the same. Measuring the lengths of objects which one has never measured before is *not* applying the rule for the use of 'metre' in a new way. One lays down the rule alongside the new object in exactly the *same* way as hitherto. This is what is called 'measuring'. (But measuring the distance to the moon *is* applying concepts of measurement in a new way!) The point of the notion that in learning to add I grasp a rule is not that the rule mysteriously determines a unique answer for indefinitely many *new* cases in the future (let alone that my intentions do). Rather should we say that the point is that it is of the nature of stipulating rules that future cases (typically) *are old cases*, that each application of a rule is doing the same again."

87. See G. P. Baker & P. M. S. Hacker, *Rules, Grammar and Necessity* 133 (1985). Baker and Hacker define the relationship between the interpretation and the use of rules as follows: "[A]n interpretation is powerless to bridge the gap between a rule and one's action. It is just another formulation of the rule, and hence it is no 'closer' to one's action than the original rule-formulation was. If the latter hangs in the air, then so does the former. . . . Like other mental acts of understanding which are alleged to breathe life into dead signs, interpretations of rules do not determine meanings. Rather the meanings of rules, like those of all symbols, lie in their *use*." (citation omitted).

88. For an account of the connections between legal interpretation and objectivity, see David Millon, "Objectivity and Democracy," 67 *N.Y.U. L. Rev.* 1 (1992) (arguing that objectivity in legal interpretation depends on "a system of shared understandings that are cultivated by the legal profession through the individual interpretive activities of its members").

89. For discussion of this point, see Benjamin F. Armstrong Jr., "Wittgenstein on Private Languages: It Takes Two to Talk," 7 *Phil. Investigations* 46, 54 (1984) ("Words . . . cannot mean whatever an individual happens to 'think they mean' . . . if they are to be words.").

90. Andrei Marmor also understands Fish's view in this way: "The only way in which the 'text' 'is there' to be read or interpreted is determined by the convictions constituting the prior understandings of a given interpretive community. Furthermore, this body of shared convictions

standing. There does appear to be *something* in Fish's view that is right. People *do* disagree in their readings of texts (especially legal texts); and these disagreements seem to be a function of conflicting presuppositions about how the meaning of texts is generated or, to put the matter more succinctly, what it is "to read" a legal text. Thus, we need to examine more closely Fish's account of disagreement to see where it goes wrong.

To do this, let us consider Fish's discussion of that jurisprudential chestnut, *Riggs v. Palmer*.[91] The question in *Riggs* was whether Elmer Palmer could inherit under the will of his late grandfather, notwithstanding the fact that Elmer had brought about his grandfather's demise by fatally poisoning him.[92] In reaching its decision that Elmer could not inherit under his grandfather's will, the New York Court of Appeals grounded its decision in the principle that no person should profit by his own wrongdoing.[93] In basing its decision on this principle, the court rejected Elmer's argument that the statute be read "literally," finding the stated principle a better statement of the law.[94]

Discussions of *Riggs* tend to portray the case as a battle between two opposing principles.[95] On the one hand is the principle stated by the majority that no person should profit from his own wrongdoing; on the other is the principle, cited by the dissent in *Riggs*, that no person should be twice punished for the same offense.[96] In his discussion of the case, Fish sees the question posed by *Riggs* in a rather different light.[97] For him, the case poses not a choice from among principles but, ultimately, one of competing purposes.[98] To appreciate fully Fish's view in all its complexity, let us begin with his view of clarity and ambiguity.

Ambiguity and clarity are normally thought to be properties of sentences. Fish does not disagree with this view. However, his agreement is supplemented by a unique perspective on the relationship between ambiguity, clarity, and purpose. He states:

> If it is assumed that the purpose of probate is to ensure the orderly devolution of property at all costs, then the statute in this case will have the plain

---

reflects nothing more than a convergence of beliefs, attitudes, etc., which can change in time or from one community to the other. There is nothing in the 'texts' themselves, Fish contends, to warrant the conclusion that the prior understandings of one interpretive community are more correct than those of another; there are no textual facts, that is, facts which can be identified independently of particular interpretive strategies." Andrei Marmor, "Coherence, Holism, and Interpretation: The Epistemic Foundations of Dworkin's Legal Theory," 10 *L. & Phil.* 383, 401 (1991) (footnotes omitted).

91. 22 N.E. 188 (N.Y. 1889).

92. *Id.* at 189.

93. See *id.* at 190.

94. *Id.* at 189.

95. See, e.g., Ronald Dworkin, *Taking Rights Seriously* 23–45 (1977) (noting that when legal principles intersect, the relative weight of each must be taken into account).

96. *Riggs*, 22 N.E. at 193 (Gray, J., dissenting) (contending that once the law has "vindicated itself" for the wrong, "further judicial utterance upon the subject of punishment or deprivation of rights is barred").

97. See Fish, *supra* note 6, at 278–81.

98. *Id.* at 279.

meaning urged by the defendant; but if it is assumed that no law ever operates in favor of someone who would profit by his crime, then the "same" statute will have a meaning that is different, but no less plain. In either case the statute will have been literally construed, and what the court will have done is prefer one literal construction to another by invoking one purpose (assumed background) rather than another.[99]

For Fish, the ambiguity or plain meaning of a sentence or statute is a function not of the sentence or statute but of the purposes the reader chooses to bring to bear on the sentence. As he states repeatedly, the sentence *by itself* has no inherent meaning—the only meaning (or clarity or ambiguity) the sentence can have is the meaning the reader gives it.[100] And the reader gives the sentence this meaning (thereby bestowing the property of clarity or ambiguity) by choosing an interpretive grid (here a purpose) that gives the sentence whatever meaning it enjoys.[101]

On its own terms, Fish's account of clarity, ambiguity, and sentence meaning makes perfect sense. If you assume that a statute has a certain purpose, and make that purpose a definitive grid against which some text (here a statute) is to be read, then the statute will be clear in the light of that purpose. However, this picture of the activity of reading a statute (or any text) is wildly inaccurate. The most obvious deficiency with Fish's account of what is at stake in *Riggs* is that both the majority and dissent recognize *not* that only one purpose informs the statute but that there are competing purposes in play.[102] The problem is not to isolate one purpose over others; rather, the problem is that both purposes are perfectly valid juridical values, and given the fact that they conflict, a choice has to be made as to which is the overriding value.[103] Thus, the problem is not that

---

99. *Id.* at 280.

100. See, e.g., *id.* at 274 (arguing that the text has meaning only "wherever and however long a particular way of reading is in force").

101. This reading of Fish is a commonplace. For example: "Fish begins by making the very obvious point that judges are members of an interpretive community bound by shared understandings of what counts as appropriate interpretation. He adds that interpretation is never determined by the text itself, in the sense of a causal chain whereby text precedes interpretation. On the contrary, interpretation *constitutes* the text. According to this view, the truth of legal propositions is always contingent on the nature of the relevant community rather than being a property of particular texts." Brendan Edgeworth, "Reading Dworkin Empirically: Principles, Policies and Property," in *Reading Dworkin Critically* 187, 199 (Alan Hunt ed., 1992).

102. Compare *Riggs v. Palmer*, 22 N.E. 188, 190 (N.Y. 1889) (majority opinion) (noting that the purpose of will statutes is to carry out the legally expressed wishes of testators and the purpose of the law of fraud is to prevent the acquisition of property via one's own crime) with *id.* at 192 (Gray, J., dissenting) (observing that some rules of law are intended to annul testamentary provisions that benefit those who are unworthy of them and that others prevent the imposition of multiple punishments for the same crime).

103. Charles Altieri describes well the very aspect of *Riggs* that Fish's analysis ignores: "Although purposes are not objective, they may have considerable support in traditional and conceptual forms of going on in legal institutions (although often never literally present 'in' the specific law). The problem is clearest in Fish's apparent assumption that both purposes facing the court have no value connection independent of the specific existential moment of choice. Both purposes seem to exist on the same level. But this is not how law or society works. The law must

the majority and dissent are working from *different* grids of intelligibility. The problem is that each is trying to make sense of the question posed against *the very same grid*. What they disagree over is how lexically to order the competing juridical values.

This point may seem to be academic, but it is not. Like Dworkin, Fish claims that interpretation, not understanding, is the nerve of legal argument. This view, I have argued, is fundamentally mistaken. For Dworkin, the mistake manifests itself in his failure to make sense of either the ordinary aspects of lawyering or the distinctive qualities of interpretation. For Fish, the difficulty lies in his inability to make sense of the notion of disagreement. Let me explain.

According to Fish, it is reasonable to claim that within the framework of each purpose, the majority and dissenting opinions in *Riggs* make perfect sense because "[i]t is not that we first read the statute and then know its purpose; we know the purpose first, and only then can the statute be read."[104] Because purpose precedes understanding, it makes perfect sense "to deny that ambiguity is a property of some sentences and not of others."[105] Again, ambiguity and clarity are a *function* of assumed purpose, not sentences themselves. As Fish argues: "[I]f meaning is a matter of what a speaker situated in a particular situation has in mind (precisely the thesis of speaker-relative presupposition), one can only determine it by going behind the words to the intentional circumstances of production in the light of which they acquire significance."[106]

The error in this logic is easy to see if we begin at the point of disagreement between the majority and the dissent in *Riggs*. Fish writes as if the question posed

---

have, and society tends to have, levels of embedding among priorities and principles that allow recursive justifications that are not all subject to change at the same rate and thus not all equally dependent on the same kinds of purposes. Law must work like Quine's network, not like Barthes's onion. So finding implicit intentions based on higher, inclusive principles is not merely one among possible choices or priorities but one based on the fundamental possibility of ever resolving competing interpretations without pure arbitrariness—that is, on the very idea of law. Fish is right that inheritance law could outweigh an unlawful-gain provision if the highest priority of law were the disposition of property, but the embedded principles would be different; we would then have another kind of society, again with levels of embedding. What Fish ignores brings us to the heart of Wittgenstein's vision—that for some of the basic principles in social institutions to change, the society itself would have to emphasize different forms of life. In this particular case, for the property consideration to outweigh constraints against violent gain, one would have to envision a society bound procedurally to versions of the person and of fairness very different from those commonly affirmed in Western culture. Such changes are possible, but they will not alter as fashions do or as Nietzschean wills desire, nor will they depend on or explain the choices of a single judge." Charles Altieri, *Canons and Consequences: Reflections on the Ethical Force of Imaginative Ideals* 86–87 (1990).

104. Fish, *supra* note 6, at 280. Here, it seems, Fish has matters exactly backwards. *Qua* individuals, we do not give meaning to texts. True, we each have intentions, which find verbal expression. However—and here is the point Fish misses—"the intelligibility of individual intentions rides on publicly shared meanings implicit in social practices." Amélie O. Rorty, "How to Interpret Actions," in *Rationality, Relativism and the Human Sciences* 81, 89 (J. Margolis et al. eds., 1986). It bears repeating that the point is *not* that persons lack intentions; rather, the point is that those intentions make no normative contribution to textual meaning.

105. Fish, *supra* note 6, at 281.

106. Fish, *supra* note 1, at 7.

in *Riggs* is merely linguistic: Is the statute clear or is it not? His argument is that the statute is clear on *both* accounts. The problem is that both purposes produce equally clear texts (plain meaning), but the purposes are produced by totally irreconcilable interpretive perspectives. In other words, the trouble is not with the texts produced by each but with the independence and incommensurability of the purposes that inform each competing interpretation. Is there a better way to make sense of the disagreement? Surely.

Had Elmer not murdered his grandfather, the meaning of the New York law of wills would never have been in question.[107] This is not because everyone would agree or did agree about the "purpose" of the statute. The requirements of the statute would never have been in question because the meaning of the statute was clear. This clarity is the product of nothing—not interpretation, not political theory—save the meaning of the words. Doubt is actuated by some fact (e.g., the murder of Elmer's grandfather) which puts that meaning in question. This is the moment at which the need for interpretation arises.

Interpretation is possible only against a background of unreflective linguistic practice.[108] Interpretation is one of a number of reflective activities we engage in when conventional meanings are called into question. In the activity of interpretation, participants advance proposals for taking our conventional meanings one way rather than another. In addition to the reflective practice of interpretation— adjudicating various proposals in accordance with criteria of interpretation—we may put the criteria themselves in question. Throughout all of this, the point of the activity is to advance interpretations in the hope of reaching agreement about how to go on with our practices (legal and otherwise). In this way, we see that, far from being foundational, interpretation is dependent upon conventional understanding and practice. Thus, interpretation is best seen as a therapeutic activity; one for reaching understanding, not explaining it.

Fish Replies

Hoist with One's Own Petard

Fish has taken issue with the characterization of his position just given.[109] He states: "Patterson gets my position wrong in a number of related ways."[110] In fact, Fish asserts not only that I attribute to him a position he does not hold, but also that the view I attribute to him is "precisely the view [he has] been arguing

---

107. Cf. Wittgenstein, *supra* note 34, at § 1 ("But what is the meaning of the word 'five'?— No such thing was in question here, only how the word 'five' is used.").

108. See Tully, *supra* note 40, at 196 ("[T]he condition for engaging in interpretation is that a wide range of ways of acting with words is not in doubt at all, but is followed as a matter of course in the activity of interpretation.").

109. Dennis M. Patterson, "The Poverty of Interpretive Universalism: Toward the Reconstruction of Legal Theory," 72 *Tex. L. Rev.* 1 (1993) [the text of the present chapter is largely taken from this article].

110. Stanley Fish, "How Come You Do Me Like You Do? A Response to Dennis Patterson," 72 *Tex. L. Rev.* 57, 57 (1993).

against for more than fifteen years now."[111] Interestingly, Fish sets about proving the truth of his assertion[112] by appealing to a text, specifically the corpus of his work produced over the course of the last fifteen years.[113] But when one examines that corpus, one finds the following description of the plight of two critics, each of whom seeks to resolve an interpretive disagreement about a text by appeal to the text in question:

> One cannot appeal to the text, because the text has become an extension of the interpretive disagreement that divides them; and, in fact, the text as it is variously characterized is a consequence of the interpretation for which it is supposedly evidence. . . . It follows, then, that when one interpretation wins out over another, it is not because the first has been shown to be in accordance with the facts but because it is from the perspective of its assumptions that the facts are now being specified. It is these assumptions, and not the facts they make possible, that are at stake in any critical dispute.[114]

With this passage, Fish places out of bounds the very strategy he adopts in response. Additionally, he employs precisely the false dichotomy that is his signature—that of "facts" (objectivity) on the one hand and "assumptions" (subjectivity) on the other.[115] In the passage just quoted from *Is There a Text in This*

111. *Id.* (emphasis omitted).

112. Fish once claimed that being interesting was more important than being right. See Fish, *supra* note 6, at 180. He wrote: "Affective criticism is arbitrary only in the sense that one cannot prove that its beginning is the right one, but once begun it unfolds in ways that are consistent with its declared principles. It is therefore a superior fiction, and since no methodology can legitimately claim any more, this superiority is decisive. . . . My fiction is liberating. It relieves me of the obligation to be right (a standard that simply drops out) and demands only that I be interesting (a standard that can be met without any reference at all to an illusory objectivity). Rather than restoring or recovering texts, I am in the business of making texts and of teaching others to make them by adding their repertoire of strategies. I was once asked whether there are really such things as self-consuming artifacts, and I replied: 'There are now.' In that answer you will find both the arrogance and the modesty of my claims." *Id.* Fish is reported to have since retracted this position. David Lehman notes: "Stanley Fish . . . made the ultimate statement of his position (which he would later retract). Fish asserted that critical theory 'relieves me of the obligation to be right . . . and demands only that I be interesting': literary criticism as a personal liberation front." David Lehman, *Signs of the Times: Deconstruction and the Fall of Paul DeMan* 75 (1991).

113. Fish relies upon two works: *Is There a Text in This Class?, supra* note 6, and *Doing What Comes Naturally, supra* note 1.

114. Fish, *supra* note 6, at 340 (emphasis omitted); see also Fish, *supra* note 1, at 87–91 (discussing Dworkin's view that legal and critical practice involves "chain enterprises" in which interpretation is an extension of an institutional history).

115. Terry Eagleton writes: "What if the literary work were not a determinate structure containing certain indeterminacies, but if everything in the text was indeterminate, dependent on which way the reader chose to construct it? In what sense could we then speak of interpreting the 'same' work? Not all reception theorists find this an embarrassment. The American critic Stanley Fish is quite happy to accept that, when you get down to it, there is no 'objective' work of literature there on the seminar table at all. *Bleak House* is just all the assorted accounts of the novel that have been or will be given. The true writer is the reader. . . . What the text 'does' to us . . . is actually a matter of what we do to it, a question of interpretation; the object of critical attention is the structure of the reader's experience, not any 'objective' structure to be found in the work itself. Everything in the text—its grammar, meanings, formal units—is a product of interpretation, in no sense

Class? one finds all the elements of Fish's theory of reading texts. The reader creates the meaning of the text. She does this, as Fish states, by bringing interpretive assumptions to bear on the text. Her assumptions transform the printed page from an inert script into an object of meaning. No one can claim that her reading is "wrong" because all differences in interpretation are differences in interpretive assumptions. And, because no set of assumptions is more "right" than another in any way, "wrong" can only mean proceeding from a different set of assumptions.[116] Unhappily for Fish, when it comes to my reading of his text, the most he can rightly accuse me of is having different interpretive assumptions. Because I do not share Fish's view of what it means to read a text, I can respond to him on the merits.

From Solipsism to the Interpretive Community

Fish claims that the root cause of my misreading of him lies in my "misunderstanding of the key notion of the 'interpretive community.'"[117] I agree with Fish that a proper understanding of the idea of an interpretive community is the key to his position. I believe, however, that it is Fish who fails to understand adequately the status of that notion in his own thought. In Fish's hands, an "interpretive community" is not one idea but two. This partially explains why Fish's conception of interpretive community cannot be a part of my position, with which he is so eager to agree.

One cannot fully understand the role of the interpretive community in Fish's thought without understanding what brought him to the idea in the first place. While he fails to mention this fact, the problems I raise with Fish's theory of reading were noticed long ago.[118] Despite prodigious effort on his part, Fish has been unable to surmount the many and varied criticisms of what, in the end, is an implausible account of meaning and interpretation.

Fish's position took root in response to the literary theory of New Criticism, which demanded that reading be cognitive rather than focused on the author's intentions or biography.[119] Through the end of the fifties, the New Critics in-

---

'factually' given; and this raises the intriguing question of what it is that Fish believes he is interpreting when he reads. His refreshingly candid answer to this question is that he does not know; but neither, he thinks, does anybody else." Terry Eagleton, *Literary Theory* 85 (1983).

116. See Fish, *supra* note 6, at 340. Such corollaries have led critics to describe Fish's position as one of "naive idealism." See, e.g., Frank Lentricchia, *After the New Criticism* 146 (1980). Lentricchia states: "[F]rom [his] rejection of naive realism Fish leaps to an equally naive idealism: aside from presently operating contexts for reading, there are neither textual nor historical constraints on the reader's consciousness; the text itself is radically indeterminate—though how a critic of Fish's disposition can allow himself that objectivist claim is never made clear. The rejection of realism leads in Fish's argument to the structuralist notion that any meaning of the text is wholly a construction of the reader. Hence it follows that all interpretations, since they cannot be matched to an objective norm, are equally arbitrary, equally available but not (Fish adds this twist) equally acceptable."

117. Fish, *supra* note 110, at 57.

118. See *infra* notes 125, 133, 156 and accompanying texts.

119. See, e.g., John A. Cuddon, *The Penguin Dictionary of Literary Terms and Literary Theory* 582 (3d ed. 1991) (describing New Criticism's preference for close textual analysis instead of analysis

sisted that the literary work be taken on its own terms.[120] A movement known as reader-response theory attempted to turn New Criticism on its head[121] with the argument that not only is the role of the reader important to an understanding of the reading process, but the reader's experience is identical to the text.[122] Fish, who is credited as "the first critic to propose this theory of reading,"[123] said as much: "[T]he reader's response is not *to* the meaning; it *is* the meaning."[124]

Fish's particular formulation of reader-response theory—affective stylistics— came in for sharp criticism on grounds of paradox[125] and solipsism.[126] In reaction to the spate of criticism, Fish moved away from identification of the text with the reader's experience of it to a view of reading as the product of a dialectical interaction between reader and text. However, this emendation to the theory of reader-as-writer was not without its problems, which a sympathetic reader of Fish summarized this way:

> When the reader's experience is the object of analysis, the integrity of the text is threatened; when the text becomes the focus, Fish's programme reverts to a closet formalism, in which the concept of the reader is only an extension of textual constraints or authorial intention.

---

of the writer's personality or the social implications of a text); W. K. Wimsatt Jr., *The Verbal Icon: Studies in the Meaning of Poetry* 3–18 (1954) (claiming that all ideas in a poem must be ascribed to the dramatic speaker's intent instead of that of the author).

120. In the classic New Critical description of a poem, Cleanth Brooks declared that "[t]he essential structure of a poem . . . resembles that of architecture or painting: it is a pattern of resolved stresses." Cleanth Brooks, *The Well-Wrought Urn: Studies in the Structure of Poetry* 203 (1947). In this view, the poem is seen as a formal object that can be analyzed as a self-contained, self-referential series of internal relations separate from the contexts of history or biography.

121. New Criticism's dismissal of the historical context of a literary text had already come under attack in the "archetypal" criticism of Northrop Frye, arguably the most influential North American critic of the late fifties and sixties. See Lentricchia, *supra* note 116, at 17 (detailing Frye's attack on New Criticism as rooted in a restricted historical context).

122. See Jane P. Tompkins, Introduction to *Reader-Response Criticism* at ix, x (Jane P. Tompkins ed., 1980) ("Reading and writing join hands, change places, and finally become distinguishable only as two names for the same activity.").

123. *Id.* at xvi.

124. Fish, *supra* note 6, at 3.

125. See, e.g., David C. Hoy, *The Critical Circle: Literature, History, and Philosophical Hermeneutics* 158 (1978). Hoy's attack is summarized in the following passage: "Fish takes the notion of response so far that the text has indeed entirely disappeared into the reader's context. Yet a response theory or reception theory that has nothing to respond to or to receive is indeed paradoxical. While the text may not be an independently given thing-in-itself, there is no need to infer that it is nothing, or that it does not exist." (citations omitted).

126. As a thesis or position in general philosophy, solipsism is the view that "I alone exist independently, and that what I ordinarily call the outside world exists only as an object or content of my consciousness." Antony Flew, *Dictionary of Philosophy* 330 (2d rev. ed. 1979). Jonathan Culler highlights the solipsistic nature of Professor Fish's version of reader-response theory in the following passage: "In [two of his earlier books], Stanley Fish claimed to report what readers actually experience when reading and argued that critics reach different conclusions because their erroneous theories . . . lead them to forget, distort, or misconstrue their actual experience of the work. Many were skeptical of this claim, suggesting that Fish was merely reporting his own experience, and at times Fish has conceded the point that he 'was not revealing what readers had

. . . The upshot of this inconclusive portrayal of the reader's role is that author, text and reader remain locked in dubious battle for the authority of meaning.[127]

Both New Criticism and reader-response theory evince preoccupation with questions of authority: Is authority for meaning in the text, as New Criticism would have it, or is it in the reader, as reader-response theory maintained? Despite the efforts of reader-response critics to overthrow the orthodoxy of New Criticism, the problems with reader-response theory were never eradicated, and the theory fell from prominence.[128]

In 1980, Fish published *Is There a Text in This Class?*, a collection of his essays from the seventies. In the introduction to this book, entitled "How I Stopped Worrying and Learned to Love Interpretation,"[129] Fish narrates the history of his several formulations of reader-response theory, in Freund's words, "from its beginnings, in the assertion of reader power, through a classical Aristotelian reversal of fortunes which puts in doubt not only the text's objectivity and the reader's autonomous selfhood but also the feasibility of the entire undertaking."[130] All the problems that plagued affective stylistics would now be overcome with the idea of the interpretive community. In this introduction, Fish describes the promise of this new development in his thought: "[I]t is interpretive communities, rather than either the text or the reader, that produce meanings and are responsible for the emergence of formal features. Interpretive communities are made up of those who share interpretive strategies not for reading but for writing texts, for constituting their properties."[131]

As I have mentioned, Fish embraced the idea of an interpretive community[132] to solve problems engendered by undue emphasis on the private mental processes

---

always done but trying to persuade them to a set of community assumptions so that when they read they would do what I did.' Yet the situation is not so simple. There are good reasons to suspect that his so-called experience of reading is more complex than the stories he tells. For one thing, Fish's reader never learns anything from his experience. Time after time he is discomfited to see the second half of a sentence take away what the first half had seemed to assert. Time after time he is bewildered to see the self-consuming artifact he is reading consume itself. What distinguishes Fish's reader is this propensity to fall into the same traps over and over again. . . . The conclusion seems inescapable: what Fish reports is not Stanley Fish reading but Stanley Fish imagining reading as a Fishian reader." Jonathan D. Culler, *On Deconstruction: Theory and Criticism After Structuralism* 65–66 (1982) (citations omitted) (quoting Fish, *Is There a Text?*, *supra* note 6, at 15).

127. Freund, *supra* note 3, at 103. For anyone with an interest in the history of Fish's views, Freund's book provides an excellent and even-handed account. *Id.* at 90–111.

128. See *id.* at 10 (concluding that reader-response theory "has a past rather than a future").

129. Fish, *supra* note 6, at 1.

130. Freund, *supra* note 3, at 105.

131. Fish, *supra* note 6, at 14.

132. The idea of an interpretive community comes from David Bleich, *Subjective Criticism* 296 (1978) ("It is not possible to 'have' an interpretation of a work of literature in isolation from a community."); see Ellen Schauber & Ellen Spolsky, *The Bounds of Interpretation: Linguistic Theory and Literary Text* 145 n.2 (1986) ("Fish apparently adapts the notion of speech community or social network from sociolinguistic usage. Bleich has an earlier discussion of the notion of communities of interpretation.").

of individual readers.[133] The authority for meaning lies neither in the reader nor in the text, but in the interpretive communities that provide strategies for readers. To achieve membership in a community, one must pass "through a professional initiation or course of training,"[134] the effect of which "is to homogenize persons who were disparate and heterogeneous before entering—and becoming inhabited by—the community's ways."[135]

Despite his claim that the idea of an interpretive community represents an advance over earlier formulations of his theory of reader-as-writer, I believe that the idea is no advance at all.[136] Instead of eradicating the problems with reader-response theory, Fish has simply exchanged one set of problems for another. In fact, Fish's conception of an interpretive community turns out to be two mutually incompatible ideas masquerading as a coherent notion.

The first idea is evident in Fish's explanation of what it means for him to speak and be understood by another professor of English:

> [T]he reason that I can speak and presume to be understood by someone like [Cornell professor M. H.] Abrams is that I speak to him *from within* a set of interests and concerns, and it is in relation to those interests and concerns that I assume he will hear my words. If what follows is communication or understanding, it will not be because he and I share a language, in the sense of knowing the meanings of individual words and the rules for combining them, but because of a way of thinking, a form of life, shares us, and implicates us in a world of already-in-place objects, purposes, goals, procedures, values, and so on; and it is to the features of that world that any words we utter will be heard as necessarily referring.[137]

I take Fish to be saying that speaking a language is a necessary but not sufficient condition for being a member of an interpretive community.[138] In addi-

---

133. John Ellis summarizes this aspect of the theory's problems in this way: "The initial step of the Reader-Response argument makes all mental processes arbitrary, so that no mental process has any necessary relation to the text that provokes it. From this it must follow that my meaning has no necessary relation to your meaning. Yet this conclusion so completely ignores the fact of our sharing common assumptions and ways of interpreting our common language that it would make communication impossible—we could only sit in our private worlds [solipsism]. But we do not; the moment we look at a piece of language and have any response whatever to its meaning, we have recognized that it is in, say, English rather than Turkish. And in so doing we are immediately sharing a convention with others, agreeing with them to use the publicly available values for linguistic structures that constitute the English language. Thus, Reader-Response criticism must destroy its own logical basis as soon as it tries to emerge from complete solipsism. If it tries to see *any* meaning in a text, it will have had to concede that meaning is constrained and not infinitely variable; but if it tries to argue that there are no constraints, it will be forced to abandon meaning—*all* meaning, not just fixed meaning but infinitely variable meaning, too." Ellis, *supra* note 3, at 121–22 (citation omitted).

134. Fish, *supra* note 110, at 58 (quoting Fish, *Doing What Comes Naturally*, *supra* note 1, at 140).

135. *Id.*

136. One reviewer of *Doing What Comes Naturally* makes the same observation. See *supra* note 14.

137. Fish, *supra* note 6, at 303–04.

138. Notice that Fish does not explain his comprehension of his colleague's verbal utterances by the simple fact that they both speak English.

tion to facility in a language, one needs to be in possession of a certain structure of interests, described by Fish as "distinctions, categories of understanding, and stipulations of relevance and irrelevance."[139] These are acquired, as we have seen, "only after one has 'passed through a professional initiation or course of training' whose effect is to homogenize persons who were disparate and heterogeneous before entering—and becoming inhabited by—the community's ways."[140]

On this first rendering of the notion, one is a member of an interpretive community when one has acquired a working knowledge of its conventions and adopted its interpretive assumptions. There are no "objects" in the world independent of the assumptions of an interpretive community, for "whatever account we have of a work or a period or of the entire canon is an account that is possible and intelligible only within the assumptions embodied in current professional practice."[141] In short, being a member of the interpretive community of lawyers means knowing how to "think like a lawyer." As Fish puts it with characteristic pith: "It is these assumptions and categories that have been internalized in the course of training, a process at the end of which the trainee is not only possessed *of* but possessed *by* a knowledge of the ropes, by a tacit knowledge that tells him not so much what to do, but already has him doing it."[142]

Up to this point, Fish's account of the homogenizing effects of professional education and training seems quite plausible. As a result of special training and homogenization, lawyers see the world through their interpretive assumptions, doctors through theirs, literary critics their own, and so on. But wait, what about the two judges in *Riggs v. Palmer*?[143] Both judges were lawyers, each went through the same process of professional homogenization, and yet they each read the text of the New York Statute of Wills differently. How does Fish's concept of interpretive community explain this difference? Here we encounter the second rendering of the idea of an interpretive community:

> If it is assumed that the purpose of probate is to ensure the orderly devolution of property at all costs, then the statute in this case will have the plain meaning urged by the defendant; but if it is assumed that no law ever operates in favor of someone who would profit by his own crime, then the "same" statute will have a meaning that is different, but no less plain. In either case the statute will have been literally construed, and what the court will have done is prefer one literal construction to another by invoking one purpose (assumed background) rather than another.[144]

This account of the judges' disparate readings of the statute is problematic. Clearly the judges in *Riggs* brought different interpretive assumptions to bear

---

139. Fish, *supra* note 110, at 58 (quoting Fish, *Doing What Comes Naturally, supra* note 1, at 141).

140. *Id.* (quoting Fish, *Doing What Comes Naturally, supra* note 1, at 140) (footnote omitted).

141. Fish, *supra* note 1, at 206.

142. *Id.* at 127 (emphasis in original).

143. 22 N.E. 188 (N.Y. 1889).

144. Fish, *supra* note 6, at 280.

on the text in question (the New York Statute of Wills). On Fish's terms, the application of distinct interpretive assumptions means that the judges in *Riggs* were members of different interpretive communities.[145] As Fish often states, "agreement is not a function of particularly clear and perspicuous rules; it is a function of the fact that interpretive assumptions and procedures are so widely shared in a community that the rule appears to all in the same (interpreted) shape."[146] Fish explains differences in interpretation as a function of differences in interpretive assumptions: "[I]t is precisely because the text appears differently in the light of different assumptions . . . that there is a disagreement in the first place."[147] But how can it be said that the judges in *Riggs* are members of different interpretive communities when they were each subjected to the same professional training?

To fully appreciate the force of this objection, consider one response available to Fish. Fish might be tempted to concede that interpretive communities can be pluralistic with respect to interpretive assumptions. For example, the professional training of lawyers makes available more than one account of the function of a statute of wills like the one at issue in *Riggs*. Similarly, the professional training of a literary critic makes available more than one account of how to read. Thus, by virtue of common training, Fish and Abrams can understand each other although they deploy radically opposed interpretive assumptions.[148] Indeed, Fish can understand himself even though he has promoted different interpretive assumptions at different times in his career.

The difficulty is that this pluralistic account of interpretive communities as held together by common experiences rather than common assumptions will not do the work demanded of it. It is important to remember that Fish embraced the idea of the interpretive community in response to the criticism that his theory of reading was solipsistic.[149] As one critic of Fish, Jonathan Culler, argues: "When Stanley Fish's claim to report the experience of all readers was challenged, he had recourse to the notion of 'interpretive communities': he was not, he admitted, reporting a universal experience but attempting to persuade others to join his interpretive community of like-minded readers."[150] Thus, the whole point of the concept of interpretive community is to ground the authority of particular readings outside of the text. Culler asserts that this formulation is "an exceedingly weak descriptive move, which leaves us with a large number of independent communities unable to argue with one another: some readers read one way—say, Fishian readers—others read another way—say, Hirschian readers—

---

145. Matters are even worse still, for according to Fish the judges in *Riggs* were not "reading" the statute; they were "writing" it. See *id.* at 14 ("Interpretive communities are made up of those who share interpretive strategies not for reading but for writing texts.").

146. Fish, *supra* note 1, at 122; see also *id.* at 300 ("[C]onstraints [on interpretation] will not inhere in the language of the text (statute or poem) . . . but in the cultural assumptions within which both texts and contexts take shape for situated agents.").

147. *Id.* at 90.

148. See *supra* text accompanying note 137.

149. See *supra* text accompanying note 137.

150. Culler, *supra* note 126, at 68 (citing Fish, *Is There a Text?*, *supra* note 6, at 15).

and so on, for as many different strategies as we can identify. . . . [T]his conception . . . separates us into monadic communities."[151]

When it comes to explaining the nature of disagreement in a practice such as law or literary criticism, Fish's dilemma is to account for disagreement without subdividing the community of lawyers or critics into a congeries of interpretive communities. My contention is that Fish has not accomplished this task. In short, I believe that Fish's appropriation of the idea of an interpretive community fails to escape the criticisms leveled against previous formulations of his view.

The central problem with Fish's account of interpretive communities is that in the course of articulating the view, Fish moves back and forth between two incompatible expressions of this central notion. Let us call the first of these conceptions the "homogeneous conception."[152] Under the homogeneous conception, the interpretive community is a group of people, each of whom has completed roughly the same process of socialization or professionalization. Some differences in interpretation can be explained in terms of differences in socialization. But the homogeneous conception fails to explain disagreement among similarly socialized subjects such as the judges in *Riggs*.

For this task, Fish introduces a second conception of the interpretive community, the "pluralistic conception." The pluralistic conception of the interpretive community explains interpretive disagreement in terms of differences in interpretive assumptions. Again Fish explains the divergent readings of the statutory text in *Riggs* in terms of incompatible assumptions about the purpose of the New York Statute of Wills. Seen through the lens of each assumption, the text of the statute is "clear." Regrettably, this clarity is purchased at the price of the unity that is the basis of the homogeneous conception. The central weakness of the pluralistic conception of the interpretive community is that it renders mysterious communication among similarly socialized actors like the judges in *Riggs* or professors in English departments. Because disagreement is commonplace in practices like law, no account of disagreement can be plausible if the community is lost in the course of the explanation. But that loss is precisely what happens when Fish goes pluralistic: He reduces an interpretive community to a collection of "people who already agree with one another."[153] In short, Fish's conception of an interpretive community is an idea at war with itself.

151. *Id.*; cf. Lentricchia, *supra* note 116, at 257 (describing the work of E. D. Hirsch as opposed to the "subjectivism and relativism" of New Criticism).

152. I think it fair to say that Fish does not purport to advance a full-blown account or theoretical sociology of practices. His is a more relaxed, narrative account of some of the more general features of professionalization. See, e.g., Fish, *supra* note 1, at 163–311 (discussing in general terms his theory of the interpretive community as it relates to professionalism).

153. Bleich, *supra* note 132, at 125. As Fish's colleagues in literary theory have noticed, such nominalism about interpretive communities renders the notion vacuous. See Schauber & Spolsky, *supra* note 132, at 146. Schauber and Spolsky noted: "If we generalize from Fish's statement about himself and Abrams [see *supra* text accompanying note 137], we have to assume that Fish and [Abrams] are in fact in the same community because both could (ultimately) understand both interpretations of the question with no great difficulty. Thus we draw two conclusions from Fish's example: first (a point that he has often made), that the first response one has to a statement depends on the context in which it is embedded; second, that since a teacher in a college English

The homogeneous and pluralistic conceptions of the interpretive community are advanced as explanations of what it means to participate in a practice like law. The presupposition behind each conception of the interpretive community is that practices must be grounded either in training (the homogeneous conception) or interpretive assumptions (the pluralistic conception). To approach law in this way is to see it as a certain sort of product. For Fish, law results from training or interpretive assumptions. As I have endeavored to show, this view of law is fundamentally misconceived.

Conclusion

Given their mutual commitment to the primacy of interpretation, I would like to close this chapter with some observations on the positions of both Fish and Dworkin. Of all the shared features of their respective positions, the one that is of the first importance to Dworkin and Fish is the claim that our primary cognitive stance toward the world is interpretive. At bottom, Dworkin and Fish have the same theory of legal truth because each has the same theory of understanding. That theory, interpretive universalism, suggests that our fundamental mode of being-in-the-world—the way in which we continually make sense of the world—is interpretive. From the interpretation of the speech of our fellow humans to deciphering script on a page, we are at every moment engaged in an activity that is profoundly hermeneutic in nature. For Dworkin and Fish, to understand anything—be it a social practice or the words of another person—is to interpret. Dworkin and Fish agree with Nietzsche that humans "are interpretation all the way down."[154]

This view of the human condition is fundamentally mistaken. It is not by virtue of interpretation that we have a common world. Rather, we have a world in concert with others because we understand the manifold activities that constitute that world. Catching on to and participating in these activities—knowing *how* to act—is the essence of understanding.[155]

---

department might at first understand things differently from a colleague but can be brought to see things as that colleague sees them, teachers in college English departments must form one community. But as Fish well knows, putting people who disagree as fundamentally as Abrams and Fish in one community robs the notion of 'community" of much of its usefulness and interest. One will merely have come back to the starting point, needing some way to describe the differences between Fish and Abrams. The determination of subcommunities within the community of academic literary scholars is therefore hardly a minor problem. If, on the one hand, every variation in interpretive perspective or strategy indicates a new community, then the notion of community loses its force. If, on the other hand, major variations in perspective do not mark community boundaries, then again the notion has little use."

154. Friedrich Nietzsche, *The Will to Power* 283 (Walter Kaufmann ed., Walter Kaufmann & R. J. Hollingdale trans., 1968).

155. This, of course, was the central message of Karl Llewellyn, at least in his early thought. See Karl Llewellyn, *The Case Law System in America* 77 (Paul Gewirtz ed., Michael Ansaldi trans., 1989) (declaring that legal certainty is a matter of "practice, not norm; way of acting, not verbal formula").

If understanding is primordial, then interpretation is of necessity a secondary endeavor; the very existence of practices of interpretation is dependent upon understanding already being in place. As we saw, interpretation cannot begin where there is no understanding, for every interpretation of a sign simply "hangs in the air" with that which it interprets.[156] *By themselves*, interpretations take us nowhere.

Despite their apparent differences, Dworkin and Fish are both committed to a picture of legal justification where each appeals to "something" which makes propositions of law true. In the previous two chapters, I have tried to show that this "something"—interpretation—is an implausible account of the nature of truth in law. Nothing "makes" propositions of law true. The realist and the anti-realist are, thus, both locked into a debate framework that generates pseudoquestions and, regretably, pointless debates. The debate over the centrality of interpretation to law is just such a debate.

---

156. See Joachim Schulte, *Wittgenstein* 119 (William H. Brenner & John F. Holley trans., 1992) ("To interpret a rule means simply to replace one formulation of the rule with another.").

7

Truth in Law: A Modal Account

> My type of thinking is not wanted in this present age, I have to swim so
> strongly against the tide.
>
> Ludwig Wittgenstein[1]

In one way or another, each of the perspectives considered in the earlier chapters of this book attempts to explain the truth of propositions of law in terms of conditions (e.g., communal agreement) or states of affairs (moral reality) that make the proposition in question true. For various but quite related reasons, this approach to the nature of truth in law has been rejected. The present chapter starts us down the road to an alternative account of the nature of truth in law.

The specific context for this chapter is constitutional argument. As will be seen, the argument under consideration sweeps far more broadly than—and is in no way limited to—constitutional law. The argument begins with the central problematic of constitutional law, the legitimacy of judicial review.[2] In his first book of constitutional theory, *Constitutional Fate*,[3] Philip Bobbitt argued that the debate over the legitimacy of judicial review proceeds from a faulty premise. Despite seemingly deep and irreconcilable divisions of opinion, all sides to the debate are wedded to a false premise: that the key to the propriety of judicial review lies in a theory of legitimacy. In other words, in the absence of a theory of legitimacy, judicial review cannot be justified.

In *Constitutional Fate*, and later in *Constitutional Interpretation*,[4] Bobbitt shows that the way out of the intractable question over the legitimacy of judicial review begins in the recognition that a theory of legitimacy is not only not needed but is positively injurious to clear thinking with respect to the nature of legitimacy in constitutional law. The legitimacy of judicial review does not depend on the merits of a particular theory; rather, legitimacy is maintained by recourse to the forms of argument (Bobbitt refers to them as "modalities") appropriate to constitutional law. It is in the use of the modalities that the truth of a proposi-

---

1. M. O'C. Drury, "Some Notes on Conversations with Wittgenstein," in *Ludwig Wittgenstein: Personal Recollections* 79 (Rush Rhees ed., 1981).
2. See Marbury v. Madison, 5 U.S. (1 Cranch) 137, 175 (1803).
3. Philip Bobbitt, *Constitutional Fate: Theory of the Constitution* (1982).
4. Philip Bobbitt, *Constitutional Interpretation* (1991).

tion of constitutional law is shown. In this way, the need for a theory of legitimacy disappears and with it the debate over the legitimacy of judicial review.

The present chapter begins with a description of the debate over the legitimacy of judicial review. Bobbitt believes the debate to be fueled by a certain picture of the nature of legal argument, one driven by a distinct conception of the relationship of theory to legal practice. Despite its aspirations, contemporary legal theory has yet to free itself from the scientist pretensions of the nineteenth century.

From here we move to Bobbitt's account of the modalities of constitutional law. In addition to appreciating the wrong-headed character of the debate over the legitimacy of judicial review, we consider the merits of Bobbitt's approach in another context, that of the failed nomination of Robert Bork for a seat on the Supreme Court of the United States.

Finally, we consider a problem perhaps endemic to the modal approach to legal argument, that of conflict among the modalities. Bobbitt's solution to the dilemma of modal conflict is resort to individual conscience. This is criticized on a number of grounds, leaving to the final chapter further consideration of this nettlesome problem.

The Conventional Picture
Legitimacy and Judicial Review

In *Constitutional Fate*, Bobbitt argues that the controversy over the legitimacy of judicial review is a pseudodebate, driven largely by a false picture of the nature of argument in constitutional law. In brief, Bobbitt argues that the practice of constitutional law is a matter of using six forms of argument to show the truth of propositions of constitutional law. A judge decides a case by employing one or more of the modalities. To be legitimate, a constitutional argument must not veer from use of the modalities. The modalities themselves, either alone or in combination, can never be legitimate, for they are the means by which legitimacy is maintained (through their use in argument).

The question of the legitimacy of judicial review has stimulated a number of important and sophisticated accounts of the nature of the Constitution and its interpretation, not to mention theories of the nature of the judicial process itself.[5] Despite the merits of these many interesting and important works, Bobbitt argues that none has noticed that the debate is a pseudodebate, driven by a mistaken picture of the nature of truth in constitutional law.

The key to the "problem" of judicial review lies in the relationship between legitimacy and justification. The conventional wisdom is that judicial review cannot

---

5. Of course, these questions have occupied generations of scholars. Two leading, recent examples are Jesse H. Choper, *Judicial Review and the National Political Process* (1980) (arguing that the Supreme Court must exercise judicial review to protect human rights), and John H. Ely, *Democracy and Distrust: A Theory of Judicial Review* (1980) (outlining a theory of representation-reinforcing judicial review).

be justified unless it can be legitimated.[6] To this end, constitutional theorists have advanced an array of theories of legitimacy.[7] Once the preferred theory is proffered, it is employed as a measure of the legitimacy of specific acts of judicial review. In short, judicial review is justified to the degree it is congruent with the preferred theory of legitimation. Bobbitt's position is that all attempts to find a normative foundation outside the conventions of legal argument misunderstand the nature of legitimacy in law. Neither the Constitution, the conventions of legal argument, nor judicial review requires legitimation. Legitimacy obtains when the conventions of legal argument (the modalities) are adhered to. A constitutional argument in support of the truth of a proposition of constitutional law is legitimate to the extent it employs the modalities. To the degree it does not, it is illegitimate.

The defenders of judicial review advance various arguments in support of the legitimacy of the practice.[8] Originalists, for example, contend that judicial review gives voice to the original intent of the framers. These intentions, they argue, must be the overriding normative justification for judicial review, lest judges go about their business without the appropriate degree of restraint on their interpretive activities.

Another "justification" for judicial review, one close in spirit to originalism, is that offered by so-called textualists. The Supremacy Clause provides: "This Constitution . . . shall be the supreme Law of the Land; and the Judges in every State shall be bound thereby, any Thing in the Constitution or Laws of any State to the Contrary notwithstanding."[9] This, it seems, implies the following:

1. All judges, when asked to apply any law, must do so in conformity with "supreme" law; that is the common import of the word "supreme."
2. The laws and constitutions of the states, even when construed by state judges, must give way to the provisions of the United States Constitution in case of conflict; "giving way" is . . . the common inference drawn from the use of the term "do as here instructed anything to the contrary notwithstanding."
3. Insofar as the same article also carefully provides that only those federal laws "which shall be made in pursuance" of the Constitution are the law of the land, this language indicates that federal laws that conflict with the Constitution cannot be given effect as law."[10]

6. As Alexander Bickel put the objection, "[W]hen the Supreme Court declares unconstitutional a legislative act or the action of an elected executive, it thwarts the will of representatives of the actual people of the here and now; it exercises control, not in behalf of the prevailing majority, but against it." Alexander M. Bickel, *The Least Dangerous Branch* 16–17 (1962).

7. Each of these theories of legitimacy is a response to the question "What justifies judicial review?" It is to confuse the relationship between legitimacy and justification to argue that judicial review cannot be legitimate unless it is justified by the dictates of a normative or political theory.

8. It turns out that in their effort to legitimate judicial review, each of these theories of legitimacy grabs hold of a form of legal argument and elevates it to the level of a theory of legitimation. For example, the reason arguments of text are appropriate in constitutional practice is that we have a written Constitution. The forms of legal argument are the means by which a proposition of law is shown to be true. A form of argument can no more legitimate legal argument than a ruler can justify or legitimate measuring.

9. U.S. Const. art. VI, cl. 2.

10. Bobbitt, *supra* note 4, at 25–26.

Yet a third "justification" for judicial review lies in the positive effects of the practice and is advanced by what Bobbitt terms "the prudential advocate."[11] Judicial review, the prudential advocate argues, has the salutary effect of serving "a goal (or goals) with which the advocate associates himself. These goals may be: the protection of minorities; the exercise of vigilance on behalf of civil liberties; the taming of revolution into reform or the fanning of reform into revolt (consciousness raising); and so on."[12]

Each of these three forms of argument is a response to the question of what legitimates judicial review. Judicial review, it seems, is legitimate because the intentions of the framers, the text of the Constitution, or the effects of judicial review each justify the practice.

Each of these justifications certainly has its detractors. The power of originalism as a normative justification for judicial review is totally dependent upon the ability of present-day interpreters of the Constitution to ascertain correctly the precise content of original intentions. This is no simple task, if only because historical evidence of intention often points in more than one direction, or sometimes in no direction at all.[13] More telling, perhaps, is the question of why the polity of the present should be governed by the dead hand of the past. Originalists have had difficulty formulating an acceptable answer to this objection.

For textualists, the situation appears even more grim. To claim that judicial review is legitimate because the text of the Constitution makes it so is, in effect, to assert that the language of the constitutional text speaks free from the individual perspective of the reader.[14] From Paris,[15] to Durham,[16] to Berkeley,[17] contemporary critics assert that there is no author and that it is the reader who produces the meaning of a text. For the textualist, it seems, there is no escape from the semantic vortex of signs and subjectivity.

Prudentialists—those who argue that judicial review is legitimate because it produces effects worth having—are represented on both the Right[18] and the

---

11. *Id.* at 26.

12. *Id.*

13. See generally Paul Brest, "The Misconceived Quest for the Original Understanding," 60 *B.U. L. Rev.* 204 (1980) (rejecting strict textualism and strict interpretivism as untenable in constitutional decision making).

14. That constitutional language is rarely this unambiguous is evidenced by Judge Easterbrook's contention that a sentence containing the number "thirty-five" may not mean what it says: "When the Constitution says that the President must be thirty-five years old, we cannot be certain whether it means thirty-five as the number of revolutions of the world around the sun, as a percentage of average life expectancy (so that the Constitution now has age fifty as a minimum), or as a minimum number of years after puberty (so the minimum now is thirty or so)." Frank H. Easterbrook, "Statutes' Domains," 50 *U. Chi. L. Rev.* 533, 536 (1983).

15. See generally Michel Foucault, *The Archaeology of Knowledge* (A. M. Sheridan Smith trans., 1972) (arguing that all knowledge is produced within an "episteme" or grid).

16. See generally Stanley E. Fish, *Doing What Comes Naturally* (1989) (collection of essays from the perspective of reader-response theory).

17. See generally Avital Ronnell, *The Telephone Book* (1989) (deconstruction of the telephone as a technological presence in discourse).

18. See Michael J. Perry, *The Constitution, the Courts, and Human Rights* 99–119, 225 (1982) (arguing for an active role for the Supreme Court in the "moral evolution" of the polity).

Left.[19] Each side argues for the legitimacy of judicial review on the basis of the values the practice promotes. Naturally, there is little agreement over what those values are or should be, but all forms of the prudentialist argument invite a well-known criticism: the problem of the infinite regress of justification. By answering the skeptic's question "What justifies judicial review?" with a response that identifies one's preferred normative agenda, the prudentialist invites the further question, "What, then, justifies that value?" To proffer yet another preferred value (for example, that vigilant protection of First Amendment guarantees is a good thing because the proliferation of viewpoints tends to produce the truth) is not an answer to the skeptic, but serves only to put her off. For every answer to the question "What justifies *X*?" the skeptic simply takes the answer, fills in the blank, and poses the question anew. More often than not, the infinite regress of justification ends not because some primordial value has been identified,[20] but because no further answer to the skeptic can be given. What this shows, the skeptic argues, is that the prudentialist justification for judicial review is really nothing more than the articulation of a personal, political preference that has been elevated to the status of law.

On the surface, it would appear as if the originalist, the textualist, and the prudentialist disagree deeply over the legitimate ground of constitutional practice. In a sense they do, for each provides a separate and distinct account of its legitimate normative foundations,[21] and their answers partake not at all of a shared or common point of view on the nature of the explanatory or justificatory matrix for constitutional law. These disagreements, however, are only superficial. What is truly important about these various approaches to constitutional argument are not the differences but a striking similarity, one that has even gone unnoticed by the combatants themselves.

The similarity is the one noticed earlier. Proponents of theories of judicial review all start from the premise that in the absence of a theory of legitimation, no act of judicial review can be justified. Bobbitt's point is that resort to a theory of legitimacy only has the effect of asking a question about law from the point of view of some other enterprise (for example, political theory, history, or moral philosophy). To argue that judicial review is legitimate by the lights of the argumentative standards of the preferred discipline may be interesting, but it is legally irrelevant; for what interests us are not propositions of morality, philosophy, or political theory, but legal propositions. And for these, only legal conventions of argument are appropriate.

19. See generally Mark Tushnet, *Red, White and Blue* (1988) (addressing five forms of constitutional argument from a prudentialist perspective).

20. But see John Finnis, *Natural Law and Natural Rights* 85–97 (1980) (a natural law jurisprudence based on a theory of basic human needs).

21. To this point, I have limited discussion to the question of judicial review. However, Bobbitt's argument is not constrained by any particular topic. He uses the debate over the legitimacy of judicial review to make a larger jurisprudential point about the nature of justification in constitutional law—that is, that the conventional picture misunderstands the relationship between legitimacy and justification.

Legal Argument and the Ghost of Langdell

The conventional wisdom treats propositions of constitutional law as if they were propositions about the world (empirical propositions). Armed with a theory of legitimacy, the conventional theorist turns her attention to the evaluation of propositions of constitutional law (e.g., "The Constitution prohibits busing school children to parochial schools"). If the proposition is consistent with ("corresponds" to) the dictates of the preferred theory of legitimacy, then the proposition is true; to the degree it does not, it is false. This approach, Bobbitt argues, treats legal propositions as if they were statements "about the world,"[22] verifiable in the same ways as empirical propositions. This confusion of legal and scientific modalities lies at the heart of contemporary constitutional jurisprudence.

To reveal the common ground shared by the divergent camps in contemporary constitutional theory, Bobbitt turns to an unlikely source: Christopher Columbus Langdell, universally regarded as the father of legal formalism[23] and a strong proponent of the use of scientific method in law.[24] Owing to his belief that law could be scientific, Langdell held the task of legal theory to be the discovery of principles that underlie legal doctrine.[25] Langdell's scientific view of law had two methodological presuppositions. First, the number of fundamental principles is small, and second, for that reason, exhaustive knowledge of reported decisions is simply unnecessary.[26] Once the fundamental principles were identified, they were all one needed to "think like a lawyer."

Bobbitt organizes his argument around the question "What is the nature of a legal proposition?" There are two answers: his own account (the modalities) and the "Langdellian" answer, which is a form of "causal" explanation embraced by many approaches to constitutional law and theory. The Langdellian approach attempts to explain constitutional law by identifying "ideological and political commitments [that] are somehow 'behind' or 'beneath'"[27] the surface play of constitutional argument. These approaches

> simply assume an epistemological attitude that is highly controversial, i.e., they undertake to explain events in the world by reference to ideas that allegedly cause such events while maintaining that the explanatory scheme itself is outside the otherwise pervasive causal influence it allegedly describes. No doubt there are many persons who continue to believe that class, or race, or sex or personal history determine "how we see the world"—as though these were spectacles that are put on at a certain age and could be removed, indeed have been removed by the clear-sighted analyst. This is only a modern version of the claim that such influences determine how we behave. But to

22. Bobbitt, *supra* note 4, at 34.

23. By "formalism," I mean the view that legal conclusions can be generated solely by rigorous use of law's distinct methodological tools.

24. See Thomas Grey, "Langdell's Orthodoxy," 45 *U. Pitt. L. Rev.* 1, 5 (1983).

25. See Christopher C. Langdell, "Address to the Harvard Law School Association" (1886), quoted in Grant Gilmore, *The Ages of American Law* 42 (1977) (comparing law to zoology).

26. See Christopher C. Langdell, *Selection of Cases on the Law of Contracts* viii–ix (2d ed. 1879).

27. Bobbitt, *supra* note 4, at 23.

a growing number this will seem naive. The world is a human idea, inseparable from our perceptions of it, and thus something we can apprehend only
with the spectacles of humanity firmly in place. Nor are our faculties de-
tachable from the perspectives they enable or the world without which they
are disabled.[28]

In this paragraph Bobbitt distinguishes causal and normative forms of explanation.[29] He thinks many theorists make the mistake of advancing causal accounts
of law when legal statements are not statements about the world: hence, the
"explanations" miss the target and leave the theorist, as they say in New England,
"shingling into the fog." Because law is a normative practice, only an account of
argument appropriate to law's character as a normative practice will suffice.
Bobbitt explains:

> Although most people may to some extent hold the view . . . that there must
> be some sublime explanatory mechanism that allows our ideas to interact with
> the world—there is no reason to think so.
>
> . . .
>
> Law is something we do, not something we have as a consequence of some-
> thing we do. Sometimes our activities in law—deciding, proposing, persuad-
> ing—may link up with specific ideas we have at those moments; but often they
> do not, and it is never the case that this link must be made for the activities
> that are law to be law. Therefore the causal accounts of how these inner states
> come into being, accounts that lose their persuasiveness in contact with the
> abundance of the world, are really beside the point. If we want to understand
> the ideological and political commitments in law, we have to study the gram-
> mar of law, that system of logical constraints that the practices of legal activi-
> ties have developed in our particular culture.[30]

While resort to principle as an explanatory method is an important element
in Langdell's approach to law, there is another aspect of the approach that is of
far greater importance. The resort to principle is motivated by a particular conception of what it is to explain legal thinking. Langdell's model is driven by the
demand to explain legal doctrine by resort to "the unifying theories that underl[ie]
the rationales of these cases."[31] Thus, the holdings of cases are not to be explained
as the consequence of legal reasoning; rather, they are simply phenomena that
themselves stand in need of "explanation."[32] From this observation, Bobbitt renders the following diagnosis:

---

28. *Id.*
29. A causal form of explanation tells you why something happened. For example, one could
give an account of the physical processes involved in stopping an automobile at a red light. One
could say that the red light sets off a causal reaction in the driver, which itself is the product of
training, physical processes, neural firings, etc. A normative explanation tells you what the physical
acts amount to (e.g., why stopping at a red light is the "correct" way to drive an automobile).
30. Bobbitt, *supra* note 4, at 24.
31. *Id.* at 46.
32. For a survey of recent law and economics scholarship with particular emphasis on the question of explanation of legal doctrine, see Jason S. Johnston, "Law, Economics, and Post-Realist
Explanation," 24 *Law & Soc'y Rev.* 1217 (1990).

Every significant casebook and law review reflects this approach, though few of their authors and editors would subscribe to Langdell's description of law as a science. Despite such up-to-date agnosticism, however, these authors and editors usually do in fact share the main consequence of Langdell's description, namely that legal holdings are propositions about the world. As such, they can be verified, if they are *law*, by reference to some feature of the world, some fact outside the control of the verifying judge or scholar. And so the "progressive" casebooks add dubious historical and social science materials, while the "conservative" casebooks confine themselves to reprints of notable cases. But whatever the excerpt, one will always find it followed by a set of leading questions designed to elicit the relevant "fact" and to invite the reader to compare that fact with the holding and rationale of the doctrine. In his lecture, the law professor will, by the use of other cases and hypotheticals, adroitly or fecklessly, demonstrate the competing values and rationales at stake. The more vain the professor, the more it will appear that the court's opinion is a hopeless series of ill-conceived assertions that can be effortlessly shown to contradict the past (precedent) as well as the future (those hypotheticals).[33]

Bobbitt argues that contemporary juridical pedagogy and sophisticated legal theory are still within the grip of the Langdellian picture of legal-as-causal explanation. Sustaining such a claim requires further comment about Bobbitt's assertion that what lies at the root of the Langdellian picture of law is the presupposition that legal propositions are, as Bobbitt puts it, "propositions about the world."[34] If the claim is true, then Bobbitt is right about the continuing hold of the Langdellian picture of law. But Bobbitt's argument cuts deeper still. As Bobbitt sees it, legal propositions are not propositions about the world. If he is right about the continuing hold of the Langdellian picture, then virtually the whole of contemporary jurisprudence is locked into a hopeless epistemology, one that fuels such complex but ultimately vacuous debates as the one surrounding the indeterminacy of law, the question of whether law is reducible to politics, and, of course, the ascendancy of the idea that law is an "interpretive" practice.[35] We turn now to Bobbitt's account of the nature of legal argument in constitutional law.

Rethinking Legitimacy: The Modalities of Constitutional Argument

Bobbitt is convinced that contemporary legal theory misconceives the nature of argument and truth in law. Time and again, a new paradigm for understanding law is announced and, upon examination, turns out to be the same old form of argument (i.e., a version of the Langdellian picture) merely in a new or more fashionable mode of expression. Bobbitt is eager to avoid both the foundationalism

33. Bobbitt, *supra* note 4, at 47.
34. *Id.* at 47.
35. See generally Ronald Dworkin, *Law's Empire* (1986) (theory of law as an interpretive concept). See also Fish, *supra* note 4, at 141–42, 149 (arguing that law is a congeries of "interpretive communities").

that demands a firm ground for law and the skepticism that ceaselessly exploits the appetite for certainty.

The crux of Bobbitt's argumentative strategy is to separate legitimacy from justification. The key is to see that the practice of judicial review—or, more broadly, constitutional law—requires no justification.[36] The answer to the skeptic's question of what justifies judicial review is "Why, nothing, of course."[37] But if nothing justifies judicial review, then can we ever know that our juridical practices are legitimate? In short, is there no connection between law and justice?

Nothing in Bobbitt's approach precludes the evaluation of a judicial decision from the point of view of one's preferred theory of justice. As he states, "[W]e assess the justice of a particular decision by reference to some external standard, a system of evaluation outside the operation of the modalities of argument."[38] The oft-repeated mistake of contemporary jurisprudence is to treat the conventions of legal argument as if they were just another theory of justice. Law is not a theory: it is a practice, and the modalities are the tools of the trade.

In *Constitutional Fate*, Bobbitt addressed the issue of the truth of propositions of law. Recognizing that different disciplines each have their own ways of assessing the truth or falsity of substantive claims, Bobbitt described the six forms (modalities) of argument that, taken together, constitute the argumentative matrix of constitutional law:[39]

36. The problem with virtually all constitutional theory, and much of general jurisprudence, is the continuing need to legitimate law by resort to some external source. For an illuminating discussion of this problem in modern jurisprudence, see Gunther Teubner, "How the Law Thinks: Toward a Constructivist Epistemology of Law," 23 *Law & Soc'y Rev.* 727, 743 (1989). As Teubner describes the problem; "From a constructivist perspective, there is no way to challenge the epistemic authority of law, neither by social realities themselves, nor by common sense, nor by scientifically controlled observation. A social epistemology on a constructivist basis can explain why law appears to be an 'essentially self-validating discourse' which one should expect to be 'largely impervious to serious challenge from other knowledge fields.' It is simply naive to invoke social 'reality' itself against legal conceptualism, against the 'heaven of legal concepts' or against the law's 'transcendental nonsense.' There is no direct cognitive access to reality. There are only competing discourses with different constructions of reality" (citations omitted).

37. Bobbitt states: "What is the fundamental principle that legitimizes judicial review? There is none. It follows from what I have said thus far that constitutional law needs no 'foundation.' Its legitimacy does not derive from a set of axioms which, in conjunction with rules of construction, will yield correct constitutional propositions." Bobbitt, *supra* note 3, at 237.

38. *Id.* at 163.

39. It is essential to understanding Bobbitt's central contention to realize that there is nothing more to constitutional argument than the six modalities. As he argues repeatedly, there simply is nothing more for "philosophy" to do than describe accurately the *practice* of constitutional argument, for that practice is constitutional law. If there is nothing more nor less to constitutional law than the six modes of argument, then there is nothing more to talk about other than how the forms are employed to sustain claims that some proposition of law is either true or false. The question nearly everyone else wants to ask about any and all aspects of constitutional law is "Is this argument legitimate?" The question makes no sense if it is a question about whether someone is making a valid argument, for the forms of argument answer any question concerning what is being done. The essential point of the argument is that the very idea of a "legitimate" form of argument is unintelligible. What would it be like to ask "Is this a legitimate way to play chess?" or "Is this a legitimate way to paint in a neoimpressionist style?" It is not clear that these sorts of questions are amenable to answer.

Historical (relying on the intentions of the framers and ratifiers of the Constitution);

Textual (looking to the meaning of the words of the Constitution alone, as they would be interpreted by the average contemporary "man on the street");

Structural (inferring rules from the relationships that the Constitution mandates among the structures it sets up);

Doctrinal (applying rules generated by precedent);

Ethical (deriving rules from those moral commitments of the American ethos that are reflected in the Constitution); and

Prudential (seeking to balance the costs and benefits of a particular rule).[40]

The most important aspect of the modalities is that it is only through their use that the truth or falsehood of legal claims is shown. Unlike the conventional perspective, which sees the truth of law as a function of something lying outside the law (for example, politics, moral philosophy, etc.) the unique and, if correct, compelling aspect of Bobbitt's account of our constitutional practice is that nothing is hidden. There is nothing more to constitutional law (or any other body of doctrine) than the use of the six modalities of argument. For jurisprudence, both constitutional and general, the lesson is clear: the essential task of jurisprudence is the accurate description of our legal practices of argument. Theory[41] is banished not because it is wrong, but because it is irrelevant. If law is an argumentative practice composed of the six modalities of argument, then the key to understanding law lies in understanding how these forms are deployed in legal argument.[42]

What, then, justifies a judicial decision? And how is justification related to legitimacy? The judicial decision is legitimate to the extent that it is rendered according to law. A decision is made "according to law" when one or more of the six modalities is employed to reach the decision.[43] The law, it turns out, is an activity—the use of the six modes of constitutional argument. Decision is an activity in which one reaches the conclusion that some proposition of law is true or false. The modalities are "the way[s] in which a proposition is true; constitutional modalities determine the way in which a constitutional proposition is true."[44] What then of legitimacy? For Bobbitt, a legal decision is legitimate to the extent that its argumentative character remains within the modalities.[45]

40. Bobbitt, *supra* note 4, at 12–13.

41. By "theory" I mean to follow Bobbitt's usage—that is, a "sublime explanatory mechanism." *Id*. at 24.

42. It is in the use of the forms of argument that legal propositions are shown to be true or false. *Id*. at 12. Bobbitt's argument in this connection is consistent with the last writings of Wittgenstein on this point: "But I did not get my picture of the world by satisfying myself of its correctness; nor do I have it because I am satisfied of its correctness. No: it is the inherited background against which I distinguish between true and false." Ludwig Wittgenstein, *On Certainty* § 94 (G. E. M. Anscombe & G. H. von Wright eds., Denis Paul & G. E. M. Anscombe trans., Harper Torchbook 1972 (1969)).

43. Bobbitt, *supra* note 4, at 182–84.

44. *Id*. at 34.

45. *Id*. at 151.

Legitimacy is not something a system of law can achieve writ large. The legitimacy of a legal system is an accretion; it develops over time and is maintained only by adherence to the legal forms of argument. To the extent that these modalities are compromised or ignored, particular decisions are illegitimate, and, over time, the legitimacy of the system as a whole is undermined.

Application of the Modalities: The Bork Hearings

Bobbitt uses the modalities to analyze the failed nomination of Robert Bork for a seat on the United States Supreme Court. Was Bork the victim of an unscrupulous media attack, or was his rejection a vote of no confidence in the originalism he so staunchly defended before, during, and after[46] the hearings on his confirmation? Bobbitt's answer is "both and neither." Bork clearly made more than a few after-dinner speeches and wrote several articles arguing that the intent of the framers should be regarded as the sole criterion of constitutional interpretation, and many in the media indeed mischaracterized his views if not his person. But the dichotomy of archdefender of the oracles of intent versus maligned media victim fails to capture the true picture. Let us take a closer look at what there is to be found.

A recurring issue in Supreme Court nomination hearings, one much discussed during the last half-dozen nominations, is the question of whether and to what extent the Senate Judiciary Committee may inquire into the so-called *political* views of the nominee. The terms within which this question is usually discussed are, to say the least, simplistic.[47] On the one hand there are the nominee's judicial abilities, candor, and judicial philosophy. On the other are the nominee's political views—his or her views about what the law on any given subject or topic might or ought to be. Bobbitt notes that, among recent nominees to the Court, there has developed a trend "of refusing to comment on matters that might come before the Court on which the nominee would sit if confirmed."[48] Of course, history shows that Judge Bork, far more than anyone before or after him, was all too willing to discuss his views on almost any subject. But this is not what Bobbitt finds interesting in the hearings. Bobbitt is not interested in the question of whether Bork ought or ought not to have been confirmed, but rather in using the modalities as a way of understanding the confirmation hearings. His rather surprising conclusion is that Robert Bork does not understand his own judicial philosophy because he is not really an originalist, but rather a prudentialist. In his opening statement, Bork said the following about his own judicial philosophy:

> The judge's authority derives entirely from the fact that he is applying the law
> and not his personal values. . . . How should a judge go about finding the law?

46. See Robert H. Bork, *The Tempting of America: The Political Seduction of the Law, passim* (1990).

47. An exception is Ronald Dworkin's essay on the Clarence Thomas nomination. See Ronald Dworkin, "Justice for Clarence Thomas," *N.Y. Rev. Books,* Nov. 7, 1991, at 41, 42–45.

48. Bobbitt, *supra* note 4, at 83.

The only legitimate way, in my opinion, is by attempting to discern what those who made the law intended. The intentions of the lawmakers [of the Constitution] are those [of the persons] who ratified our Constitution and its various amendments. The judge's responsibility is to discern how the framers' values, defined in the context of the world they knew, apply in the world we know. If a judge abandons intention as his guide, there is no law available to him and he . . . goes beyond his legitimate power.[49]

From the moment Bork finished his opening statement, the hearings never focused on the question of the utmost importance: the nominee's conception of how judges should decide cases. Both the nominee and the members of the Senate Judiciary Committee failed to see the important distinction between the substantive content of our constitutional rights and the ways in which courts decide cases regarding the question of what rights we have. The distinction is revealed in the following exchange between Senator Joseph Biden and Judge Bork:

> *Senator*   Judge, I agree with the rationale offered in the [*Griswold*] case. Let me just read it to you . . . I happen to agree with it. It said, in part, "would we allow the police to search the sacred precincts of marital bedrooms for telltale signs of contraceptives? The very idea is repulsive to the notions of privacy surrounding the marriage relationship. We deal with the right of privacy older than the Bill of Rights. Marriage is a coming together for better or worse, hopefully enduring, and intimate to the degree of being sacred. The association promotes a way of life, not causes. A harmony of living, not political face. A bilateral loyalty, not a commercial or social project."
>
> *Bork*   I could agree with . . . every word you read but that is not . . . the rationale of the case. That is the rhetoric at the end of the case. What I objected to was the way in which this right of privacy was created.
>
> *Senator*   As I hear you, you do not believe that there is a general right of privacy that is in the Constitution.
>
> *Bork*   Not one derived in *that* fashion.[50]

This exchange also illustrates another fatal flaw in the hearings. Every time a question was put to Bork in the form of "Do you believe there is a constitutional right to *x*?" Bork would respond in a manner consistent with his belief that the important question was not what rights we have but the manner in which those rights are derived. Repeatedly, "Bork tried to draw the obvious distinction between ways of deriving constitutional arguments and substantive decisions. His questioners typically did not accept the distinction, prompting him repeatedly to reassert it."[51] When it came to discussing precedent, Bork sealed his fate with his own words:

49. *Id.* at 88–89 (quoting from Nomination of Robert H. Bork to be Associate Justice of the Supreme Court of the United States: Hearings Before the Senate Comm. on the Judiciary, 100th Cong., 1st Sess. 104 (1987)) [hereinafter Senate Hearings].
50. Quoting Senate Hearings at 117.
51. Bobbitt, *supra* note 4, at 212 n.23.

> [T]he role of precedent in constitutional law is less important than it is in a proper common law or statutory model . . . So if a constitutional judge comes to a firm conviction that the courts have misunderstood the intentions of the founders, he is freer than when acting in his capacity as an interpreter of the common law or of a statute to overturn a precedent . . . [and so] an originalist judge would have no problem whatever in overruling a non-originalist precedent, because that precedent by the very basis of his judicial philosophy, has no legitimacy.[52]

Everyone understood what Bork meant by these words. If intention was to be the sole measure of legitimacy, Bork was stating forthrightly that the weight of precedent could be ignored and, if found wanting by the measure of an originalist yardstick, overturned. As Bobbitt explains,

> It meant that decisions like *Roe v. Wade* (the abortion case), *Reynolds v. Sims* (the re-districting opinion that mandated one-man-one-vote), *Shelley v. Kramer* (outlawing racially restrictive real estate covenants), even *Brown* itself—all of which the nominee had criticized at one time or another—could be overturned even if the nominee was careful not to say he would do so. Bork's implicit demand that such holdings be re-examined for legitimate support was enough to cause an avalanche of public disapproval.[53]

What conclusions are we to draw? Is it the case that "in the end, the Senate rejected the nominee because it rejected the judicial philosophy of constitutional intentionalism with which Judge Bork had associated himself"?[54] The answer must be that the vote against Bork was, indeed, a rejection of what was perceived as his particular brand of intentionalism. But was the perception accurate? "[W]as this really Bork's view?"[55]

Before proceeding, it is important to ponder just what it is in the constitutional philosophy of intentionalism that many find troublesome. Like many other approaches to the interpretation of the Constitution, intentionalism is a theory of legitimacy: to the intentionalist, the very act of reading the Constitution cannot itself be legitimate unless that act is underwritten by something outside itself—legitimation flows from the recovery of the intentions of the drafters of the document. Correlatively—and this is the worrisome point—any precedent not so generated is illegitimate, and hence subject to being overruled. It is this last aspect of intentionalism that, in the end, was Judge Bork's undoing.

It did not have to be this way, for Bork is not a thoroughgoing intentionalist. In objecting to *Roe v. Wade*, Bork noted that the principal failing of the opinion is that it "does not have legal reasoning in it that roots the right to an abortion in constitutional materials."[56] When Bork made this statement at his confirmation hearings, Senator Orin Hatch queried: "I presume that your concerns about the reasoning of the . . . case do not necessarily mean that you would automati-

---

52. Senate Hearings at 370.
53. Bobbitt, *supra* note 4, at 93.
54. *Id*. at 94–95.
55. *Id*. at 95.
56. Senate Hearings at 185.

cally reverse that case as a Justice of the Supreme Court?"[57] Bork's answer to this question is most interesting. After rehearsing the line of questioning an intentionalist might take on the legitimacy of prior precedent and the right to privacy, Bork replied: "[T]here are cases we look back on and say they were erroneous or they were not compatible with original intent, but we don't overrule them *for a variety of reasons.*"[58]

What might be some of the reasons that would cut against overruling an illegitimately derived precedent? Bork offered a few to his senatorial questioners:

> I suppose the passage of time by itself is not important. The only reason it is important is that if expectations and institutions and laws and so forth have grown up around the decision in that passage of time. That certainly weighs in favor of not overruling the decision.[59]

> I will be glad to discuss my general approach to stare decisis and the kinds of factors I would consider. . . . It has to be in the first place clear that the prior decision was erroneous. I mean, not just shaky but really wrong in terms of constitutional theory. . . . But that is not sufficient to overrule. I have discussed these factors before. . . . For example, the development of private expectations on the part of the citizenry. . . . The growth of institutions, governmental institutions, private institutions around a ruling. . . . The need for continuity and stability in the law. . . . The need for predictability in legal doctrine.[60]

Bork then put statements such as these together with his originalism. The mix made for a heady brew:

> From the beginning of these hearings, Senator, I have said that . . . the ultimate touchstone for a judge . . . in constitutional law . . . is the original understanding; that means what the ratifiers understood when they ratified the Constitution. But I have also said that the law has developed, and the nation has developed, and decisions have been made around which too much has been built, and around which too many expectations have clustered, for them to be overruled. . . . The commerce clause cases cannot be overruled. You cannot cut the commerce clause back. . . . The equal protection cases cannot be overruled. . . . I have mentioned some first amendment cases that cannot be overruled, I have mentioned a lot of cases that I think are now part of our law, and whatever theoretical challenges might be levelled at them, it is simply too late . . . for a judge to overrule them. . . . Incorporation doctrine [by which the Bill of Rights is applied to the states, the source for the principal due process decisions of the Warren Court] I mentioned . . . is also something that is now thoroughly established.[61]

57. *Id.*
58. *Id.*
59. *Id.* at 264–65.
60. Bobbitt, *supra* note 4, at 97 (quoting Senate Hearings at 292–93).
61. Bobbit, *supra* note 4, at 99 (quoting Senate Hearings at 465). Of course, one sees the same point of view at work in the plurality opinion of Justices O'Connor, Kennedy, and Souter in Planned Parenthood v. Casey, 112 S. Ct. 2791, 2804–16 (1992) (pointing out that for two decades people have relied on the availability of abortions in organizing their relationships and lives, and that the cost of upsetting these expectations cannot be dismissed in reexamining the abortion

What do these quotations really show? Could they not be read as yet another instance of "confirmation conversion"? Many choose so to read them, and there is nothing in the substance of Bork's remarks that completely rules out such a reading.[62] Yet this reading misses the fact that even so ardent an intentionalist as Bork has a hard time maintaining allegiance to a single constitutional modality. Like his teacher and fellow prudentialist, Alexander Bickel, Bork realizes that constitutional law cannot be an axiomatic exercise. But Bork, driven as he is by a narrow (but not irrelevant) conception of constitutional law, manages to deceive even himself about his own theoretical commitments. In his testimony, Bork showed himself to be something more than the knee-jerk intentionalist many took him to be. Yet he seemed unable to put together his philosophical commitment to original intention with his quite pragmatic view of the role of entrenched precedent. When read against the background of the modalities, Bork's jurisprudence becomes as clear as it has ever been and turns out to be more complicated than even Bork himself realized. It is perhaps this lack of self-knowledge that, in the end, cost Bork his place on the Court.

Modal Conflict and the Recursion to Conscience

Bobbitt's singular contribution to constitutional jurisprudence is in drawing attention to the fact that the modalities are the argumentative grammar of constitutional law. The six modalities are the ways in which propositions of constitutional law are shown to be true or false. The modalities are not true by virtue of something outside the practice of argument that provides the practice's normative foundations. There is also no sublime logic to constitutional argument that theory might somehow disclose. There is only the practice and nothing more.

But what happens when the modalities conflict?[63] Richard Fallon, who follows Bobbitt in a descriptive approach to constitutional jurisprudence, analyzes the problem this way:

---

issue). For a different reading of the implications of the opinion, see Ronald Dworkin, "The Center Holds!," *N.Y. Rev. Books*, Aug. 13, 1992, at 29, 31–33 (casting the opinion as an example of law as integrity).

62. The following statement by Senator Strom Thurmond is representative of the sort of opinion many Americans no doubt developed during the hearings: "[Y]ou have criticized certain . . . decisions, [but] you have also indicated that some of these decisions are accepted law, and should not be disturbed by the Supreme Court. This has been taken by some as change in your views, in order to enhance the probability of your confirmation." Bobbitt, *supra* note 4, at 98 (quoting Senate Hearings at 465). It is precisely to statements such as these that Bork had to respond, and respond well. He did not. The trick was to appear principled yet pragmatic. Bork had a far easier time with one task than the other.

63. Bobbitt states: "What I did not see [when I wrote *Constitutional Fate*] was that the possibility of conflict between forms [modalities] would resuscitate the debate over legitimacy and encourage an eager resort to 'ideologizing' preferred modalities to provide the external referent that such legitimacy was, mistakenly, thought to require." Bobbitt, *supra* note 4, at xiv. Bobbitt's failure to address this problem was a central criticism of *Constitutional Fate*. See Sanford Levinson, "The Audience for Constitutional Meta-Theory (Or, Why, and to Whom, Do I Write the Things

Constitutional law has a commensurability problem. The problem arises from the variety of kinds of argument that now are almost universally accepted as legitimate in constitutional debate and interpretation.[64]

[I]t is impossible to reason or argue about the correct decision in hard cases— cases made hard by the actual or apparent tendency of different kinds of arguments to point to divergent results—without a theory of how different kinds of constitutional argument appropriately contribute to a single decision.[65]

For Fallon, the problem of modal conflict—which he identifies as "the commensurability problem"—is "among the most important in constitutional law."[66] In sharp contrast to Fallon, Bobbitt not only does not see modal conflict as a problem, he regards it as a distinct virtue of constitutional law. He states:

The space for moral reflection on our ideologies is created by the conflict among modalities, just as garden walls can create a space for a garden.[67]

The recursion to conscience is the crucial activity on which the constitutional system of interpretation that I have described depends. It is the purpose of this book to remind the Reader of this fact. This particular sort of recollection is the very thing that the current commentary on constitutional decision-making seeks to dispense with by insisting on the illegitimacy of our practices and the need for a particular decision process.[68]

These quotations contain the essentials of Bobbitt's solution to the problem of modal conflict, albeit in compressed form. The solution has two parts. The first is a negative aspect, which denies both the need for and the coherence of metatheoretical legitimation of constitutional practice. The second, positive aspect of the position is the role of the six modalities in the practice of constitutional argument. As these passages show, there are two components to the positive position: the modalities of argument and the recursion to conscience. The question is whether these two elements cohere. It is not at all clear that they do.

The central difficulty with the positive aspect of the position is the role Bobbitt assigns to the exercise of individual conscience. As mentioned, Bobbitt sees modal conflict as a distinct virtue of his approach. The reason this conflict is a virtue is that such conflict provides "[t]he space for moral reflection."[69] For recursion to conscience to succeed as a solution to the problem of modal conflict, it must be

---

I Do?)," 63 *U. Colo. L. Rev.* 389, 398 (1992): "[I]t is a notorious truth about *Constitutional Fate* that it does not remotely offer a way of choosing among the six legal-grammatical modalities that Bobbitt discusses—text, history, structure, doctrine, prudence, and ethos. When, for example, one concludes that history and doctrine, or text and prudence lead to conflicting results, Bobbitt does not in fact present a hierarchy that allows resolution."

64. Richard H. Fallon Jr., "A Constructivist Coherence Theory of Constitutional Interpretation," 100 *Harv. L. Rev.* 1189, 1189 (1987).

65. *Id.* at 1191–92.

66. *Id.* at 1191.

67. Bobbitt, *supra* note 4, at 177.

68. *Id.* at 184. The problem with the metaphor of the garden is that without a public practice of gardening, it is impossible to tell whether someone is gardening or merely moving plants around.

69. *Id.* at 177.

possible to wed to the exercise of individual conscience an account of constitutional argument that relies so heavily on a public, intersubjective practice of legal argument.[70] It is far from clear that this is even possible.[71]

Consider any proposition of constitutional law. To the question of how one settles the truth or falsity of a proposition of constitutional law, Bobbitt answers that one employs the modalities. The use of the modalities is a practice—they (and the ways they are used) are public, cultural property. This means that the truth of a constitutional proposition is not a function of what anyone thinks or believes about the proposition; rather, one uses the modalities of argument to show the truth of the proposition. Because the modalities of constitutional argument are public coin, no private meanings are possible.[72]

Recursion to the private realm of conscience is necessary only in the event of modal conflict. Because modal conflict is resolved by conscience, individuals—most importantly judges—must make moral choices. Thus, it is individual conscience that decides the truth and falsity of controversial propositions of constitutional law. The process of decision in easy constitutional cases (cases in which the modes do not conflict) will be public, but in "hard cases" (those of modal conflict), individual conscience is the only analytical apparatus at work.[73]

Were Bobbitt true to the force of his own argument, he would have to admit that the inevitable conflicts among the modalities can only be settled in the public sphere.[74] Conflicts among the modalities are resolved not by what individuals

---

70. The problem is that conscience, as Bobbitt describes it, is supremely private—"hidden from view," as it were. Interestingly, Ronald Dworkin's "interpretive" approach to legal practice suffers from precisely the same difficulty. See Gerald Postema, "'Protestant' Interpretation and Social Practices," 6 *Law & Phil.* 283, 296–97 (1987): "There is nothing in Dworkin's meta-theory of interpretation . . . that requires attention to the interpretive activities of fellow participants. Herein lies the strong 'protestantism' of Dworkin's theory. Not only is each participant encouraged to take up the interpretive enterprise . . . but each individual participant also has access to the truth, as it were, about what the practice is and requires, through private interpretation of the practice-text. While Dworkin seems to recognize that the practice is common, he counsels participants to live as if each had a private understanding of his own."

71. Bobbitt takes issue with my claim that "conscience" is another name for interpretation. See Philip Bobbitt, "Reflections Inspired by My Critics," 72 *Tex. L. Rev.* 1869, 1966 (1994) ("'Conscience' is a name for the act of deciding among incommensurables. It is not a language game.").

72. See Wittgenstein, *supra* note 51, at §§ 243–315, 348–412; Ludwig Wittgenstein, *The Blue and Brown Books* 46–74 (2d ed. Basil Blackwell 1960) (demonstrating the imposssibility of a private language).

73. Of course, there is no public access to this inner realm, for by its very nature, conscience is a function of "individual moral sensibility." Bobbitt, *supra* note 4, at 168.

74. By way of contrast, Richard Fallon handles the problem of modal conflict by resort to a theory of coherence. See Fallon, *supra* note 64, at 1237–51. The problem with appeal to a general theory of coherence is that the form of the argument is prudential. Thus, modal conflict is eliminated but at the cost of reductionism: all modes of justification are reduced to one, the prudential. (For an analysis of this shortcoming, see Bobbitt, *supra* note 4, at 1301–02.) It is perhaps unfair to characterize Fallon's endeavor as reductionist, for he does not seek to bring all the modalities under control by resort to one. Rather, his effort is to identify "a decision calculus that assesses the rightness or wrongness of possible conclusions along more than one dimension." Fallon, *supra* note 64, at 1241 n.230. Fallon does not identify or produce such a calculus, instead claiming that

decide, but by what they ultimately accept as an adequate resolution of modal conflict.[75] No particular resolution of modal conflict springs forth from conscience as a fully formed resolution, as persuasion—not conscience—ultimately drives choice.[76] In a passage we considered earlier, in discussion of Ronald Dworkin's jurisprudence, Charles Taylor put the matter this way:

> What if someone does not "see" the adequacy of our interpretation, does not accept our reading? We try to show him how it makes sense of the original nonsense or partial sense [or, in Bobbitt's terms, modal conflict]. But for him to follow us he must read the original language as we do, he must recognize these expressions as puzzling in a certain way, and hence be looking for a solution to our problem. If he does not, what can we do? The answer, it would seem, can only be more of the same. We have to show him through the reading of other expressions why this expression must be read in the way we propose. But success here requires that he follow us in these other readings, and so on, it would seem, potentially forever. We cannot escape an ultimate appeal to a common understanding of the expressions, of the "language" involved.[77]

What is missing in Bobbitt's otherwise compelling account of the practice of constitutional law is some description of the practice of persuasion that is so much a part of constitutional law and law generally.[78] How is it that lawyers convince one another of a particular reading of the law when the meaning of law is put in

---

"constructivist coherence theory assumes a decision calculus." *Id.* at 1240–41 n.230. Instead, Fallon advances a hierarchy of arguments, with arguments from text at the top of the list. His reason for giving pride of place to the textual modality "follows from the settled proposition that it is the Constitution we are interpreting." *Id.* at 1244. This states, rather than solves, the problems under consideration.

75. Bruno Latour makes a parallel observation in the sociology of science. See Bruno Latour, *Science in Action* 42 (1987): "[A] fact is what is collectively stabilised from the midst of controversies when the activity of later papers [for our purposes, judicial opinions, law review articles, addresses, etc.] does not consist only of criticism or deformation but also of confirmation. The strength of the original statement does not lie in itself, but is derived from any of the papers that incorporate it."

76. See generally Brian Simpson, "The Common Law and Legal Theory," in *The Common Law and Legal Theory* 14 (William Twining ed., 1986) ("[C]ommon law rules enjoy whatever status they possess not because of the circumstances of their origin, but because of their continued reception.").

77. Charles Taylor, "Interpretation and the Sciences of Man," in 2 *Philosophy and the Human Sciences (Philosophical Papers)* 15, 17 (1985) (emphasis added). Compare Geertz's evaluation of the importance of persuasion in anthropological writing: "This capacity to persuade readers (most of them academic, virtually all of them at least part-time participants in that peculiar form of existence evasively called "modern") that what they are reading is an authentic account by someone personally acquainted with how life proceeds in some place, at some time, among some group, is the basis upon which anything else ethnography seeks to do—analyze, explain, amuse, disconcert, celebrate, edify, excuse, astonish, subvert—finally rests." Clifford Geertz, *Works and Lives: The Anthropologist as Author* 143–44 (1988).

78. To be quite specific, and to make the point on the same plane as Bobbitt's argument, one wants to know where a discussion or argument goes after the individual decision makers resolve a modal conflict differently. In the present formulation of his position, Bobbitt resorts to conscience as the next step in the process. For the reasons given, I think this move fails.

question? Why is one rendering of a modal conflict followed by some courts or judges and not others? It is an obvious and important feature of law that the merits of a single judicial decision play no role in the wider discourse of law unless and until another judge or court finds the reasoning persuasive.[79] The cultural methods and resources for persuasion simply cannot be ignored. By leaving the resolution of modal conflict to the uncharted realm of conscience, Bobbitt leaves for another day further discussion of a central aspect of the practice of constitutional law that he has otherwise described so well.[80] Why does he do so? I shall close this chapter by considering this question.

Justification, Legitimacy, Justice, and Truth

The modalities are the grammar of law, the ways in which propositions of law are shown to be true. Legitimacy is not a property of legal modalities. Rather, legitimacy is an "accretion," maintained over time by adherence[81] to (the use of) the modalities. Further, employment of the modalities does *not* guarantee justice: "[J]udicial review that is wicked, but follows the forms of argument, is legitimately done; and review that is benign in its design and ameliorative in its result but which proceeds arbitrarily or according to forms unrecognized within our legal culture, is illegitimate."[82]

If the use of the modalities does not guarantee justice, then what, if anything, does? Bobbitt advances a two-part answer to this question. In the law, Bobbitt writes, "justice arises from law practices [the use of the modalities in argument]; in the absence of legal practices there would be no just legal decisions. . . . This makes justice useful all right—since it provides the standards against which we can test alternative decisions."[83] But whence come the standards of justice?

> [W]e assess the justice of a particular decision by reference to some external standard, a system of evaluation outside the operation of the modalities of argument. That is how *justifying* is done; but not, I will argue, *deciding*.
>
> . . .

79. See generally Richard Bronaugh, "Persuasive Precedent," in *Precedent in Law* 217, 217–47 (Lawrence Goldstein ed., 1987) (providing a philosophical account of persuasion in appeal to precedent).

80. It may be the case that, from the legal point of view, there is nothing more to be said about justification in constitutional law. The modalities of justification are the ways in which propositions of law are shown to be true or false. When a judge decides a case, she employs the modalities. The decision may require resort to conscience, but conscience does not do any normative work (Bobbitt seems to say that it does, but he has not made a convincing case for this central claim). The reasoning is either persuasive or it is not. Conscience does not persuade, nor is it persuaded: only argument can do that.

81. By "adherence" I mean maintenance of the grammar of constitutional argument through continued use of the modalities. The Supreme Court's decisions, for example, would lose their legitimacy were the Court to abandon the modalities as the discourse of constitutional argument and decision.

82. Bobbitt, *supra* note 4, at 28.

83. *Id.* at 148.

Whether a particular decision is just is a matter judged by the critical standards of the day; but the employment of those standards is a part of the decision only to the extent that the modalities of argument incorporate them by reference.[84]

From these passages, it seems fair to say that the "justice" of a particular decision is assessed from the point of view of a given theory or account of justice. For example, consider the following case: B saves the life of A but in the course of doing so B is severely injured. In gratitude for his self-sacrifice, A promises B an annuity for life. Is the promise enforceable?[85]

One might assess the justice of a decision enforcing such a promise from the point of view of utility. The "justice" of the particular decision, however, is inseparable from the language of justice chosen to evaluate it (e.g., efficiency, utility, wealth maximization, egoism, Kantian moral philosophy, Rawls's two principles of justice).

What is gained by the insight that the justice of a particular decision may be assessed variously, relative to diverse theories or accounts of justice? Little, if anything. Why? The answer lies in the lesson Bobbitt himself draws from his characterization of the forms of legal argument as modalities. The modalities themselves are neither true nor false: they are the means by which propositions of law are characterized as "true" or "false." Is not the same true of the forms of argument in the many languages of justice? For instance, outside the discourse of utilitarianism, the assertion "A's promise to B ought to be enforced on grounds of efficiency" would be neither true nor false. The forms of economic argument are the ways in which the claim "this decision promotes efficiency (and, thus, justice)" is shown to be true or false.

The lesson to be drawn is that the languages of justice have the same (modal) status as the language (grammar) of law. Just as the law takes the facts of a case as its object (e.g., what A said to B), so too do the languages of justice take the law as their object. In this, the languages of justice enjoy the same status as the law. These languages may be employed to show the truth of propositions of justice. In this, Bobbitt seems to agree:

> [In law] legitimacy is . . . separate from justification, whereas in literary criticism the forms of evaluation embody the critic's values. To say that *The Grapes of Wrath* exposes the class structure may be an observation laden with significance for critics of a certain school; to say the same thing of *Maher v. Roe*, which denied women a right to abortion funding, may be to say something important, *but it is not legal argument and has no legal consequences* (though of course it may have important consequences for the law and the respect due it).[86]

In this paragraph, and others, Bobbitt relies upon the distinction between propositions *of* law and propositions *about* law. Before considering this distinction in

---

84. *Id.* at 163.
85. See Webb v. McGowan, 27 Ala. 82, 168 So. 196 (1935), *cert. denied*, 232 Ala. 374, 168 So. 199 (1936).
86. Bobbitt, *supra* note 4 at 40.

the context of constitutional argument, let us work through a nonlegal example. Take bicycle riding. This is a common activity, one that is governed by rules of various sorts. Bicycling is the sort of thing that may be done well or poorly. It is teachable, and it is learnable. In these things, bicycling is no different than a great many other activities (e.g., playing the cello, archery, painting, and fiction writing).

Consider the following claim: "Riding a bicycle is good for the cardiovascular system." I take this to be a proposition *about* bicycling; one that is true. The proposition can be shown to be true by resort to medical evidence such as the connection between exercise and the condition of the heart. Contrast this proposition with the following: "Moving the pedals in a clockwise fashion causes the cycle to move forward." This proposition is a proposition *of* bicycling, one that states a truth intrinsic to that activity. The movement of the pedals is something accomplished in bicycling; the movement of the pedals in a clockwise fashion is *how* one bicycles in a forward direction.

Nothing about the truth of the medical proposition contributes to the truth of the bicycling proposition (or vice versa). The justification advanced in support of the medical proposition connects not at all with that preferred in support of the bicycling proposition. Were one to justify the medical proposition by appeal to the means used to justify the bicycling proposition, I would say that the purported justification is illegitimate. Legitimacy is a matter of using the form of argument appropriate to the proposition in question.[87] Illegitimacy in justification results from the use of forms of argument from one discourse to justify a proposition of another discourse.[88]

It is simply a confusion to justify propositions *of* law with the justificatory tools of other disciplines (thereby justifying claims *about* (but not *of* law)). Apropos of Bobbitt's comment above regarding *The Grapes of Wrath* and *Mayer v. Roe*, to say something of *legal* significance, one must speak in the language of the law. Even in translation, the languages of justice do not show us which propositions are true and which false as a matter of law.

---

87. "Legitimacy" may be used in two senses. First, an argument is legitimate if it employs the forms of argument appropriate to the question. For example, an argument to the effect that a painting is beautiful is legitimate if the argument employs aesthetic modes of argument. A second use of the word "legitimate" asks whether a certain action is licensed. In the context of the default rules debate, the question is whether it is legitimate for the state to fill gaps in contracts in accordance with given criteria. The second use of the word "legitimate" raises questions of moral, political, or social philosophy. Starting from premises about efficiency, justice, rationality, or politics, the contract theorist sets out to evaluate contract law from the perspective of her preferred theory. To the degree contract law is found to fall short of the demands of the preferred theory, it will be found to be "illegitimate." But forms of argument as such are neither legitimate nor illegitimate, they are the grammar with which the exercise of justification proceeds. See generally, Brian Langille, "Revolution Without Foundations: The Grammar of Scepticism and Law," 33 *McGill L. J.* 451 (1988). An argument—justifying a claim that a proposition of law is true—is legitimate to the extent it employs appropriate modes of argument. Illegitimacy is a condition of an argument which employs modes of argument inappropriate to the proposition at hand.

88. Illegitimacy is a confusion or conflation of modes or forms of argument.

This analysis may tell us how law and justice are "related," but it tells us nothing about how justice arises in law or, as Bobbitt puts the question, "If a legitimate system does not ensure justice, how can it be justified?" Bobbitt's unique answer to this question lies in his account of the role of conscience in adjudication.

As we saw previously, resort to conscience results from conflict among two or more of the modalities. Bobbitt draws a sharp distinction between justifying and deciding.[89] We use the modalities to decide a case and the languages of justice to assess the justice of particular decisions. But are judicial outcomes themselves just? Bobbitt provides the following answer: "[T]he system is just, not because it produces just outcomes, but because it permits an opportunity for justice consistent with the freedom of conscience to decide matters."[90] In other words the American constitutional system is just precisely *because* it creates a space for the exercise of individual conscience.[91]

How, then, does conscience go about its work? Bobbitt suggests it does this through the languages of justice: "To summarize: a particular decision will be deemed just according to the prevailing practices of moral theory [the then-current languages of justice]. These *may* legitimately influence a constitutional decider when faced with a modal conflict but such a role is irrelevant to their role as evaluative standards once the decision is made."[92] "Conscience," it seems, is another name for the languages of moral theory. These, Bobbitt argues, may legitimately be employed to solve the problem of modal conflict. Legitimacy is maintained by limiting resort to extralegal sources of argument to cases of modal conflict.

The problem with this argument is that Bobbitt seems to be ennobling conscience at the price of clarity. It may very well be the case that in hard cases judges have resort to so-called extralegal forms of argument. This seems to be a case of interpretation, where the question is what we are to do when our practice of legal justification breaks down. Additionally, Bobbitt provides no account of justice (or the "justness" of the system) apart from an identification of conscience with justice. But it is far from self-evident that the exercise of conscience is consistent with—or guarantees—justice.

Conclusion

Despite misgivings over the role of conscience in cases of modal conflict, one cannot but conclude that Bobbitt's account of constitutional argument repre-

---

89. See Bobbitt, *supra* note 4, at 163. ("[W]e assess the justice of a particular decision by reference to some external standard, a system of evaluation outside the operation of the modalities of argument. That is how *justifying* is done; but not, I will argue, *deciding*.").

90. *Id.*

91. See *id.*, at 168 ("The United States Constitution formalizes a role for the conscience of the individual sensibility by requiring decisions that rely on the individual moral sensibility when the modalities of argument clash.").

92. *Id.* at 168

sents a major jurisprudential advance. The significance of his account lies in the recognition that truth in law is a matter of the forms of legal argument, not the conditions that make propositions of law true. The next and final chapter develops an account of legal argument consistent with Bobbitt's insight into the nature of legal truth. Additionally, that insight is put in a wider context, that of a complete account of the nature of truth in law.

8

Postmodern Jurisprudence

To understand a sentence means to understand a language.
Ludwig Wittgenstein[1]

There is nothing outside of the text.
Jacques Derrida[2]

In previous chapters, I have considered the leading contemporary answers to the question of what it means to say that a proposition of law is true. With one exception,[3] all the views discussed proceed from a "modernist" perspective on the question of truth. From the modernist point of view, "truth" names a relation between an asserted proposition and some state of affairs that makes the proposition true.[4] The view I identify as "postmodern" rejects the project of unraveling the connection between propositions and what makes them true. From a postmodernist point of view, to say that some proposition is true is to say that "a sufficiently well placed speaker who used the words in that way would be fully warranted in counting the statement as true of that situation."[5] The first part of this chapter is devoted to providing an account of modernism and postmodernism.

In the second part of this chapter, I explore the role of language and its relationship to truth. The story of philosophy of language in the late-nineteenth and the first half of the twentieth century is one of the rise of reference as the key to meaning. As reference came to dominate philosophical discourse, nonreferential forms of speech such as aesthetics and ethics were relegated to a second-class status as mere expressions of speaker preferences. The latter part of this chapter recounts the relevant history and explains why the strict dichotomy between language as reference and language as expression cannot be sustained.

Having set up the need for and an outline of a postmodern account of language, we return to law. In the third and final part of this chapter I present my answer to the question "What does it mean to say that a proposition of law is

---

1. Ludwig Wittgenstein, *Philosophical Investigations* § 199 (G. E. M. Anscombe trans., 3d ed. 1958).

2. Jacques Derrida, *Of Grammatology* 158 (Gayatri Spivak trans., 1976).

3. That being the position of Philip Bobbitt, discussed in chapter 7.

4. Robert Brandom refers to this point of view as "representationalist." See Robert Brandom, "Truth and Assertibility," 73 *J. Phil.* 137 (1976).

5. Hilary Putnam, *Representation and Reality* 115 (1988).

true?" The answer is not that it is true if it names a relation between a proposition and some state of affairs but that it is true if a competent legal actor could justify its assertion. Doing this requires the speaker to employ the forms of legal argument. In short, "true" is a term of commendation or endorsement. The forms of argument are the answer to the question "What is the justification for saying the proposition in question is 'true'?"

But the forms of legal argument are only part of the story. In addition to the use of forms of argument to show the truth of a legal proposition, lawyers often engage in the related but distinct activity of interpretation. Interpretation is an activity occasioned by a breakdown in our argumentative conventions—the forms of argument. Because interpretation has been a central focus of attention in previous chapters, the present moment will be used to pull together several strands from earlier discussions. Interpretation in law manifests itself in three distinct ways. The most obvious example is the case of conflict among forms of legal argument. The question here is how one defends the choice of one form over another. In addition, interpretive questions may arise over just what is to count as a particular form of argument. In this chapter we shall consider one such interpretive question, in the context of historical argument. Lastly, the forms of argument employed by lawyers in the distinct activities of justification and interpretation may themselves sometimes be called into question.

Modernism and Postmodernism

Modernism

Modernism is the form of thought identified with the spirit of the aspirations of the Enlightenment, whose familiar story is captured by Jeffrey Stout's felicitous phrase "the flight from authority."[6] Spurred on by the power of science and its control over nature, philosophy replaced the medieval emphasis on custom, ritual, authority and cosmology with a self-conscious preoccupation with legitimacy, progress,[7] autonomy,[8] rationality,[9] and human emancipation.

---

6. See Jeffrey Stout, *The Flight From Authority: Religion, Morality, and the Quest for Autonomy* 2–3 (1981): "[M]odern thought was born in a crisis of authority, took shape in flight from authority, and aspired from the start to autonomy from all traditional influence whatsoever; that the quest for autonomy was also an attempt to deny the historical reality of having been influenced by tradition; and that this quest therefore could not but fail."

7. See Hans Blumenberg, *The Legitimacy of the Modern Age* (R. Wallace trans., 1983) (a defense of the idea of progress as a secular notion).

8. If any single theme runs through the whole of modernity it is the idea of autonomy. In politics, the subject is free to decide her own conception of the good, in art the work of art must be allowed to "speak for itself," literature has the same hopes for itself, as does law. When the tradition starts to slip away, and the autonomy of the text thereby threatened, the anxiety may be expressed in terms of fetishization. For discussion of this phenomenon in music, see Harold Brown, "Pedantry or Liberation? A Sketch of the Historical Performance Movement," in Nicholas Kenyon, *Authenticity and Early Music* 27–56 (1988).

9. For discussion of rationalism, see *infra*, notes 14–16.

Modernism is exemplified by three axes which, taken together, provide a three-dimensional perspective:[10]

1. Epistemological foundationalism—Knowledge can only be justified to the extent it rests on indubitable foundations.
2. Theory of language—Language has two functions: it represents ideas or states of affairs, or expresses the attitudes of the speaker.
3. Individual and community—"Society" is best understood as an aggregation of "social atoms."[11]

These three components of the modernist picture should not be understood simply as parts of a whole. Each represents not an idea or element in a picture but an axis which, when taken with the others, enables one to see a broad range of thinkers as all of a piece.

As the label suggests, epistemological foundationalism is a knowledge axis, with foundationalism[12] at one end and skepticism[13] at the other. The representative rationalist foundationalist[14] is the philosopher, René Descartes.[15] In essence, Descartes saw the problem of knowledge as a problem about certainty. Separating belief from illusion required a method. For this, Descartes invented the "method of doubt."[16] The process of validating belief required that the belief be

10. See Nancey Murphy & James McClendon, "Distinguishing Modern and Postmodern Theologies," 5 *Mod. Theology* 191 (1989) (describing modernity by reference to three axes). See also Nancey Murphy, "Scientific Realism and Postmodern Philosophy," 41 *Brit. J. Phil. Sci.* 291 (1990) (describing postmodern philosophy of science).

11. Murphy, *supra* note 10, at 292.

12. See D. W. Hamlyn, *The Theory of Knowledge* 10 (1970): "There is a tendency to think of the corpus of knowledge as a building that is rising upward and that those who increase the stock of knowledge are building additional stories on to the existing fabric. If the foundations are not secure the whole building will eventually come crashing to the ground."

13. See *id.* at 7–8 ("Philosophical skepticism . . . raises fundamental doubts about the possibility of knowing anything at all."). For a broad essay on skepticism in the tradition of analytic philosophy see Skorupski, "The Intelligibility of Scepticism," in *The Analytic Tradition* 1–29 (D. Bell & N. Cooper eds., 1990).

14. For the rationalist, the flux of experience cannot be made sense of without resort to ideas, for it is through ideas that experience is organized and knowledge achieved. But which ideas are the correct ones and which illusory? Rationalists of whatever stripe take this question seriously; however, they take it seriously in a way that cannot go unnoticed. For the rationalist, there is no need to consult other people in getting an answer to the question "How do I know my beliefs are true?" Through introspection, an individual can gain knowledge of the world by methodological discernment of ideas. True beliefs are those which are in accordance with clear and distinct ideas. In short, "one could define rationalism as the view that knowledge about the world is the development of what, in some sense, we already know in the form of clear, distinct, and mutually consistent ideas present to our consciousness." Robert Ackermann, *Data, Instruments and Theory* 7 (1985).

15. For an interesting essay on Descartes's account of subjectivity and the relationship of his thought to modernity, see Dalia Judovitz, *Subjectivity and Representation in Descartes: The Origins of Modernity* (1988).

16. For discussion, see John Cottingham, *A Descartes Dictionary* 51 (1993): "'Descartes' method of doubt' is the label often applied to the procedure whereby Descartes attempts to clear away the rubble of prejudices or preconceived opinions, in order to lay down a reliable metaphysical base for his new science. 'I realized that it was necessary, once in the course of my life, to

submitted to an inner (mental) tribunal wherein the belief was interrogated. Ideas which survived this process of questioning earned the label "clear and distinct." That which could not be doubted—the indubitable—was valid and, thus, "knowledge."[17] The emphasis on method and validation led, not surprisingly, to the valorization of mathematics, science, and geometry, for it was in these areas that Descartes found that which was most certain: axiom, system, and deduction.

The other foundationalist approach to knowledge is empiricism, which replaces the rationalist emphasis on the formal relations between and among ideas with an appeal to our ordinary, commonsense understanding of experience. When we see an object, we have a retinal impression of a thing which exists in space and time or, to put it more colloquially, we have an experience of another body. Providing an explanation of such an experience (e.g., how it is possible, what is involved in "having" the experience) without resort to anything "in" the mind is the gravamen of empiricism. Empiricism is foundationalist in that, for the empiricist,

> verification and justification, telling whether something is true and backing up one's claims about what is true, must eventually rely upon the evidence of one's senses; not in the first instance, maybe, but at the end of the day. What else could we appeal to, to tell us whether something is true, than the evidence of our senses? This is a good sound empiricist question. So the evidence of our senses is what we start from when we need to construct a justification for our beliefs, on this approach.[18]

Skepticism[19] is not a necessary corollary of either the rationalist or the empiricist account of knowledge. In other words, it is a mistake to see the skeptic as

---

demolish everything and start again right from the foundations if I wanted to establish anything at all in the sciences that was stable and likely to last'. Although Descartes was sometimes maliciously accused of being a sceptic, he made it clear, right from the first public presentation of his metaphysics, that his purpose in raising systematic doubts was to eliminate doubt and find something secure and indubitable: 'since I wished to devote myself solely to the search for truth, I thought it necessary to do the very opposite and reject as if absolutely false everything in which I could imagine the least doubt, in order to see if I was left believing anything that was entirely indubitable'. Doubt, in short, is a means to an end, not an end in itself. And at the end of the Meditations, it is striking that the mediator is able, with relief, to dismiss his earlier doubts as 'laughable' and 'exaggerated'." (citations omitted).

17. See Roy Boone, *Foucault and Derrida: The Other Side of Reason* 42 (1990): "For Descartes, when the understanding perceives something clearly and distinctly, we can be sure that it perceives truly, because God, who is not a deceiver, gave us the powers that we have, and it is inconceivable that where we perceive something clearly God intended that we should be deceived. It follows from this that corporeal things 'possess all the properties which I clearly and distinctly understand'." (citation omitted).

18. Jonathan Dancy, *Introduction to Contemporary Epistemology* 86 (1985).

19. The great critic of skepticism is, of course, Immanuel Kant. Kant takes seriously the skeptical claim that we can never "know" the truth of any proposition by advancing a "Critical Philosophy" of transcendental idealism. See Immanuel Kant, *Critique of Pure Reason* (Norman Kemp Smith ed. & trans., 1929); Immanuel Kant, *Critique of Practical Reason* (Lewis White Beck trans., 1956); Immanuel Kant, *Critique of Judgment* (William Pluhar trans., 1987). A recent treatment of Kant's theory of knowledge is Herbert Schwyzer, *The Unity of Understanding* (1990). For a brilliant analysis of the aporias of judgment, and Kant's solution to them, see Howard Caygill, *The Art of Judgment* (1989).

one who denies the rationalist or the empiricist account of knowledge. The skeptic does not deny that what is described (on either account) as knowledge is in fact knowledge; she denies that we ever *have* knowledge. For example, David Hume believed that, although we had to assume its existence, we could not prove the existence of the external world.[20] All we have to base our knowledge of causation on is a constant conjunction of sense impressions. Sense impressions—raw input from the outside world—are the only available "ground" of knowledge.[21] In our own century, the idea that knowledge is built up from simple elements in sensory experience was taken to new heights by the Vienna Circle. Led by the philosopher Rudolf Carnap, the Circle advanced a wide-ranging program for the constitution of knowledge in fields as diverse as philosophy, sociology, architecture, and language studies.[22]

In sum, knowledge on the modernist view (rationalism or empiricism) is foundational. For modernists, the only question is whether the foundations are themselves adequate and whether the "logic of construction" from foundations is itself adequate. "Taking epistemology seriously" does not require a commitment to one or the other ends of the axis; it merely requires that one be captivated by the questions that infuse the poles of the axis.

The two poles of the language axis stand for the two functions of language: language refers to objects or facts in the world, or is expressive of the attitudes,

---

20. See David Hume, *A Treatise of Human Nature* 187 (L. A. Selby-Bigge ed., 1888) ("What causes induce us to believe in the existence of a body? but 'tis in vain to ask, Whether there be a body or not? That is a point, which we must take for granted in all our reasonings.").

21. Modern philosophy had wrestled with the relationship between epistemology and vision long before the Vienna positivists turned their attention to the matter. See 2 Arthur Schopenhauer, *The World as Will and Representation* (E. Payne trans., 1958) (criticizing Kant's aesthetics and epistemology for inattention to the physiology of apperception). For discussion of vision as a theme in modernity, see Jonathan Crary, *Techniques of the Observer: On Vision and Modernity in the Nineteenth Century* (1990).

22. Underlying the subject matter divisions of the Circle's broad program was a simple, yet powerful approach to knowledge, one having philosophical, cultural, and political dimensions. Peter Galison describes the details of the program in two seemingly disparate arenas: science and architecture. The Vienna positivists' program "sought to instantiate a modernism emphasizing what I will call 'transparent construction,' a manifest building up from simple elements to all higher forms that would, by virtue of the systematic constructional program itself, guarantee the exclusion of the decorative, mystical, or metaphysical. There was a political dimension to this form of construction: by basing it on simple, accessible units, they hoped to banish incorporation of nationalist or historical features. From simple observation reports ('protocol statements') and logical connectives (such as 'if/then,' 'or,' 'and'), the logical positivists sought to ground a 'scientific,' antiphilosophical philosophy that would set all reliable knowledge on strong foundations and isolate it from the unreliable. Since all valid inferences would be built out of these basic statements, the sciences would be unified by their starting points. For their part, the Bauhäusler hoped to use scientific principles to combine primitive color relations and basic geometrical forms to eliminate the decorative and create a new antiaesthetic aesthetic that would prize functionality. So close had the two groups come in their shared vision of modernism that, when the Bauhaus reconvened as the New Bauhaus in Chicago after fleeing the Nazis, the New Bauhaus imported the Vienna Circle's logical positivism as a fundamental component of its basic design program." Peter Galison, "Aufbau/Bauhaus: Logical Positivism and Architectural Modernism," 16 *Critical Inquiry* 709, 710–11 (1990).

preferences, or emotions of the speaker. One pole, that of representationalism, is closely linked with epistemological foundationalism. If language is a medium for referring to objects in the world, then knowledge of what something is can be gleaned from the object's representation in language. The point of studying language is to study the ways in which words refer to things.

In their philosophical heyday, modernist philosophers advanced theories of language that saw words as placeholders for things.[23] In the twentieth century, the work of Ludwig Wittgenstein before 1929 stands as the paradigmatic expression of the program of "logical atomism," which emphasizes the reduction of the elements of sentences to their constituent parts in the world. In describing Wittgenstein's quintessentially modern *Tractatus*,[24] David Pears puts it this way:

> We evidently do succeed in using this language to describe the world, but how is this done? His answer is that we succeed only because there is a fixed grid of possible combinations of objects to which the structure of our language conforms. The grid must exist and connections must be made with it if language is going to work. But it clearly does work and so the metaphysical conclusions follow.[25]

To see language as a structure or grid is a way of answering the question "How does language represent the world?" A related and, for law, more important question, is "How can one see a variety of situations as 'the same'?" Put another way, the question is about the role language plays in connecting up a variety of factual contexts that, despite their differences, can be said to be "the same."[26]

If language is not a means of referring, then what else can it do? If one accepts the claim that language does refer to things in the world—the representationalist view—then what is one to do with ethical discourse? The Vienna Circle recommended that ethics, together with the whole of "continental philosophy," be dismissed as "bad poetry." The only alternative is to develop an account of language as a mode of expression. Thus, moral judgments cannot be "true", for they do not "represent" the world; rather, they are "expressions of preference, expressions of attitude or feeling, insofar as they are moral and evaluative in character."[27]

Now to the third modernist axis. To the individualist, society is composed simply of "social atoms,"[28] each endowed with needs and desires the existence

---

23. See Richard Rorty, *Philosophy and the Mirror of Nature* 257–312 (1979).

24. Ludwig Wittgenstein, *Tractatus Logico-Philosophicus* (David Pears & Brian McGuinness trans., 1974).

25. 1 David Pears, *The False Prison* 6 (1987).

26. For example, in contract law, an offer can be accepted orally, in writing, by telegram, smoke signal, etc. What makes all these different ways of acting "the same thing," that is, "acceptance"?

27. Alasdair MacIntyre, *After Virtue* 11 (1981).

28. See generally Elizabeth Wolgast, *The Grammar of Justice* 1–27 (1987) (discussion of the ontological and conceptual foundations of liberalism, specifically the theory of individuality as social atomism).

and identity of which are known (internally) to each.[29] Political economy is best understood from the perspective of individual motivation.[30] All talk of public values, group norms, or "structures" is eschewed. Methodological individualism is the explanatory model for understanding.

The collectivist counters that far more foundational than the individual is the *class* to which that person belongs. Class is one of many constitutive social facts that shape the individual—make her what she is. At its most radical expression, the individual is not in control of her fate, she is produced by forces beyond her control. At the individual level, agents are capable of making free and rational decisions with respect to their own preferences only to the extent they are able to become aware of and break free from the structures that shape their choices.

Taken together, these three axes give us the following picture of modern thought:[31]

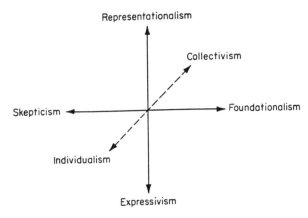

29. There are two "spaces" which, taken together, comprise the individual. The realm of right, which is created by reason, is divided into two spheres, the public and the private. The public realm is the realm of right. In this realm, private action is restricted to the extent it impacts on the right of others to act similarly. The private realm is the realm of individual choice about which actions are, from the perspective of the individual, good. This account of the relationship between reason, agency, and normativity was first worked out in the philosophy of Immanuel Kant. See Immanuel Kant, *Groundwork of the Metaphysics of Morals* (H. J. Paton trans., 1964). For discussion of this perspective in the light of the postmodern critique of agent-centered reason, see John McGowan, *Postmodernism and Its Critics* 31–43 (1991).

30. See Adam Smith, *The Wealth of Nations* 119 (1970): "It is not from the benevolence of the butcher, the brewer or the baker that we expect our dinner, but from their regard to their own self interest. We address ourselves not to their humanity but to their self-love, and never talk to them of our own necessities but of their advantages."

31. This diagram is taken from Murphy & McClendon, *supra* note 10, at 196. As mentioned above, with respect to modernism our focus is on the question "What does knowledge consist in?" The position advanced here is that knowledge is the demonstrable ability to move within a linguistic practice. This view is advanced *both* as a substantive position on knowledge and as an alternative to the views of knowledge identified as modernist or (often) postmodernist. One can be skeptical to the claims about being in postmodernity without forsaking a position in the modern/postmodern debate about knowledge.

Postmodern Thought

Postmodern thought may be defined as "any mode of thought that departs from the three modern axes described above without reverting to premodern categories."[32] Postmodernism is not about the reconstitution of any or all of these axes. As we shall see, the movement from the modernist picture of knowledge to the postmodern view was a gradual shift in perspective. Not surprisingly, the shift begins on modernist terms.

The story of science from the seventeenth to the twentieth century is best told as the rise of experiment as the central focus for philosophical debates over the ground of knowledge.[33] This is due to the empiricist basis of the most influential theory of scientific knowledge, that of positivism.[34] During the 1950s and sixties, the positivist picture of knowledge received close scrutiny and was found wanting. The first chink in the positivist armor resulted from a blow that came from within its own ranks, in the thought of the philosopher and logician, W. V. O. Quine.[35] In Quine's view, the whole idea of knowledge as a process of

32. Murphy & McClendon, *supra* note 10, at 199. These premodern categories are authority, specifically religious authority, and cosmology—understanding the world on the basis of an explanation of why the universe exists at all, and then explaining that by postulating the existence of a deity. See Antony Flew, *A Dictionary of Philosophy* 77–79 (2d ed. 1979). For a broader telling of the story of modernism, *see* Stephen Toulmin, *Cosmopolis: The Hidden Agenda of Modernity* (1990); Martin Berman, *All That's Solid Melts into Air: The Experience of Modernity* (1982, 1988). For a recent work concentrating on the cultural aspects of postmodernism, see Fredric Jameson, *Postmodernism, or, The Cultural Logic of Late Capitalism* (1991). An excellent bibliography on postmodernism is found in *After the Future: Postmodern Times and Places* 333–50 (Gary Shapiro ed., 1990).

33. This is only a recent realization, first brought to light in Ackermann, *supra* note 14. See also Peter Galison, *How Experiments End* (1987) (detailed review of experiments on gyromagnetic effects and the production of scientific knowledge). The usual story of the growth in scientific knowledge goes like this: "It has become usual in recent history of science to rehearse the shortcomings of standard textbook presentations of scientific progress: observations not in accord with previous conceptions of the world accumulate until they force a new set of theoretical views on the scientific community. Even now it is not hard to find physics textbooks that recount the origins of special relativity in terms of the inexorable march of optical ether-drift experiments. According to these potted versions of history, Einstein 'simply' generalized the clear observational fact that motion with respect to the ether could not be observed. In this way the strength of physical argumentation is rhetorically linked to its connection with observation (or experiment) and the historical sequence is described in such a way as to enhance the role of experience and denigrate the corresponding theoretical analysis." Peter Galison, "History, Philosophy, and the Central Metaphor," 2 *Sci. in Context* 197, 198–99 (1988).

34. See David Oldroyd, *The Arch of Knowledge* 168–262 (1986) (tracing the origins of the positivist model of knowledge).

35. See W. V. O. Quine, "Two Dogmas of Empiricism," in *From a Logical Point of View* 20–46 (1953) (arguing against the idea of a "basic" unit of knowledge and urging instead a view of knowledge as embedded in "the whole of science"); Galison, *supra* note 33, at 203 ("Quine strongly opposed the total separation of observation from other forms of knowledge; for him, all were up for evaluation."); Murphy, *supra* note 10, at 294 ("Quine not only replaced the foundationalist theory of knowledge with a holist account, but also provided a new picture or metaphor—that of a web or network of beliefs—to replace the 'layer-cake' model."). For a very quick tour through Quine's thought, see Hilary Putnam, "Misling," *London Review of Books*, Apr. 21, 1988, at 11–13.

building from the simple to the complex, and the concomitant notion that knowledge is a matter of correspondence between word (concept) and world, had to be scrapped. In its place, Quine substituted holism, the view that the truth of any one statement or proposition is a function not of its relationship to the world but of the degree to which it "hangs together" with everything else we take to be true. Quine stated his view this way:

> The totality of our so-called knowledge or beliefs, from the most casual matters of geography and history to the profound laws of atomic physics or even of pure mathematics and logic, is a man-made fabric which impinges on experience only along the edges. Or, to change the figure, total science is like a field of force whose boundary conditions are experience. A conflict with experience at the periphery occasions readjustments in the interior of the field. Truth values have to be redistributed over some of our statements. Reëvaluation of some statements entails reëvaluation of others, because of their logical interconnections—the logical laws being in turn simply certain further statements of the system, certain further elements of the field. Having reëvaluated one statement we must reëvaluate some others, which may be statements logically connected with the first or may be the statements of logical connections themselves. But the total field is so underdetermined by its boundary conditions, experience, that there is much latitude of choice as to what statements to reëvaluate in the light of any single contrary experience. No particular experiences are linked with any particular statements in the interior of the field, except indirectly, through considerations of equilibrium affecting the field as a whole.
>
> If this view is right, it is misleading to speak of the empirical content of an individual statement—especially if it is a statement at all remote from the experiential periphery of the field. Furthermore it becomes folly to seek a boundary between synthetic statements, which hold contingently on experience, and analytic statements, which hold come what may. Any statement can be held true come what may, if we make drastic enough adjustments elsewhere in the system.[36]

Quine's picture of knowledge of the external world changed the way people thought about the construction of knowledge. The breakthrough was to see knowledge not as a matter of foundations—building up from bedrock—but a function of one's being able to move about within a holistic web (be it a web of theory or intersubjective practice). It is in the move from simplicity, reductionism, and foundations to holism, network, and totality that Quine's epistemology is rightly described as "postmodern."[37] Quine's embrace of holism, together with his pragmatism on questions of truth,[38] invite comparison with the second of the three aspects of modernism that are displaced in postmodernism, that of the referential theory of language.

36. Quine, *supra* note 35, at 43.

37. See Murphy, *supra* note 10, at 294 ("As candidate for the title of postmodern epistemologist I nominate Willard V.O. Quine.").

38. For discussion of this aspect of Quine's thought, see Christopher Hookway, *Quine: Language, Experience and Reality* 50–58 (1988).

Language—its powers, its secrets—is a central preoccupation of contemporary philosophy.[39] But how does language do its work? Are we lost in the laby-
rinth of language, as Nietzsche seems to have thought,[40] or is language simply a
medium within which the world is represented or, to put the emphasis where it
should be, *re*-presented? Does language have the power to represent nature as it
is in itself, *sub specie aeternitatis?* In other words, do words represent in language
states of affairs in the world in such a way that the truth of any proposition may
be discerned by the comparison of the proposition with the state of affairs it
depicts?

Postmodern approaches to language[41] do not present arguments *against* the
modern, representationalist view.[42] Rather, postmodernist conceptions of the
word-world relation see the modernist picture of propositional, representation-

---

39. See Richard Rorty, *Consequences of Pragmatism* xiii–xlvii (1982).

40. See Friedrich Nietzsche, "On Truth and Lies in a Nonmoral Sense," in *Philosophy and
Truth: Selections from Nietzsche's Notebooks of the Early 1870's* 79–100 (Daniel Breazeale ed. & trans.,
1979).

41. For discussion of the relationship between language and representation in modernism
and postmodernism, see Scott Lash, *Sociology of Postmodernism* 12 (1990) ("Modernism . . .
had clearly differentiated and autonomized the roles of signifier, signified, and referent. Post-
modernization on the contrary *problematizes* these distinctions, and especially the status and relationship of signifier and referent, or put another way, representation and reality.").

42. The postmodern emphasis is on the question of what can be done with language. See 2
Richard Rorty, *Philosophical Papers (Essays on Heidegger and Others)* 58 (1991): "[Donald]
Davidson's account of human linguistic behavior takes for granted, as the later Wittgenstein also
did, that there are no linguistic entities which are intrinsically relationless—none which, like the
'simple names' of the *Tractatus*, are by nature relata. But Davidson's holism is more explicit and
thoroughgoing than Wittgenstein's, and so its antiphilosophical consequences are more apparent.
Whereas in the *Philosophical Investigations* Wittgenstein still toys with the idea of a distinction
between the empirical and the grammatical, between nonphilosophical and philosophical inquiry,
Davidson generalizes and extends Quine's refusal to countenance either a distinction between
necessary and contingent truth or a distinction between philosophy and science. Davidson insists
that we not think either of language in general or a particular language (say, English or German)
as something which has distinct edges, something which forms a bounded whole and can thus
become a distinct object of study or of philosophical theorizing." Rorty's claim that "Davidson's
holism is more explicit and thoroughgoing that Wittgenstein's" is a red herring. Davidson's account of understanding is, in the vocabulary here in use, thoroughly modernist and empiricist—
a far cry from the holist and pragmatist reading advanced by Rorty. The central reason Rorty's
characterization of Davidson's position cannot be sustained is that, for Davidson, understanding
is a matter of an empirical theory. See Donald Davidson, "A Nice Derangement of Epitaphs," in
Truth and Interpretation: Perspectives on the Philosophy of Donald Davidson 433–46 (Ernest LePore
ed., 1986): "[C]laims about what would constitute a satisfactory theory are not . . . claims about
the propositional knowledge of an interpreter, nor are they claims about the details of the inner
workings of some part of the brain. They are rather claims about what must be said to give a satisfactory description of the competence of the interpreter. *We* cannot describe what an interpreter
can do except by appeal to a recursive theory of a certain sort." *Id.* at 438. Thus, understanding
another person is a matter of having a theory about the sounds that emanate from her mouth.
These sounds are interpreted by reference to a grid that is recursively mapped onto the audible
output of the interlocutor. This, Rorty, claims, is pragmatism! For a Wittgensteinian critique of
the shortfalls of Davidson's account of understanding, see Stephen Mulhall, *On Being in the World:
Wittgenstein and Davidson on Seeing Aspects* 91–122 (1990).

alist truth[43] as unintelligible; a project that never gets off the ground.[44] The locus of the dispute is the modernist theory of correspondence, specifically the sentence-truth-world relation. To put the postmodern alternative in a nutshell, the modernist picture of sentence-truth-world is replaced with an account of understanding that emphasizes practice, warranted assertability, and pragmatism.

In his synthesis of the thought of Dewey, Wittgenstein, Heidegger, and Davidson, Richard Rorty has rethought the American pragmatist project in philosophy. This rethinking, which ranges across areas as divergent as philosophy of mind and political theory, returns again and again to the argument that the modernist approach to truth just is not worth the effort to keep it afloat. Rorty summarizes his position this way:

> For the pragmatist, the notion of "truth" as something "objective" is just a confusion between
>> (1) Most of the world is as it is whatever we think about it (that is, our beliefs have only limited causal efficacy)

---

43. See Joseph Rouse, *Knowledge and Power* 154 (1987): "[The realist] takes as already determined both the way the world is and our understanding of how our interpretations take it to be. The realist of course recognizes that we do not know in advance how the world is. But once we have some definite interpretations of the world, we can use them as the basis for our actions, which in turn test the adequacy of our interpretations. If our actions fail to achieve their aims, something must be wrong with the interpretations they were based on. If our actions succeed, this success of course does not entail that their underlying interpretations do accord with the reality they interpret. But if a wide variety of actions in differing circumstances generally succeed, the best explanation for their success is that those interpretations at least approximately accord with the way those objects really are. But where do we acquire our understanding of what our various interpretations do say about the world and of what would count as success in our actions? The realist needs to give some account of understanding such that we can understand how our interpretations take the world to be independent of how the world actually is. Otherwise the alleged independence of object and interpretation can never get off the ground. Sentences and practices do not have ready-made meanings, nor do they acquire meaning by convention. (How could the parties involved understand what they were agreeing to?) They acquire meaning only in their performance or use."

44. The following summary of the cumulative effect of Quine, the later Wittgenstein, and like-minded philosophers, speaks to this point: "When it comes to deciding between theories constructed within different conceptual schemes it is possible in Quine's view to have a situation of under-determination—that is, of there being no factually objective way to decide between them. Because ontology is relative to conceptual schemes there is no decisive fact of the matter. But Quine did wish to emphasize the importance of empirical enquiry to our understanding of the world. Empirical enquiry takes place at the boundaries of holistic networks or structures of theory—where they meet the world—and those boundaries gradually change, so altering the conceptual structure, but not in any sudden or pervasive way. A corollary of this position was a radically different conception of epistemology: seeing it not as the reconstruction of first principles of all knowledge, being transcendent of particular discourses, but rather as *psychology*, being the study of particular acts or behavioural patterns of knowing. This fundamental questioning of the nature of epistemology, associated with the later work of Wittgenstein and to some extent with the later work of [Rudolf] Carnap, had a profound but unfortunate effect. In Quine's words, it 'loosed a wave . . . of epistemological nihilism', reflected partly, as he says, in a tendency 'to belittle the role of evidence and to accentuate cultural relativism.'" Christopher Lloyd, *Explanation in Social History* 73 (1986) (citation omitted).

and

> (II) There is something out there in addition to the world called "the truth about the world" (what James sarcastically called "this tertium quid intermediate between the facts *per se*, on the one hand, and all knowledge of them, actual or potential, on the other").

The pragmatist wholeheartedly assents to (I)—not as an article of metaphysical faith but simply as a belief we have never had any reason to doubt—and cannot make sense of (II). When the realist tries to explain (II) with

> (III) The truth about the world consists in a relation of "correspondence" between certain sentences (many of which, no doubt, have yet to be formulated) and the world itself

the pragmatist can only fall back on saying, once again, that many centuries of attempts to explain what "correspondence" is have failed.[45]

Risking repetition, it must be emphasized that the modernist picture of what makes communication successful is not being *replaced* with another explanatory picture. The postmodern approach to language eschews advancement of explanations in favor of descriptions of localized linguistic practices. The reason the later Wittgenstein's approach to language is so revolutionary[46] is the fact that his attack on modernist philosophical methods breaks down the distinction between explanation and the phenomenon to be explained. All understanding occurs *in language*.[47] Language is the universal medium within which we think, act, and understand. The idea of language "corresponding" with something outside itself can never be cashed out because all talk about language is still *use of language*: no part of language can be torn apart from the whole and valorized as a "metalanguage," a superlanguage or "language about language." As Wittgenstein put the matter in the book of his first recorded thoughts about the language-world relation:

> But is *language*: the *only* language?
>
> Why should there not be a mode of expression through which I can talk *about* language in such a way that it can appear to me in co-ordination with something else?
>
> Suppose that music were such a mode of expression: then it is at any rate characteristic of *science* that *no* musical themes can occur in it.

---

45. Rorty, *supra* note 39, at xxvi.

46. For a discussion of Wittgensteinian "language philosophy" in the context of modernism and postmodernism, see Albrecht Wellmer, *The Persistence of Modernity* 65 (David Midgley trans., 1991) ("Wittgenstein's skeptical question is: 'How can I know what I am talking about? How can I know what I mean?' Language philosophy's critique destroys the subject as author and as the final judge of his meaning and intentions.").

47. This undercuts the idea that "understanding" can occur in any "private" sense. Owing to its character as a public medium, language—and thus, meaning—can never be relegated to a private realm. For discussion of this point in the context of the philosophy of consciousness, see Ernst Tugendhat, *Self-Consciousness and Self-Determination* 77–97 (P. Stern trans., 1986) (discussion of Wittgenstein on private language and its relationship to self-consciousness).

I myself write only sentences down here? And why?

How is language unique?[48]

So what does all of this mean for truth? If the modernist conception of "truth" is abandoned, are we not left with abject relativism?[49] Is not every claim to truth, every description of a state of affairs as good or acceptable as any other? This is what the purveyors of "truth" would have us believe. The fact that we cannot demonstrate how language "cuts reality at the joints"[50] does not mean that we cannot come up with better and worse ways of carrying on our practices. At least this is the claim to be sustained.

Language and Truth

Modernism and Language

Of the three axes that comprise the modernist framework, the one that is of paramount importance for law is the linguistic axis. In this section I will first sketch this axis in more detail. I shall then advance a postmodern conception of the relationship of language to the world. This then leads to the final section of the present chapter, which is a detailed account of legal justification from the postmodern point of view.

Speaking broadly, one might say that philosophy of language in the modernist tradition takes its basic task to be disclosure of the relationship between the word and the world. In the modernist tradition, the principal function of language is representational: it depicts the way things are. States of affairs, which exist independently of mind, can be portrayed or represented accurately in speech or thought to the degree their depiction in expression correctly or accurately reflects these states of affairs. In modernist terms, the question "What does this sentence mean?" may be translated as "What state of affairs does the asserted proposition purport to represent (depict)?"

Wittgenstein's picture theory of language[51] is a good example of a representationalist theory of language. Wittgenstein believed that sentences were statements of possible states of affairs.[52] For example, the sentence "I am sitting at

48. Ludwig Wittgenstein, *Notebooks 1914–1916* 52 (G. H. von Wright ed., G. E. M. Anscombe ed. & trans., 1969).

49. Rorty provides an answer from the perspective of epistemology: "[T]he thing to do is to marry truth and meaning to nothing and nobody but each other. The resulting marriage will be so intimate a relationship that a theory of truth will *be* a theory of meaning, and conversely. But that theory will be of no use to a representationalist epistemology, nor to any other sort of epistemology. It will be an explanation of what people *do*, rather than of a non-causal, representing, relation in which they stand to non-human entities." Richard Rorty, "Representation, Social Practise, and Truth," in 1 *Philosophical Papers (Objectivity, Relativism, and Truth)* 154 (1991).

50. Richard Rorty, "Texts and Lumps," in Rorty, *supra* note 49, at 80.

51. See Wittgenstein, *supra* note 24, at 1–3.144.

52. For an excellent description of the picture theory, as well as an introduction to the thought of Wittgenstein, see Anthony Kenny, *Wittgenstein* (1973). See also Joachim Schulte, *Wittgenstein: An Introduction* (1992).

my computer" expresses a proposition, which can correlate with a "state of affairs." Wittgenstein put it this way:

2.1   We picture facts to ourselves.

2.11   A picture represents a situation in logical space, the existence or non-existence of states of affairs.

2.12   A picture is a model of reality.

2.13   In a picture objects have the elements of the picture corresponding to them.

2.131   In a picture the elements of the picture are the representatives of objects.

2.14   What constitutes a picture is that its elements are related to one another in a determinate way.

2.141   A picture is a fact.

2.15   The fact that the elements of a picture are related to one another in a determinate way represents that things are related to one another in the same way.

           Let us call this connexion of its elements the structure of the picture, and let us call the possibility of this structure the pictorial form of the picture.

2.151   Pictorial form is the possibility that things are related to one another in the same way as the elements of the picture.

2.1511   *That* is how a picture is attached to reality; it reaches right out to it.

2.1512   It is laid against reality like a measure.[53]

The picture theory provides us with one expression of the dominant, modernist view of language as a representational medium. To the degree an asserted proposition depicts reality, the proposition may then be said to be "true." To the degree it fails accurately to depict reality, it is "false." Again, Wittgenstein: "[T]his proposition represents such and such a situation. It portrays it logically. Only in this way can *the proposition* be true or false: it can only agree or disagree with reality by being *a picture* of a situation."[54]

On a modernist, representationalist account of language, any given use of language is successful—that is, states a truth—if and only if the utterance accurately describes the facts. But what of linguistic utterances that are not factual in nature? Consider in this connection statements such as "Killing is wrong" and "This painting is beautiful." As mentioned previously, the modernist tradition characterizes all nonfactual discourse as "expressive" in nature. What is expressed are the feelings or preferences of the speaker. Thus, a statement such as "'Garden of Earthly Delights' is a beautiful painting" is merely a statement of feeling or sentiment. Because normative and aesthetic statements cannot depict facts (there being no "facts" to depict), they are nonpropositional in nature. The most one can achieve by way of their expression is a statement of individual preference.

---

53. Wittgenstein, *supra* note 24, at 2.1–2.1512.
54. Wittgenstein, *supra* note 48, at 8.

Postmodernism and Language

Postmodernist philosophy of language departs from the modernist account by rejecting the dichotomy between language as representation and language as expression. The way in which the modernist account of language is best overcome is by illustrating how the choice it presents between representation and expression is a false one. Of course, much in this description of the postmodernist account of language is controversial. For present purposes, the best way to state the position in a succinct way is to show how postmodernist philosophers have overcome the idea—so prevalent in modernism—that it is the world that fixes a reference for our concepts.

There is no better way to explore this issue than the recent renewal of the debate between realists and anti-realists. These perspectives represent the two dominant schools of thought in the contemporary philosophical debate over the question of what determines the truth of a proposition. For realists, a proposition is true in virtue of some feature of the empirical, conceptual, or normative realm that makes it true. For the realist philosopher of science, for example, a claim with respect to some unobservable aspect of nature is made true because of the way the world is.[55] The moral realist similarly asserts that any moral claim is true or false in virtue of certain features of the world, to which we refer when we employ moral concepts.[56]

The anti-realist opposes the realist picture of truth with a variety of alternative pictures. For example, conventionalists assert that there are no features of the world that make propositions true or false. Rather, truth and falsity are a function of agreement among participants in a given practice. For the anti-realist philosopher of science, the only measure of the truth of a scientific proposition is the fact of group assent. On this account, a scientific proposition is "true" if everyone agrees it is true.[57] Likewise, in ethics the anti-realist explains morality

---

55. Philosophers of science identifying themselves as realists often disagree with one another over the nature of their realism. See generally Roger Jones, "Realism About What?" 58 *Phil. of Sci.* 185 (1991). As Jones frames it: "While beyond a commitment to a 'nature of things itself' advocates of realism are seriously divided, they share the general hope that the scientific enterprise has the capacity to provide accounts of this nature-of-things-itself that are true. In what is more or less the 'classical' realist position, this hope is elevated to a belief. Indeed, such classical realists are willing to go out on a limb and claim that theories in the 'mature' areas of science should already be judged as 'approximately true', and that more recent theories in these areas are closer to the truth than older theories. Classical realists see the more recent theories encompassing the older ones as limiting cases and accounting for such success as they had. These claims are all closely linked to the claim that the language of entities and processes—both 'observational' and 'theoretical' ones—in terms of which these theories characterize the-nature-of-things-itself genuinely refers. That is, there are entities and processes that are part of the nature-of-things-itself that correspond to the ontologies of these theories." *Id.* at 186.

56. See, e.g., Alan Goldman, *Moral Knowledge* 8–12 (1988) (contrasting coherence theory of law with realism and anti-realism in ethics); Michael Moore, "Moral Reality," 1982 *Wis. L. Rev.* 1061 (1982).

57. Of course, this is also the view of Stanley Fish.

as the product of a tacit or hypothetical bargain reached by citizens of a polity. The bargain generates principles of justice that, among other things, provide a basis for the evaluation and criticism of conduct.

Having stated the realist and anti-realist positions with respect to the issue of truth generally, one must examine the question central to the present inquiry, that of what it means to say that a proposition of law is true. Michael Dummett, who first employed the term "anti-realism," elucidates the connection between the *truth* of propositions and the question of their *meaning*. Let us take a class of propositions, the truth value of which is in dispute. Dummett says that with respect to that class

> [t]he realist holds that the meanings of statements of the disputed class are not directly tied to the kind of evidence for them that we can have, but consist in the manner of their determination as true or false by states of affairs whose existence is not dependent on our possession of evidence for them. The anti-realist insists, on the contrary, that the meanings of these statements are tied directly to what we count as evidence for them, in such a way that a statement of the disputed class, if true at all, can be true only in virtue of something of which we could know and which we should count as evidence for its truth. The dispute thus concerns the notion of truth appropriate for statements of the disputed class; and this means that it is a dispute concerning the kind of *meaning* which these statements have.[58]

For both the realist and the anti-realist, knowing the meaning of a sentence means knowing its truth conditions (when, and under what conditions, the sentence would be true). Here, the anti-realist (Dummett) seems to have the upper hand; for the only way to make sense of meaning and understanding is by reference to the procedures for verifying the presence or absence of truth conditions. If all the realist can do is assert *but not adduce* (for example, due to some epistemic failure) the presence of those truth conditions, then the realist has not met her burden of proof.[59] But, the realist will counter, failure to meet the burden of proof on any one occasion does not preclude meeting it on another, nor does it prove that a right answer could not or does not exist.

Some philosophers argue that the realism/anti-realism debate is phony, and believe it can be avoided by looking at questions of knowledge, truth, and meaning from an "antirepresentationalist"[60] point of view. The basic viewpoint against

58. Michael Dummett, "Realism," in *Truth and Other Enigmas* 145, 146 (1978).

59. Dworkin has consistently made this argument in connection with his thesis that there is a right answer to every legal question. See Ronald Dworkin, *Taking Rights Seriously* 81–130 (1977).

60. Here I follow Richard Rorty's usage. See Rorty, *supra* note 49, at 2–3. "[Anti-realism] is standardly used to mean the claim, about some particular true statements, that there is no matter of fact which they represent. But, more recently, it has been used to mean the claim that no linguistic items represent any nonlinguistic items. In the former sense it refers to an issue within the community of representationalists—those philosophers who find it fruitful to think of mind or language as containing representations of reality. In the latter sense, it refers to antirepresentationalism—to the attempt to eschew discussion of realism by denying the notion of 'representation,' or that of 'fact of the matter,' has any useful role in philosophy. Representationalists typically think that controversies between idealists and realists were, and controversies between skeptics and antiskeptics are, fruitful and interesting. Antirepresentationalists typically think both sets of

which antirepresentationalism is deployed is that of language set apart from and "over and against" reality. The realist asserts that something in the world is referred to or implicated by a proposition, and it is this that *makes* the proposition true. The anti-realist counters that there is nothing out there beyond our conventional assessments of truth and falsity. Despite their differences, both the realist and the anti-realist claim that the meaning of our propositions *comes from somewhere*; the disagreement is not over the question of how there is meaning, only of its *source*: the world (realism) or conventional criteria (anti-realism).

A philosopher whose recent work points a way out of the realism/anti-realism debate is Hilary Putnam. Putnam has devoted a substantial portion of his career to arguing for the superiority of realism as a form of explanation in science and morals. Not long ago, Putnam radically changed course and recast his view of the relationship between meaning and truth in ways germane to the present discussion. The position, described as "antirepresentationalist," is directed at the view of language as something set "over and against reality"—against the idea that reality is something that can be captured by language, much as a cookie cutter captures dough. Putnam argues that the cookie cutter metaphor is undermined by the fact that

> [w]hat is (by commonsense standards) the same situation can be described in many different ways, depending on how we use the words. The situation does not itself legislate how words like "object," "entity," and "exist" must be used. What is wrong with the notion of objects existing "independently" of conceptual schemes is that there are no standards for the use of even the logical notions apart from conceptual choices. What the cookie-cutter metaphor tries to preserve is the naive idea that at least one Category—the ancient category of Object or Substance—has an absolute interpretation.[61]

What Putnam describes here is the realist position on the relationship between meaning and truth: a statement (proposition) is true if the words used to express the proposition (the cookie cutter) capture some feature of reality (in the dough) that subsists independently of all conceptual schemes. The anti-realist counters

---

controversies pointless. They diagnose both as the results of being held captive by a picture, a picture from which we should by now have wriggled free."

61. Hilary Putnam, *Representation and Reality* 114 (1988). Putnam's way of approaching questions of interpretation and meaning highlights the error in Fish's approach to these questions (see chapter 6). Fish agrees with Putnam, Rorty, Sellars, and Davidson that situations can be described, as Putnam puts it, "in many different ways." *Id.* The problem with Fish is that he does not wish to stay within a given language of description, since, he claims, any description of a situation is always up for grabs. But this claim is false. It is one thing to say that the effects of pollution on riparian owners may be described either in legal terms (e.g., duty, fault, and causation) or in economic terms (e.g., in light of the Coase theorem). However, once one adopts a language of description, one either uses the language correctly or one does not. As I have argued here, the question whether one is using words correctly or not has nothing whatsoever to do with interpreting the intentions of another (Fish) or with the personal interpretation of political theory (Dworkin). This does not preclude the possibility of disagreement, but rather makes disagreement possible. See Paul Feyerabend, *Three Dialogues on Knowledge* 145 (1991) ("Poems are not without constraints. As a matter of fact, the constraints poets impose on their work are often more severe than the constraints accepted by a botanist, or a birdwatcher.")

with "the view that it's all *just* language."[62] Is there any escape from the anti-realist's claim that "the world" is merely a function of our categories? Putnam answers thus:

> We can and should insist that some facts are there to be discovered and not legislated by us. But this is something to be said when one has adopted a way of speaking, a language, a "conceptual scheme." To talk of "facts" without specifying the language to be used is to talk of nothing; the word "fact" no more has its use fixed by the world itself than does the word "exist" or the word "object."[63]

But if the world does not fix the reference of our words, what does? It is at this point that Putnam makes a very interesting move:

> "Is the tree identical with the space-time region it occupies?" or "Is the chair identical with the mereological sum of the elementary particles that make it up?" . . . "Is a space-time point a concrete individual, or is it a mere limit, and hence an abstract entity of some kind?" [These questions] can all be handled in much the same way. "Identical," "individual," and "abstract" are notions with a variety of different uses. The difference between, say, describing space-time in a language that takes points as individuals and describing space-time in a language that takes points as mere limits is a difference in the choice of a language, and neither language is the "one true description."[64]

But this seems to confirm the anti-realist claim that "the world" is relative to a given conceptual scheme and that there are different worlds to the extent that there exist different languages of description. In short, that truth is simply relative to a conceptual scheme. Putnam responds in this way:

> The suggestion I am making, in short, is that *a statement is true of a situation just in case it would be correct to use the words of which the statement consists in that way in describing the situation.* . . . [W]e can explain what "correct to use the words of which the statement consists in that way" means by saying that it means nothing more nor less than a sufficiently well placed speaker who used the words in that way would be fully warranted in counting the statement as true of that situation.[65]

Putnam's analysis harkens back to our earlier discussion of the limits of legal positivism.[66] When Congress produces a statute, there are many ways to talk about their product. Law is a linguistic practice that provides one of several languages of description. In light of what Putnam refers to as "commonsense standards," the statute is "in the world." But *how* is it in the world? What does it mean? How do we make sense of it?

Rorty has a wonderful image for this question. He writes:

62. See Putnam, *supra* note 61, at 114.
63. *Id.*
64. *Id.* at 114–15.
65. *Id.* at 115.
66. See chapter 4.

The pragmatist meets this point by differentiating himself from the idealist. He agrees that there is such a thing as brute physical resistance—the pressure of light waves on Galileo's eyeball, or of the stone on Dr. Johnson's boot. But he sees no way of transferring this nonlinguistic brutality to *facts*, to the truth of sentences. The way in which a blank takes on the form of the die which stamps it has no analogy to the relation between the truth of a sentence and the event which the sentence is about. When the die hits the blank something causal happens, but as many *facts* are brought into the world as there are languages for describing that causal transaction. As Donald Davidson says, causation is not under a description, but explanation is. Facts are hybrid entities; that is, the causes of the assertibility of sentences include both physical stimuli and our antecedent choice of response to such stimuli. To say that we must have respect for facts is just to say that we must, if we are to play a certain language game, play by the rules. To say that we must have respect for unmediated causal forces is pointless. It is like saying that the blank must have respect for the impressed die. The blank has no choice, nor do we.[67]

The investigation of truth in law turns out to be the effort to describe what lawyers *do* with language. The modernist, referential approach preoccupies itself with the ways in which legal language represents, depicts, and captures the world. Those who deny such a referring relation have left themselves little in the way of alternatives to relativism or crass conventionalism. We need not embrace these two unpalatable alternatives. But if jurisprudence is to be an account of what lawyers do, what is to be said of truth? Let us now turn to that question.

Postmodern Jurisprudence: The Truth of Propositions of Law

The central claim of a postmodernist account of language is that the truth of our statements is not the result of the relationship between our linguistic acts and some state of affairs. Putnam's point is that "reality" does not come prepackaged. We make sense of the world linguistically. Owing to the fact that language does not "cut things at the joints,"[68] "knowledge" will not be the grasp of a relation (truth condition) between word and object; rather, knowledge will be unpacked in terms of linguistic competence, facility in the languages of man.

What postmodernism achieves is a shift from a concept of language as representation to language as practice (meaning as use). It is a move from picturing to competence, with competence being a manifested ability with and facility in a language. Of course, our immediate concern is with the special language of law. If it makes little sense to theorize whether legal propositions are true in virtue of mind-independent truth conditions (the realist) or depend solely upon conventional (positivism) and, for some, "arbitrary" (Fish) criteria, then in what can truth in law consist?

---

67. Rorty, "Texts and Lumps," in Rorty, *supra* note 49, at 81.
68. *Id*. at 80.

In the previous section, I characterized the postmodern view of language as emphasizing language as a social practice rather than a representational medium. A shift from language as a medium of representation to a social practice also marks a fundamental change in the nature of epistemology. For the modernist, knowledge is knowledge of referring relations (the grasp of truth conditions). For the postmodernist, knowledge is an ability, manifested in linguistic practices.[69] Understanding a linguistic practice, having the ability to say something true, is a learned ability. What is it that is learned?

Law is an activity driven by assertion. As Dworkin puts it so well, propositions of law—"statements and claims people make about what the law allows or prohibits or entitles them to have"[70] can be quite general or quite specific. Propositions of law may range from "The Fourteenth Amendment prohibits the denial of equal protection" to "Jones has violated the motor vehicle code by exceeding the speed limit." How in the law do we go from assertion to truth? To answer this question, we need to know something about the nature of legal argument.[71]

Claims in law are assertive in nature. The claim "Ordinance S is unconstitutional" asserts a purported truth. To ask what it is about S which prompts one to assert its unconstitutionality is to ask for the *ground* of the claim "S is unconstitutional." Suppose S states the following requirement: "Any assembly of twelve persons or more requires a parade permit." This fact is the ground for the claim that S is unconstitutional. The ground is advanced in support of the claim. This relation may be represented thus:

But, one might ask, what connects the ground to the claim? This is to ask how the ground is *relevant* to the claim. What is sought is the *warrant*. The warrant is the connection between the ground and the claim for which the ground is marshaled. In the case of S, the warrant is the First Amendment. The First Amendment, which provides for the right to peaceable assembly, is the warrant that provides the connection between the ground and the claim. This connection may be represented in the following way:

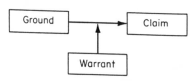

69. See Wittgenstein, *supra* note 1, at § 199 ("To understand a sentence means to understand a language. To understand a language means to understand a technique."). See also Peter Winch, *Trying to Make Sense* 75 (1987) ("The notion of a 'technique' of using the picture replaces that of a 'rule of projection' on which the Tractatus had relied. 'The connection between the picture and what is pictured' is what we might call the lines of projection; but so too might we call the technique of projection.").

70. Ronald Dworkin, *Law's Empire* 4 (1986).

71. The typology of argument developed in the balance of this chapter was first articulated in Stephen Toulmin, *The Uses of Argument* 94–118 (1958). For an application in the context of theology, see Nancey Murphy, *Reasoning and Rhetoric in Religion* (1994).

Of course, the text of the First Amendment is not self-executing. There is more to the move from ground to claim than resort to a warrant. In addition to invoking a warrant, the warrant must be used in the right way. This is where the forms of argument come into play. The forms of argument are culturally endorsed modes for the use of warrants. The forms of argument are the *backings* for warrants. The structure of legal argument may be depicted thus:

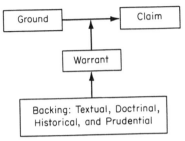

In the case of the proposition "*S* is unconstitutional," *S* is an assertion having the status of a claim (proposition) of law. The ground of the claim is the fact that the ordinance contains a parade permit requirement. The First Amendment warrants the move from the ground to the claim that *S* is unconstitutional. The backing for the warrant is the ordinary meaning of the language of the First Amendment (textual argument), perhaps backed with appeal to precedent (doctrinal argument). Of course, this typology of legal argument does not tell us everything we need to know about legal argument, but it does tell us a great deal. Having described the basic framework for legal argument, let us expand the scheme to bring in other activities.

In chapter 7, we considered the problem of conflict among what we are here referring to as the backings for warrants (the forms of argument). Bobbitt's solution to the problem of conflict—the recursion to conscience—was rejected because it relegated this occasion for interpretation to a hidden realm. How, then, does interpretation in the face of conflict among the forms of argument proceed?

The first thing to notice is how the typology of argument sketched above must now be expanded to reflect the need for interpretation. In cases of conflict among forms of argument, the typology now looks like this:

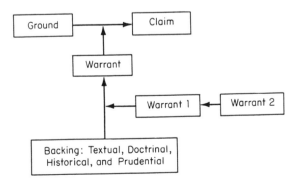

In this expanded schema, "Warrant 1" represents the criterion for choosing among forms of argument in cases of conflict. But what *is* the criterion? How, in law, do we move from contradiction to truth? I have suggested[72] that Quine's metaphor of science as "a total field of force" is the best way to think about legal interpretation. Quine's contribution to the philosophy of science was to suggest that "it is misleading to speak of the empirical content of an individual statement."[73] Likewise, in law, it is misleading to speak of the truth of a proposition of law in isolation from other propositions within the legal "web of belief."

In choosing between different interpretations, we favor those that clash least with everything else we take to be true. In law, as in all matters, "[w]e convince someone of something by appealing to beliefs he already holds and by combining these to induce further beliefs in him, step by step, until the belief we wanted finally to inculcate in him is inculcated."[74] In law, we choose the proposition that best hangs together with everything else we take to be true.

Riggs v. Palmer nicely illustrates this thesis.[75] *Riggs* is less about matters of principle than it is a dispute over how to read a statutory text. Neither the majority nor the dissent disagreed that the statutory language was the relevant starting point for analysis. The disagreement was over the question whether it was the *terminus* of analysis as well. The dissent, of course, argued that the ordinary meaning of the statutory text was dispositive. Why is the majority's argument more persuasive (in the way Quine describes)?

The majority opinion advances two principal arguments. Owing to Dworkin's recurring use of *Riggs* to illustrate the importance of principles in law, little attention has been given to the majority's main rhetorical strategy. The majority begins by noticing that the problem of statutory construction was first discussed by Aristotle.[76] In a nutshell, if statutes were always to be read literally, absurd consequences would follow. The majority illustrates this thesis with examples drawn both from eminent thinkers[77] as well as other areas of law.[78] The following excerpt is representative of the majority's approach:

> In 1 Blackstone's Commentaries the learned author, speaking of the construction of statutes, says: "If there arise out of them any absurd consequences

72. See the discussion *supra* at text accompanying notes 33–36.
73. Quine, *supra* note 35, at 43.
74. W. V. Quine & J. S. Ullian, *The Web of Belief* 86 (1970).
75. I would say that *Riggs* is a dispute between textual (dissent) and prudential (majority) forms of argument.
76. Aristotle, *Nicomachean Ethics*, bk. 5, chap. 10 (Jonathan Barnes ed., 1984).
77. See, e.g., Samuel Pufendorf, *On the Duty of Man and Citizen According to Natural Law* (1991); Matthew Bacon, *A New Abridgment of the Law* (1813).
78. For example, insurance law. See *id.* at 512: "'It would be a reproach to the jurisprudence of the country if one could recover insurance money payable on the death of a party whose life he had feloniously taken. As well might he recover insurance money upon a building that he had willfully fired.' These maxims, without any statute giving them force or operation, frequently control the effect and nullify the language of wills. A will procured by fraud and deception, like any other instrument, may be decreed void and set aside, and so a particular portion of a will may be excluded from probate or held inoperative if induced by the fraud or undue influence of the person in whose favor it is" (citations omitted).

manifestly contradictory to common reason, they are, with regard to those collateral consequences, void. . . . When some collateral matter arises out of the general words, and happen to be unreasonable, then the judges are in decency to conclude that the consequence was not foreseen by the parliament, and, therefore, they are at liberty to expound the statute by equity and only quo ad hoc disregard it;" and he gives as an illustration, if an act of parliament gives a man power to try all causes that arise within his manor of Dale, yet, if a cause should arise in which he himself is party, the act is construed not to extend to that because it is unreasonable that any man should determine his own quarrel. There was a statute in Bologna that whoever drew blood in the streets should be severely punished, and yet it was held not to apply to the case of a barber who opened a vein in the street. It is commanded in the Decalogue that no work shall be done upon the Sabbath, and yet, giving the command a rational interpretation founded upon its design, the Infallible Judge held that it did not prohibit works of necessity, charity or benevolence on that day.[79]

It is telling, indeed, that in his dissent, Judge Gray never comes to terms with the majority's argument. It is clear that Judge Gray's insistence on fidelity to the statutory text is driven by his assertion that depriving Elmer of his legacy improperly deprives him of his property—it is tantamount to punishing him twice for the same offense:

> What power or warrant have the courts to add to the respondent's penalties by depriving him of property? The law has punished him for his crime, and we may not say that it was an insufficient punishment. In the trial and punishment of the respondent the law has vindicated itself for the outrage which he committed, and further judicial utterance upon the subject of punishment or deprivation of rights is barred. We may not . . . "enhance the pains, penalties and forfeitures provided by law for the punishment of crime."[80]

But the majority answers this assertion with an argument the force of which cannot be denied:

> Just before the murder he was not an heir, and it was not certain that he ever would be. He might have died before his grandfather, or might have been disinherited by him. He made himself an heir by the murder, and he seeks to take property as the fruit of his crime. What has before been said as to him as legatee applies to him with equal force as an heir. He cannot vest himself with title by crime. My view of this case does not inflict upon Elmer any greater or other punishment for his crime than the law specifies. It takes from him no property, but simply holds that he shall not acquire property by his crime, and thus be rewarded for its commission.[81]

---

79. 115 N.Y. 506, 510–11, 22 N.E. 188, 189–90 (1889) (citations omitted). Thus, the majority concludes: "What could be more unreasonable than to suppose that it was the legislative intention in the general laws passed for the orderly, peaceable and just devolution of property, that they should have operation in favor of one who murdered his ancestor that he might speedily come into the possession of his estate? Such an intention is inconceivable." *Id.* at 115 N.Y. at 511.

80. *Id.* at 519–20 (citation omitted).

81. *Id.* at 513–14.

The force of the majority's prudential argument does not come at the expense of the statutory text. Through careful and wide-ranging comparison with other areas of law, the majority shows the problem at issue to be long-standing and, more importantly, that its solution is consistent with other solutions to problems of textual meaning. In short, the success of the majority's argument is to be explained in terms of its showing the degree to which it can be made to cohere with everything else we take to be true about legal texts (e.g., contracts, statutes). The dissent's position suffers from a lack of adequate engagement with the majority's argument and, to some degree, a begging of the question at issue. One cannot assume that Elmer had his property taken away from him, for the issue was whether his legacy was rightly his. The majority seizes on this *petitio principii*, and exploits it to great effect.

Of course, there may be dispute over what is to count as an appropriate measure for the criterion of choice among conflicting forms of argument. This debate is indicated above as Warrant 2. As the movement back suggests, there is no natural place to stop in the regression from the site of the original difficulty (conflict among forms of argument) to the choice of criterion to resolve the conflict. At each point in the regression, appeal is made to matters not in question in an effort to reach agreement. As we have noted previously, "[T]he condition for engaging in interpretation is that a wide range of ways of acting with words is not in doubt at all, but is followed as a matter of course in the activity of interpretation."[82]

A second interpretive endeavor concerns the relationship between warrants and beliefs. We have identified four forms of argument as central to law. These forms of argument serve as backing for the warrants with which lawyers draw connections between grounds and claims. But backings may themselves be called into question. Consider the most common occasion of the historical form of argument, that of statutory interpretation. The nerve of statutory interpretation is appeal to historical facts as backing for the move from history to decision (historical argument). For example, in support of their assertion of the truth or falsity of the proposition that Title VII does or does not permit private affirmative action, the majority and dissenting opinions in *Weber*[83] each appeal to the facts of legislative history to back up their assertion of the truth or falsity of the proposition there at issue. However, if historical argument is to have any validity, beliefs about legislative history must themselves be true, for if they are false, then the move from history to judgment cannot be sustained.

Richard Posner has challenged conventional beliefs about the status of facts of legislative history. On several occasions,[84] Posner has argued that the canons of statutory interpretation are an improper guide to the meaning of statutes because they are based on false assumptions regarding the nature of the legislative process. The basic assumption Posner calls into question is an imputation of omniscience to Congress:

---

82. James Tully, "Wittgenstein and Political Philosophy: Understanding Practices of Critical Reflection," 17 *Pol. Theory* 172, 196 (1989).

83. Discussed earlier in chapters 4 and 5.

84. See Richard A. Posner, *The Federal Courts* 286–93 (1985) (hereafter *Federal Courts*); Richard A. Posner, "Statutory Interpretation—In the Classroom and in the Courtroom," 50 *U. Chi. L. Rev.* 800 (1983) (hereafter "Statutory Interpretation").

Most of the canons of statutory construction go wrong not because they misconceive the nature of judicial interpretation of the legislative or political process but because they impute omniscience to Congress. Omniscience is always an unrealistic assumption, and particularly so when one is dealing with the legislative process. The basic reason why statutes are so frequently ambiguous in application is not that they are poorly drafted—though many are— and not that the legislators failed to agree on just what they wanted the statute to accomplish in the statute—though often they do fail—but that a statute necessarily is drafted in advance of, and with imperfect application for the problems that will be encountered in, its application.[85]

As an example of a canon founded on the assumption of legislative omniscience, consider that of *expressio unius est exclusio alterius.*[86] Posner's point, one that is well taken, is that the canon would only make sense "if all omissions in legislative drafting were deliberate."[87] As an example, Posner raises the Supreme Court's decision in *Touche Ross & Co. v. Redington,*[88] where the Court used the canon as the basis "for refusing to create private remedies for certain statutory violations."[89] Posner objects:

Whether the result in the private-action cases is right or wrong, the use of *expressio unius* is not helpful. If a statute fails to include effective remedies because the opponents were strong enough to prevent their inclusion, the courts should honor the legislative compromise. But if the omission was an oversight, or if Congress thought that the courts would provide appropriate remedies for statutory violations as a matter of course, the judges should create the remedies necessary to carry out the legislature's objectives.[90]

By calling into question certain of the assumptions of the historical form of argument, Posner turns what is normally backing (historical argument) into something that *itself* requires backing. This may be represented thus:

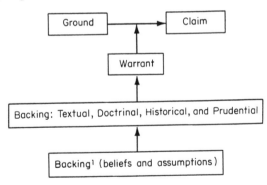

85. Posner, "Statutory Interpretation," *supra* note 84, at 811.
86. "[T]he expression of one thing is the exclusion of another." *Black's Law Dictionary* 521 (5th ed. 1979).
87. *Id.* at 813.
88. 442 U.S. 560 (1979).
89. Posner, "Statutory Interpretation," *supra* note 84, at 813.
90. *Id.*

What Posner calls into question are certain of the beliefs and assumptions of the historical form of argument. Posner is not rejecting legal argument *per se*, nor is he putting in question any other aspect of legal reasoning. His is a quite specific and localized complaint. In fact, much of the strength of his criticism is drawn from the fact that he is able to make his points about unrealistic historical assumptions without upsetting any other part of the system of beliefs.[91]

We must take matters one step further to complete our account of the typology of forms of legal argument. Consider a direct challenge to the efficacy of a form of argument. Let us stay with historical argument. Together with textual and doctrinal argument, historical argument is among the most common of the forms of argument. In American jurisprudence, lawyers often ask what motivated a legislature to draft the law as it did. The focus is often on a problem, issue, or set of historical circumstances to which the legislature or Congress was responding when the legislation in question was drafted. In short, appeal to history as a guide to purpose and intent is a cardinal move in the lawyer's argumentative framework.

Recalling the earlier discussion *United Steelworkers of America v. Weber*,[92] I want to consider William Eskridge's challenge to the conventional understanding of the historical form of argument. In "Dynamic Statutory Interpretation,"[93] Eskridge describes two perspectives that are usually brought to bear in the interpretation of statutes:

1. Textual perspective: the statutory text, which is the formal focus of interpretation and a constraint on the range of interpretive options available.
2. Historical perspective:[94] the original legislative expectations surrounding the statute's creation, including compromises reached.

To these two perspectives, which we recognize as the textual and historical forms of argument, Eskridge adds a third, the "evolutive perspective," which he describes as "the subsequent evolution of the statute and its present context, especially the ways in which the societal and legal environment of the statute has materially changed over time."[95]

In an effort to make his argument against the background of conventional understanding of legal argument, Eskridge notes that "[w]hen the statutory text clearly answers the interpretive question . . . it normally will be the most impor-

---

91. Posner is critical of Guido Calabresi's proposal "that courts ought to have the same power in dealing with statutes that they do in dealing with their own precedents . . . [because] the judgment whether a statute has outlived its usefulness is a legislative rather than a judicial judgment." Posner, *Federal Courts, supra* note 84, at 290 (criticizing Guido Calabresi, *A Common Law for the Age of Statutes* (1982)). Notice that the ground of Posner's criticism is the rule of law virtues. The *form* of Posner's criticism is that Calabresi's proposal is too inconsistent with our fundamental beliefs, specifically separation of powers.

92. 443 U.S. 193 (1979).

93. William Eskridge, "Dynamic Statutory Interpretation," 135 *U. Pa. L. Rev.* 1479 (1987). Eskridge's theory of dynamic statutory interpretation is fully discussed in William N. Eskridge, Jr., *Dynamic Statutory Interpretation* (1994).

94. *Id.* at 1483.

95. *Id.*

tant consideration."[96] Of course, the ordinary meaning of the text is not always dispositive, as was the case in *Weber*. When text is not dispositive, the door opens for dynamic statutory interpretation.

Why is *Weber* a good candidate for dynamic statutory interpretation? Eskridge regards the question in *Weber* as one particularly amenable to dynamic analysis because

> it recognizes not only that the very nature of the problem had changed since 1964, but also that the legal and societal context of Title VII had changed. In 1964, the legal culture—legislators, judges, administrators, and commentators—focused on how to root out discrimination inspired by racial animus. People thought that rooting out actual prejudice would create a color-blind society. The intellectual focus changed over the next fifteen years, as the legal community came to realize that discrimination could be just as invidious even when it could not be established that prejudice was at its root. The concept of the continuing effects of historical patterns of discrimination suggested that current institutions might perpetuate discrimination even though no one in those institutions remained personally prejudiced. This insight was not a historical concern of the 1964 Act, but it evolved into a current concern and was recognized in subsequent statues, judicial decisions, and commentary.[97]

While Eskridge labels his argument "evolutive," the argument is clearly historical in nature. The point of the argument is to put in question the conventional limits on historical argument, which preclude asking anything about history other than from the then-present perspective. Eskridge puts the historical form of argument in question by making the case for the legal significance of failed legislative aspirations. Where the text of a statute is unclear, as he argues it was in *Weber*, and history demonstrates a clear historical aspiration on the part of Congress, *subsequent* history (both social and legal) should play a justificatory role.

How are we to assess Eskridge's argument for a dynamic reading of statutes? This question is one about our current practices: do the means exist for adjudicating between rival conceptions of the historical form of argument?[98] Notice how Eskridge's argument dovetails with historical argument, conventionally understood. He is not asking that our long-standing approach to historical evidence be abandoned or even altered. In fact, the strength of this new conception of the importance of history actually builds off of historical argument, traditionally understood.

In what can only be characterized as a pragmatic argument, Eskridge claims that his dynamic conception of history is consistent with rule of law virtues,[99]

96. *Id.*

97. *Id.* at 1493.

98. This activity is, of course, interpretive in nature. See Tully, *supra* note 82, at 196: "Interpretation . . . is a practice we engage in when our understanding and use of signs is in some way problematic or in doubt. Here we attempt to come to an understanding of the sign in question by offering various interpretations (expressions) as opposed to different ones, adjudicating rival interpretations, in some cases calling the criteria of adjudication into question, and so on."

99. Eskridge, "Dynamic Statutory Interpretation," *supra* note 93, at 1483–1576.

raises no countermajoritarian difficulties,[100] enhances the legitimacy of government,[101] and assigns to judges no tasks not already within their competence. In short, dynamic statutory interpretation is appealing "because it rests upon a realistic vision of the legislative and interpretive processes *and* because it promotes more candid decisionmaking in statutory interpretation cases."[102]

Eskridge's model of dynamic statutory interpretation enables us to pull together the three distinct but related threads of a postmodern jurisprudence. He begins by employing the forms of argument to frame the issues at stake in the *Weber* case. Textual and historical arguments point in no clear direction. Something labeled "Dynamic Statutory Interpretation" is introduced, which, at first glance, appears to be something new and different. Indeed, it is different *but in a distinct way.* Our conventional understanding of historical argument is put in question and a proposal made for improving how we use history to show the truth of propositions of law. Of course, there are criteria for what is to count as an adequate historical argument, and Eskridge deftly employs those criteria to make the case that his proposed recasting of historical argument fits well with everything else we take to be true about statutory interpretation. Here we have the employment of conventional criteria of truth evaluation (the forms of argument), the reflective practice of putting a form of argument in question (recasting historical argument in dynamic terms), and appeal to conventional interpretive criteria (consistency with rule of law virtues, etc.), all in an effort to demonstrate the superiority of his enhanced understanding of the historical form of argument.

The typology of legal argument just developed starts with the observation that assertion is a central feature of legal practice. Assertion begins in the belief that a proposition is true *as a matter of law.* What does it mean for a proposition to be true as a matter of law? The typology just advanced is the answer to this question.

Looked at in this way, many activities that now appear disparate and unconnected can be seen as related. The most familiar, of course, is the role of the forms of argument as the grammar of legal justification. In the move from ground to claim, lawyers have no difficulty in reaching for the forms of argument to show the truth of propositions of law. The practice of law is conducted in the language of the forms: without them there is no law.

To describe only the forms of argument is to present an incomplete account of the nature of law. In addition to the problem of conflict among the forms of argument, the forms themselves are contested in a number of different ways. Warrants provide the basis for the move from ground to claim. As noted in the discussion of legal positivism in chapter 4, the truth of legal propositions does not consist solely in the text of the law being produced "in the right way." The forms of argument are the legal grammar of meaning-making. We use the forms of argument to show what the legislatively produced text means. To ignore these,

100. *Id.* at 1523–29.
101. *Id.* at 1529–33.
102. *Id.* at 1538.

as positivism does, is to ignore what enables us to say something true from the legal point of view.

The forms make it possible to move from ground to claim (i.e., provide the backing for warrants). Because warrants themselves involve matters of belief, these beliefs may be called into question. The discussion in this chapter of Posner's criticisms of the canons of statutory construction provided one example of the interpretive activity of calling into question beliefs about history which are basic to the historical form of argument. As mentioned, Posner uses the unchallenged portion of the field of legal argument to make his point that the falsity of beliefs about the legislative process has deleterious and measurable consequences for the integrity of legal judgment. In this way, his argument confirms an essential element of postmodern jurisprudence; that legal argument is "horizontal" in nature. When a problem in some aspect of the argumentative field arises, solutions are measured not against a practice-transcendent ideal but by the degree to which the proposed solution fits with everything not then in question.

A more wide-ranging challenge to the forms of argument is illustrated by William Eskridge's proposal for a rethinking of the *nature* of historical argument. Eskridge takes our conventional approach to resort to history as an element in the justificatory matrix of law and forces us to see history from a dynamic and not a static perspective. Again, just as in the case of Posner, Eskridge uses the elements of law not then in question to persuade us that his is truly a *legal* argument, not an import from another discipline. As with Posner, it is the *form* of the argument that is of interest.

Conclusion

This chapter has performed two principal functions. First, it provides a broad philosophical account of the shortcomings of the truth-conditional approach to meaning in law. With the exception of Bobbitt's modal analysis of constitutional argument, every view we have considered is grounded in the idea that the meaning of a proposition of law is a matter of the proposition's standing in a certain relation to some state of affairs. For realists, that state of affairs (e.g., moral essences) is a mind-independent reality. For anti-realists, the meaning-maker is the fact of communal agreement.

I have tried to show that each of these views fails to account for the normativity of law. In my view, normativity in law arises from linguistic practices. Unlike the anti-realist, I do not believe that communal agreement can explain normativity. The relation goes the other way: normativity—intersubjective linguistic practice—makes agreement possible. In this chapter, I attempted to go beyond existing accounts of law as a linguistic practice to put the debate in a wider context and to develop the position in a new way. Agreement and disagreement are distinct yet related argumentative legal phenomena. Without some description of their role in legal argument, no complete jurisprudence is possible.

Afterword

The pages of this book are devoted to a single question, "What does it mean to say that a proposition of law is true?" Put differently, this book has taken up the question of the logical status of propositions of law. I hope I have shown that each of the authors under consideration has an answer to this question. I have also tried to show that each of these seemingly different answers is, in a deep and previously unnoticed way, the same. That is, each author views propositions of law as true in virtue of "something"; each theory is an effort to identify the "truth maker." My effort has been to show the fruitlessness of such an approach to law and to point the way to a different approach.

Thus, I think it fair to say that the present work is, as one sympathetic reader put it, "a work of demolition." It was not my intention to advance yet another "theory of law," for it is just such an enterprise I wish to call into question. Rather, I hope that this work will inspire others to abandon the effort to identify the "true grounds of law" and pursue a different course. In short, when it comes to law, I wish to leave everything as it is.

Another way of putting this last point is to see this book as an attempt to answer the question of what it means to follow a legal rule. Because they have similar expectations about rule-following, most contemporary writers in jurisprudence have a similar outlook on this central normative question. I have tried to show why this approach is flawed and why there is little cost to abandoning it.

If one adopts the approach to law advanced in these pages, what is one's work? What does it mean to "render perspicuous" the grammar of law? I have argued that law is a practice of argument. As such, propositions of law do not have "grounds." The essence of law is legal argument: the forms of legal argument are the culturally endorsed modes for showing the truth of propositions of law. It is in the use of these forms that the practice is to be understood. Their use in practice *is* the law.

This point of view counsels a return to the local. Much of contemporary jurisprudence is the effort to justify the forms of argument in the various departments of law. The history of jurisprudence in this century has been an effort to identify the legitimate structure of justification. Once identified, such a structure could be brought to bear on the law, for a critical perspective was then possible. But, as I have tried to show in the final chapter of this book, such an enterprise is no longer tenable. If developments in philosophy of language, epistemology, and metaphysics in the last half century teach us anything, it is that meaning arises from human practices and that no practice or discourse enjoys a privileged position vis-à-vis others. Philosophy, the queen of the sciences, is now a local endeavor.

And what do I mean by "the local"? Skeptical as I am of jurisprudential projects that seek to underwrite the legitimacy of law by recourse to something outside law (e.g., economics or moral philosophy), I would urge more careful attention to the ways in which different areas of the law employ the forms of legal argument. Such an enterprise is not necessarily philosophical. The forms of legal argument are a historical product, an inheritance. As such, their character changes over time in response to a variety of pressures, both internal and external to the legal system. A historical account of these developments is, potentially, quite interesting.

Finally, let me respond to a potential criticism of this approach to law, one born of a mistaken understanding of the project. Law is not a "self-contained" enterprise. It is an error to read the view of law articulated in these pages as one wherein law is, as some used to say, "autonomous." The law is not isolated from the social and discursive spaces around it. However, law is an identifiable practice, one with its own argumentative grammar. The mistake of so much of contemporary jurisprudence is to think that this grammar is reducible to the forms of argument of another discipline. It has been my effort here to deny the plausibility of this approach; not because law is autonomous but because such reductionism obscures the nature of law.

Index